JAEPL, Vol. 25, 2020

JAEPL

The Assembly for Expanded Perspectives on Learning (AEPL), an official assembly of the National Council of Teachers of English, is open to all those interested in extending the frontiers of teaching and learning beyond the traditional disciplines and methodologies.

The purposes of AEPL are to provide a common ground for theorists, researchers, and practitioners to explore innovative ideas; to participate in relevant programs and projects; to integrate these efforts with others in related disciplines; to keep abreast of activities along these lines of inquiry; and to promote scholarship on and publication of these activities.

The *Journal of the Assembly for Expanded Perspectives on Learning, JAEPL*, also provides a forum to encourage research, theory, and classroom practices involving expanded concepts of language. It contributes to a sense of community in which scholars and educators from pre-school through the university exchange points of view and boundary-pushing approaches to teaching and learning. *JAEPL* is especially interested in helping those teachers who experiment with new strategies for learning to share their practices and confirm their validity through publication in professional journals.

Topics of interest include but are not limited to:

- Aesthetic, emotional & moral intelligences
- Learning archetypes
- Kinesthetic knowledge & body wisdom
- Ethic of care in education
- Creativity & innovation
- Pedagogies of healing
- Holistic learning
- Humanistic & transpersonal psychology
- Environmentalism
- (Meta)Cognition
- Imaging & visual thinking
- Intuition & felt sense theory
- Meditation & pedagogical uses of silence
- Narration as knowledge
- Reflective teaching
- Spirituality
- New applications of writing & rhetoric
- Memory & transference
- Multimodality
- Social justice

Membership in AEPL is $45. Contact Sheila Kennedy, AEPL, Membership Chair, email: kennedsh@lewisu.edu. Membership includes current year's issue of *JAEPL*

Send submissions, address changes, and single hardcopy requests to Wendy Ryden, Co-Editor, *JAEPL*, email: wendy.ryden@liu.edu. Address letters to the editors and all other editorial correspondence to Wendy Ryden (wendy.ryden@liu.edu).

AEPL website: www.aepl.org
Back issues of *JAEPL*: http://trace.tennessee.edu/jaepl/
Blog: https://aeplblog.wordpress.com/
Visit Facebook at **Assembly for Expanded Perspectives on Learning**
Production of *JAEPL* is managed by Parlor Press, www.parlorpress.com.

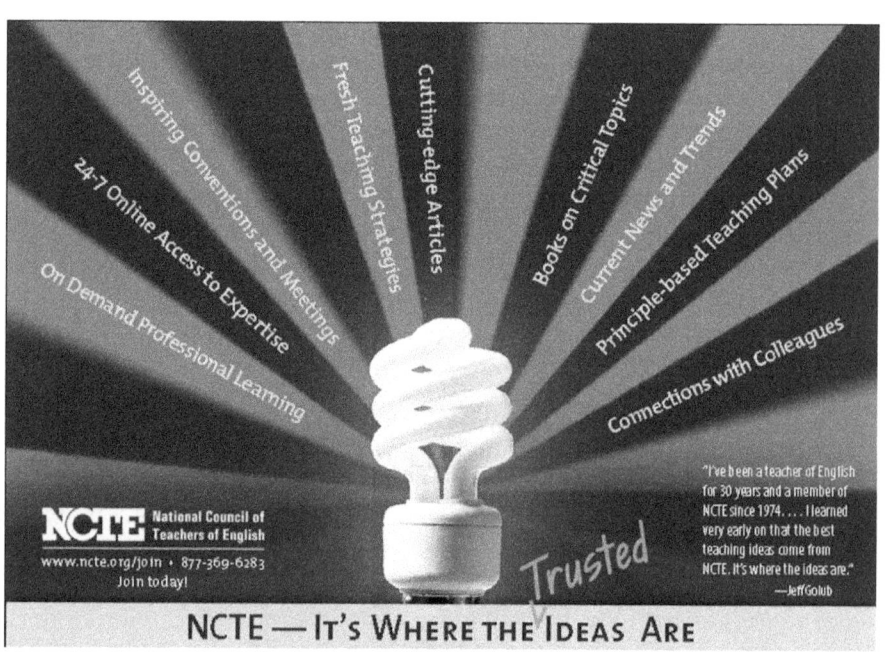

Assembly for Expanded Perspectives on Learning

Executive Board	
Chair	Bruce Novak, Foundation for Ethics and Meaning
Associate Chair	Nate Mickelson, New York University
Secretary	Bob Lazaroff, Nassau Community College, SUNY
Acting Treasurer	Nate Mickelson, New York University
Ex-officio	Marlowe Miller, University of Massachusetts, Lowell
	Vajra Watson, University of California, Davis
TRACE Website	Elizabeth DeGeorge, University of Tennessee, Knoxville
AEPL Website	Daniel J. Weinstein, Indiana University of Pennsylvania
Advisory Board	Chair: Peter Elbow, University of Massachusetts, Amherst
	Sheridan Blau, Teachers College, Columbia University
	Alice G. Brand, SUNY College at Brockport
	John Creger, American High School, Freemont, CA
	Richard L. Graves, Auburn University, Emeritus
	Doug Hesse, University of Denver
	Nel Noddings, Stanford University
	Sondra Perl, Lehman College, CUNY
	Kurt Spellmeyer, Rutgers University
	Charles Suhor, NCTE
	Peter Stillman, Charlottesville, NY
	Jane Tompkins, University of Illinois at Chicago
	Robert Yagelski, SUNY Albany
Founding Members	Alice G. Brand, SUNY College at Brockport
	Richard L. Graves, Auburn University, Emeritus
	Charles Suhor, NCTE
Membership Contact	Sheila M. Kennedy, Lewis University
JAEPL Co-Editors	Wendy Ryden, Long Island University
	Peter H. Khost, Stony Brook University

JAEPL is a non-profit journal published yearly by the Assembly for Expanded Perspectives on Learning with support from TRACE at University of Tennessee, Knoxville. Back issues are archived at: http://trace.tennessee.edu/jaepl/.

JAEPL gratefully acknowledges this support as well as that of its manuscript readers:

Jacob Babb, Indiana University Southeast
Ulrika Bergmark, Luleå University of Technology
Shane Borrowman, Univ of Montana Western
Jaclyn Fiscus-Cannaday, Florida State University
Ellen C. Carillo, University of Conneticut
Nicole I. Caswell, East Carolina University
Laura J. Davies, SUNY Cortland
Michael-John DePalma, Baylor University
Heather Graves, University of Alberta
Asao B. Inoue, Arizona State University
Tammie M. Kennedy, Univ of Nebraska at Omaha
Faith Kurtyka, Creighton University
Eric Leake, Texas State University
Paul Lynch, St. Louis University
Ian Marshall, William Paterson University
Mark McBeth, John Jay College of Criminal Justice and CUNY Graduate Center
John Muckelbauer, University of South Carolina
Deborah Mutnick, Long Island University Brooklyn
George Otte, CUNY School of Professional Studies
Michelle Payne, Boise State University
Alexandria Peary, Salem State University
Jeong-eun Rhee, Long Island University, Post
Rich Shivener, York University
Monica Stitt-Bergh, University of Hawai'i at Mānoa
Jill Swiencicki, St. John Fisher College
Geoff Taggart, University of Reading, UK
Christy Wenger, Shepherd University
Courtney Adams Wooten, George Mason University
Michael Zerbe, York College of Pennsylvania

JAEPL

The Journal of the Assembly for Expanded Perspectives on Learning

Co-Editors

Wendy Ryden
Long Island University

Peter H. Khost
Stony Brook University

Book Review Editor
Irene Papoulis
Trinity College

"Connecting" Editor
Christy Wenger
Shepherd University

Copyright © 2020
by the Assembly for Expanded Perspectives on Learning
All rights reserved

(ISSN 1085-4630)

An affiliate of the National Council of Teachers of English
Member of the NCTE Information Exchange Agreement
Member of the Council of Editors of Learned Journals
Indexed with MLA Bibliography
Website: www.aepl.org
Blog: https://aeplblog.wordpress.com/
Visit Facebook at **Assembly for Expanded Perspectives on Learning**
Back issues available at: http://trace.tennessee.edu/jaepl/

Volume 25 • 2020

Contents

Essays

Jeff Ringer	1	The Inventive Work of the Christian Mind
Jared Featherstone	19	Contemplative WAC: Testing a Mindfulness-based Reflective Writing Assignment
Hella Bloom Cohen	35	STEMM-Humanities Co-Teaching and the Humusities Turn
Keith Rhodes	47	Seeing Writing Whole: The Revolution We Really Need

Special Section
The Toil of Feeling: Education as Emotional Labor

Wendy Ryden	58	Teaching at the End of Empire
Kelly Blewett	60	FYC Students' Emotional Labor in the Feedback Cycle
Sarah V. Seeley	79	"So, that's sort of wonderful": The Ideology of Commitment and the Labor of Contingency
Anna Sicari	99	Complaint as 'Sticky Data' for the Woman WPA: The Intellectual Work of a WPA's Emotional and Embodied Labor
Kerri-Ann M. Smith, Kathleen Alves, Irvin Weathersby, Jr., and John D. Yi	118	Invictus: Race and Emotional Labor of Faculty of Color at the Urban Community College
Jesse Priest	136	Rhetoric and Emotion Save Science: Lessons from Student Eco-Activists
Natalie Davey	157	The Good Enough Teacher

Book Reviews

Irene Papoulis	173	Varieties of Solace
Nate Mickelson	174	Bradley, Burt. *After Following: Poems*
Paul Puccio	177	Khost, Peter H. *Rhetor Response: A Theory and Practice of Literary Affordance*
Erin Frymire	181	Restaino, Jessica. *Surrender: Feminist Rhetoric and Ethics in Love and Illness*
Tracy Lassiter	184	Mailhot, Terese Marie. *Heart Berries: A Memoir*

Connecting

Christy I. Wenger	187	On "Showing Up" in Teaching, Tutoring, and Writing: A Search for Humanity
Nicole Wilson, Angela Montez, and Sara Yiseul Chung	189	Sylvia Wynter Over Tea
Christina M. LaVecchia and Cristina D. Ramírez	195	The Versatility of a Rhetoric and Composition Degree: Tales from Former Postdocs Outside the Field
Patricia Pytleski	201	Writing Center Reflections: The Impact of Tutor to Tutor Teaching
	205	**Contributors to *JAEPL*, Vol. 25**
	209	**Announcement**

The Inventive Work of the Christian Mind

Jeff Ringer

Abstract: *Responding to Bizzell's 2008 JAEPL article, this article argues that the intellectual work of religious minds involves inventing arguments grounded in the religious community's ethos that advocate for new perspectives within that community. Using Katharine Hayhoe's evangelical Christian environmentalist rhetoric as an example, this article prompts rhetorical educators to rethink approaches to teaching ethos.*

> *What if there is intellectual work to be done that can only be done by what [Shannon] Carter calls the "Christian mind"—or Jewish, Muslim, or Buddhist mind?*
>
> —Patricia Bizzell, "Faith-Based World Views as a Challenge to the Believing Game"

The epigraph comes from Patricia Bizzell's contribution to the 2008/2009 special issue of *JAEPL* about Peter Elbow's believing game. In her essay, Bizzell praises the intellectual work that Elbow's believing game can accomplish while raising a key question: What happens when the believing game encounters sincere religious faith? For Bizzell, religious faith presents the believing game with its "greatest test" (30), because faith represents more than "a skeptical thought experiment in which consequences are deduced from premises" (32). Faith demands that rhetoric come to terms with emotion, which, citing Lynn Worsham, Bizzell defines as a "tight braid of affect and judgment that is socially and historically constructed and bodily lived" (qtd. in Bizzell 31). Bizzell argues that inventional strategies like Elbow's believing game cannot access religious faith's tight braids of affect and judgment, because doing so requires immersion within "a powerful web that seeks to impact every aspect of one's life" and thus exceeds the bounds of a skeptic's game (32). To demonstrate the difficulty of accessing those features of religious faith, Bizzell discusses the work of Shannon Carter and Sharon Crowley, each of whom explores the intersections of faith and invention. Carter is interested in helping evangelical Christian students engage with academic discourse; Crowley is interested in helping secular rhetors convince fundamentalist Christian citizens to change their apocalyptic ways. Neither, according to Bizzell, is able to access fully the web of affect and judgment that marks the faith of committed evangelical Christians. They can view such faith as outsiders, but they cannot inhabit it.

It is this line of thinking that leads Bizzell to frame the question I included as the epigraph. This question is provocative for a number of reasons, not the least of which is the possibility that religious minds—minds, as I'll discuss below, that are shaped by immersion within their religious communities—have access to rhetorical material bound up in tight braids of affect and judgment that other minds might not be able to access, or at least not access in the same way. As such, her question prompts rhetoricians to rethink existing assumptions about invention. While rhetorical education generally forwards invention as outward-looking—students analyze audience, purpose, *kairos*,

1

and other components of situations or ecologies—Bizzell's question suggests that students might look into their own braids of affect and judgment, which are shaped by embodied experiences within the communities to which they belong. That notion of belongingness brings us to a conception of ethos often ignored in rhetorical education. While ethos is generally taught in terms of whether the rhetor *seems* to be knowledgeable or credible, it can also be understood as the "dwelling places" or communities rhetors inhabit (Hyde; Perkins). Rhetors' minds are formed by these communities and the relations that comprise them.

Bizzell's question, though, also implies that religious minds remain relatively untapped in terms of the intellectual work they might be positioned to do, and so my purpose in this essay is to tease out an answer to her question. There is intellectual work that can best be done by religious minds, and it involves inventing arguments grounded in the religious community's belief system that advocate for new perspectives within that community. I make this argument by first exploring the possibilities for invention that religious minds can leverage and then discussing rhetorical theory about invention and ethos as located (Hyde; Jarratt and Reynolds; LeFevre; Simonson). To demonstrate the inventive work of one Christian mind, I investigate the rhetorical action of Katharine Hayhoe, a climate scientist who speaks from her evangelical Christian ethos to likeminded audiences about the dangers of climate change. Specifically, I explore how Hayhoe's ethos offers inventive possibilities for persuading evangelical Christian audiences to take climate change seriously. Hayhoe's example underscores the importance of thinking through the implications of Bizzell's question for contemporary public discourse. Climate change is one of the greatest dangers to society, and yet large segments of the population, including many evangelical Christians, view it as little more than fake news. Public rhetoric made by an evangelical Christian climate scientist aimed at persuading an evangelical Christian audience to take climate change seriously thus offers an ideal test case to explore Bizzell's question.

To benefit fully from Hayhoe's example, rhetorical studies must rethink current approaches to rhetorical education, and so I close by arguing that rhetorical educators should invite students to look inward and consider how immersion within their own dwelling places might open up paths of invention unavailable to other rhetors (Perkins 75). This argument extends work I began in *Vernacular Christian Rhetoric and Civil Discourse*, where I considered the possibility that evangelical Christian students might be able to argue from their positionality about issues of public concern in ways that foster deliberative discourse (Ringer 83-113). Such students need to be taught how to do so, though, and rhetorical education generally has held religion at arm's length, especially evangelical Christianity. Religion, the thinking goes, might serve as a worthy object of inquiry, but certainly not as a source of public argument that can serve democratic ends. However, recent scholars like Mike DePalma and Chris Earle, among others, have argued that rhetorical education should view students' religious identities as powerful resources for inventing and delivering public arguments. Realizing that potential means teaching for it, though, and in the present case it means helping students know how their own dwelling places might offer inventive means for arguing deliberatively within the communities to which they belong. While it certainly is concerning that contemporary public discourse is marked by in-group thinking (Daniell 86), rhetorical educators must perceive such realities as constraints that can be leveraged for deliberative ends. In the early twenty-first century, that is one form of intellectual work religious minds are best positioned to do—leverage the constraints of in-group thinking to invent and argue deliberatively for new perspectives.

Christian Minds, with a Difference

Understanding this intellectual work necessitates defining "religious" or "Christian" minds. On the one hand, doing so is impossible. While Christian minds certainly would hold beliefs derived from Christian faith (Medhurst "Filled"; "Religious"), there is no single conception of Christianity, and so there is no one way to define *the* Christian mind. I am not, however, attempting to make any definitive claim about what constitutes Christianity. Rather, I use the term "Christian mind" synecdochally to name individuals who have been formed by Christian communities. Religious minds are embodied and have inhabited the socio-cultural contexts, material spaces, belief systems, and braids of affect and judgment that align with a specific religious tradition and practice. This approach is consistent with Carter, who defines her use of "Christian mind" by drawing on William G. Pollard's *Physicist and Christian: A Dialogue Between Communities*. Community is the key term. Pollard notes that "all knowledge is really imparted through community, and cannot be had in isolation or alienation from the community within which a particular segment of knowledge is known" (qtd. in Carter 583-84). Carter sees Pollard's thinking as consonant with rhetorical education and explores how Christian communities are organized around shared faiths and orthodoxies that can be known but must also be applied or lived (584-85). To illustrate this difference, Carter references the words of a case study participant who distinguishes between merely going to church and being a "churchly child" (585). Community belonging constitutes the difference. Religiously committed individuals do not simply go through the motions or assent to "consequences [...] deduced from premises" (Bizzell 32). They are immersed within communities of faith in ways that shape their entire being.

This definition of religious minds—those embodied minds that are shaped by the religious communities in which they have been immersed—is consonant with Bizzell's understanding of religion, emotion, and identity. Bizzell, however, is not alone in raising the possibility that immersion within religious communities might position rhetors to do certain kinds of intellectual work. C. Jan Swearingen writes that "[s]ome of the workings of rhetoric within religion really should be explained and analyzed by the believer," because skepticism offers its own constraints that might limit what such academics can perceive (137). Similarly, Thomas Lessl argues that insiders to religious discourse "bring to [public] debate a greater depth of understanding regarding how religious minds come to grips with civic concerns" (195-6). He writes that religiously-committed rhetoricians possess a "peculiar advantage when it comes to understanding such intersections of the sacred and the secular," because they participate meaningfully within a faith tradition and community (196). Lessl likens nonreligious rhetoricians investigating religious discourse to "ethnographers who have ventured onto some remote Pacific island without being able to speak the language of the tribe they wish to study" (196). Writing about evangelical Christianity in particular, Mark Allan Steiner argues that evangelicals are "uniquely positioned" to promote civil discourse because they have at their disposal a range of values, including humility, that could inform deliberative rhetoric (291, 310-11). Swearingen, Lessl, and Steiner thus agree with Bizzell that some intellectual work might best be performed by religious—even evangelical Christian—minds.

At the end of *Toward a Civil Discourse*, though, Crowley offers a different take as to who can perform the intellectual work she calls for. Crowley invents arguments grounded in biblical values (e.g., "loving one's neighbor") that she hopes will persuade fundamentalist Christians to change their apocalyptic ways. She envisions secular, liberal academics as conducting such invention, because, in Crowley's estimation, they comprise the group of rhetors who would want to disarticulate fundamentalist Christians' destructive views. As Bizzell suggests, though, Crowley is ultimately frustrated by her task, a frustration that emerges from the binary she employs to define the two groups (DePalma, Ringer, and Webber). In Beth Daniell's words, "Crowley seems unable to use [her theorizing] to reach her stated goal of opening up space for civil exchange" (86). *Toward a Civil Discourse* is largely regarded as a tour de force of rhetorical invention, and so the fact that she admits defeat by the end should be concerning for rhetorical educators. If Crowley cannot open paths of invention through the religiously-inflected deliberative impasse that marks public discourse in the early twenty-first century, who can? Elsewhere, I have argued that evangelical Christian student writers are well-suited to do such work (Ringer 1). I make that case by theorizing vernacular religious creativity, the idea that religious believers adapt their faiths in relation to their pluralistic contexts. The upshot of vernacular religious creativity is that even devout evangelical Christians espouse perspectives that depart from what society assumes evangelical Christians believe, and that those differences can inform deliberative ends.

In one case study, I argue that "Kimberly" had the potential to argue from her ethos to convince other evangelical Christians of the importance of the HPV vaccine, which is controversial in evangelical communities. HPV is a sexually-transmitted disease, but because the vaccine is best administered to girls around age eleven, some evangelicals interpret its use as license for premarital sex. Kimberly, however, embraced a nuanced position. She was personally committed to abstinence but also believed in the importance of the HPV vaccine because she knew many girls who were sexually active. Writing for her FYW course, Kimberly argued that parents should vaccinate their daughters against HPV, though she does so without positioning herself as an evangelical Christian committed to abstinence. I argue that if she had positioned herself as an insider to evangelical Christianity due to her personal stance on abstinence, she might have gained a hearing for her argument with a family-values audience. She might then have been able to "enact deliberative discourse within [her] own enclaves" by arguing for a perspective not commonly shared within the evangelical Christian community (Ringer 110). Kimberly, however, did not fulfill that potential. She was not taught how to do so and feared that writing from a faith-based perspective at a public university would get her in trouble.

My sense when writing Kimberly's case study was that who she was as a rhetor—an evangelical Christian who supports the HPV vaccine—opened up lines of argument that would be unavailable to rhetors who do not share her faith and positionality. She struck me as the opposite of Lessl's ethnographer: fluent in the language and values of her faith-based community—and recognized as such—she had the potential to argue deliberatively for an uncommon perspective within her faith communities. But because Kimberly's case study reveals a missed opportunity, I could not make any claim about how her rhetorical action might reveal the inventive work of the Christian mind. Questions thus remain. What might such inventive work look like in actuality, particularly when it entails arguing deliberatively within a likeminded community? While Kimberly's case study underscores the possibility that invention might be tied to the rhetor's identity, what relationships exist, if any, between ethos and invention? Before offering an example that illustrates the inventive work of the Christian mind, I take up this theoretical question.

Ethos—and Invention—as Located

In his introduction to *Ethos: New Essays in Rhetorical and Critical Theory*, James Baumlin explores two schools of thought concerning ethos. The Aristotelian view emphasizes the constructed nature of ethos as a product of language and not a reflection of the rhetor's standing in society. Common in composition textbooks, this is the version of ethos which Priscilla Perkins likens to method acting (75). By contrast, the Isocratean view emphasizes the character of the rhetor as it exists prior to rhetorical action, a view that would later inform Quintilian's famous dictum of a good person speaking well (Baumlin *xiv-xv*). This second notion of ethos reflects its shared etymological root with our terms for habitus and inhabit, which is why ethos can also be defined in terms of rhetors' dwelling places (Hyde). Baumlin suggests that the complexity inherent in the two notions of ethos demands that rhetoricians ask questions about where ethos is located. Does it precede rhetorical action, or does it emerge from the rhetorical action itself?

One contribution to Baumlin's collection that explores ethos's location is Susan Jarratt and Nedra Reynolds's "The Splitting Image: Contemporary Feminisms and the Ethics of *êthos*." Responding to feminist criticisms that poststructural conceptions of the self can reify "traditional notions of the subject" (39), Jarratt and Reynolds theorize a feminist conception of ethos that values the positionality of the rhetor. They do so by responding to George Yoos's argument about ethical appeals wherein he reaffirms the "gap between the speaker and his words" that Plato advanced in *Phaedrus* (Jarratt and Reynolds 41; Baumlin *xi-xii*). Jarratt and Reynolds take issue with Yoos's appeal to "a stable, moral Self" and seek to understand ethos in ways that emphasize "the speaker having been created at a particular site within the contingencies of history and geography" (47). Emphasizing such positionality underscores "a constant awareness that one always speaks from a particular place in a social structure" (47). While Jarratt and Reynolds do not completely collapse the gap defined by Yoos, they underscore how rhetors can and should speak from their particular positionalities. Citing Fredric Jameson's standpoint theory, Jarratt and Reynolds define the difference from which rhetors speak as the "capacity for … seeing features and dimensions of the world and of history masked to other social actors" (qtd. in Jarratt and Reynolds 52). While Jarratt and Reynolds view ethos as partially constructed in discourse, they also define it as a product of the situated, embodied knower, which resonates with Worsham's conception of emotion as "socially and historically constructed and bodily lived" (qtd. in Bizzell 31). Speaking from within one's ethos or dwelling place in a likeminded community offers a degree of authority and credibility that might be unavailable to other rhetors. As Jarratt and Reynolds put it, rhetors can "speak artfully to those around them" (57).

But how does invention relate to this notion of ethos? The answer might lie in the fact that both are located. In "In[ter]vention: Locating Rhetoric's *Ethos*," Judy Holiday writes that "location underwrites all rhetorical situations, shaping and circumscribing knowledge, perception, and invention" (389). Location can be understood as material as well as social, and invention, as rhetors have long maintained, is inherently social (Lauer; LeFevre; Zulick). In *Invention as a Social Act*, Karen Burke LeFevre links invention to both notions of location. Regarding social location, LeFevre states that "the inventing writer [is] part of a community, a socioculture, a sphere of overlapping (and sometimes conflicting) collectives" (93). But LeFevre also emplaces invention within material locations, noting that "writers invent not only in the study but also in the smoke-filled chamber" (93). Rhetors are thus positioned within social and material locations, and that positionality occasions and constrains invention. In that sense invention can be understood as arising from embodied immersion within the material settings, social contexts, and discourse communities to which rhetors belong (LeFevre 93). Invention, like ethos, is located.

More recently, Peter Simonson has defined a number of interrelated media that comprise invention, including bodies, minds, experience, place, time, physical and geographic space, the social, and the cultural. Simonson defines the social as composed of "interactions, relationships, roles, social identities (e.g., race, class, gender, sexuality), small groups, publics, formal organizations, movements, communities, and institutions (e.g., educational, political, legal, religious)" (314). His acknowledgment of religion as part of the social component of invention is important as is his emphasis on culture. The cultural media of invention include "cultures and subcultures" as well as "meanings, values, ideologies, common opinion (*doxa*), rituals, genres, traditions, formalized practices, and conceptual schemes" (Simonson 314-15). Simonson's emphasis on ideology as pertinent to invention is significant in consideration of the inventive work of religious minds. But so, too, is his use of terms associated with ethos, namely "habits," which are formed by rhetors' experiences; "habitus," which is composed in large part by individuals' interactions within social contexts; and "habitats," which follow from social relationships and help to generate "words, ideas, countervailing arguments, emotions, and bodily expressions" (314, 317). Connecting several of Simonson's media allows us to define invention as the product of embodied minds situated in particular contexts that have become habitualized into ways of thinking, knowing, and doing as a result of immersion within those contexts.

What connects these conceptions of invention and ethos to the intellectual work of evangelical Christian minds is the concept that evangelical Christianity functions as a subculture (Cope and Ringer), which Simonson links to the cultural medium of invention. Evangelical Christian minds can be defined as products of evangelical subcultures and extensive experience within evangelical socio-cultural contexts. Additionally, evangelical Christian minds form ideologies or belief systems particular to those communities and the experiences and commitments that such communities privilege. Those ideologies feature certain ideologics, which Crowley defines as "connections that can be forged among beliefs within a given ideology" (75). Over time, ideologics gather into belief systems that can be woven more or less tightly (75). While Crowley does not speak favorably of densely articulated belief systems—the "more densely" they are articulated, the "more impervious they are to rhetorical intervention" (78)—she also acknowledges that "rhetorical power can be activated by people who are equipped to articulate available openings in discourse" (52). By "articulate," she means forming arguments and making connections between and among beliefs, which can serve as premises for arguments (Crowley 52, 75).

If it is true that evangelical Christian belief systems are densely articulated, then it is possible that someone who shares that belief system might be specially "equipped to articulate available openings in discourse" in arguments for a likeminded audience. An argument grounded in the particular ideologics that comprise evangelical Christian ideologies made by someone who inhabits that ethos would resonate within those densely articulated belief systems (Crowley 78-79). Certainly, a rhetor who does not inhabit an evangelical Christian ethos would be able to invent arguments drawing on similar premises. But given how densely articulated evangelical Christian ideologies tend to be, the particular ideologics would be difficult to name, identify, leverage, or channel without having formed the tight braid of affect and judgment that comes from belonging to that community. Even a non-believer who embeds herself within an evangelical Christian social context to conduct ethnographic research would lack the habitus—the "dynamic being-in-the-world" (Simonson 313)—that allows rhetors to speak authoritatively within likeminded communities. Who the rhetor is—the dwelling places she inhabits—matters for invention.

One further point about Crowley's notion of densely articulated belief systems: while the density of such belief systems suggests that they are difficult to change, it is not impossible to do so (Crowley 79). Crowley argues that "beliefs encompassed within densely articulated ideologics resonate more sympathetically, and with more intensity, than do beliefs operative within ideologics that are less tightly woven" (79). If, as is the case with evangelical Christianity, those ideologics are woven tightly into a belief system that "explains everything," then rearticulating any belief within that system represents a tall order (Crowley 79). Crowley explains: "Once one becomes a member of a desired community, the community itself offers little internal impetus for change" (195). Part of the reason why is that the rhetoric generally featured within a community is more likely to be epideictic, which praises community values, rather than deliberative, which might call those values into question (195-96). The only hope Crowley identifies for changing densely articulated beliefs is to change the context itself. However, what if an insider espoused a perspective that differs from what is commonly accepted within that community? What if such a rhetor were to reflect the community's values epideictically while also arguing deliberatively for a new perspective? This is the possibility I perceived with Kimberly, an insider who shared much of the densely articulated belief system of her faith community but who espoused a novel perspective that could be argued for from the vantage of a shared ethos. Rhetors with similar positionalities might be able to rearticulate beliefs in ways that resonate with the belief system without threatening to upend it.

The Inventive Work of Hayhoe's Christian Mind

I suggest that one such rhetor is Katharine Hayhoe, a climate change scientist and professor at Texas Tech who is also an evangelical Christian. To explore the inventive work of Hayhoe's Christian mind, I discuss representative anecdotes that feature Hayhoe, including the first episode of Showtime's documentary *Years of Living Dangerously*; a YouTube video produced and posted by Nova Science Now; and a book called *A Climate for Change: Global Warming Facts for Faith-Based Decisions* that Hayhoe co-wrote with her husband, evangelical pastor Andrew Farley. I highlight anecdotes that reveal Hayhoe's immersion within evangelical Christianity and analyze arguments about climate change she invents from her ethos as an evangelical Christian.

Viewers gain a sense of Hayhoe's Christian mind in the first episode of Showtime's documentary, *Years of Living Dangerously*, which investigates climate change as a global phenomenon with localized effects. Actor Don Cheadle, who co-hosts the episode, explores the conflict between science and faith. He travels to Plainview, Texas, a rural community dealing with the economic effects of climate change. Cheadle introduces viewers to Hayhoe, who lives in nearby Lubbock, and talks with Hayhoe about her research. As Cheadle returns to Plainview, viewers hear him say, "As I leave town, I wonder how people in Plainview would react to what she just told me." They also see a warehouse in the distance with the words "Jesus is Lord over Plainview" painted on the side, which announces a belief articulation prevalent in the community. Cheadle asks, "Would they see a conflict between her science and their faith?" The episode cuts to a scene of a lively worship service in what appears to be an evangelical church. A praise band plays on stage, while scores of worshippers sing along with lifted hands. The next scene shows Hayhoe and her husband sitting at their table, heads bowed in prayer. Cheadle continues: "But Katharine doesn't see a conflict." Viewers then hear Farley praying, "Father, thank you for this morning…." Cheadle concludes: "She's a devout Christian herself."

Viewers gain a deeper sense of Hayhoe's Christian mind when next they see her in the episode. Hayhoe states,

> Many people view science and faith as deeply divided. But for me growing up with a dad who was a scientist who was also a missionary and who was very active in the church, I grew up with the understanding that there was no conflict. By studying science, we're studying what God was thinking when he created the universe.

Hayhoe's narration provides viewers with a sense of her immersion within evangelical Christianity: she grew up in a Christian home, is the daughter of a missionary and active church member, and believes that God created the universe. Such beliefs and experiences are common within evangelical Christianity. Even if most evangelical Christians are not children of missionaries, they likely know missionaries and "missionary kids." While the belief system from which Hayhoe speaks reflects evangelical Christianity, Hayhoe links to this belief articulation the view that science and faith are complementary. Hayhoe forges this ideologic by framing her belief in terms of a common evangelical Christian view of creation, namely that the universe is a product of God's creation:

"By studying science," she says, "we're studying what God was thinking when he created the universe." While Hayhoe's Christian mind is distinctly evangelical, science is welcome within it. It is this difference that constitutes a line of argumentative force for Hayhoe's evangelical public rhetoric.

Perhaps the fullest statement about Hayhoe's Christian mind appears in the preface to *A Climate for Change*, which she co-wrote with Farley:

> Bike to work. Hug a tree. Eat granola. Live off the grid. Wear hemp. Bathe in a stream. And worship the earth.
>
> We often find ourselves labeled—just because we think global warming is a serious problem people should know about.
>
> But here's who we really are.
>
> We're Christians. We don't worship the earth. We worship the Creator of the Universe. We believe that God spoke the world into existence and sustains it by His power. We believe that Jesus Christ is the way to eternal life, that the Bible is God's Word, and that nothing compares to the importance of the gospel message.
>
> Now for what we *don't* believe. We don't believe the universe came into existence through random chance. We don't believe that life came from nothing or that humans evolved from apes.
>
> We don't believe in government running our lives or in destroying the economy to save the earth. We believe in common sense. We believe in the sensible progression from older to newer technologies. (xi)

Here we see one of the clearest iterations of Hayhoe's positionality as an evangelical Christian who speaks through the densely articulated belief system she shares with many others in the evangelical Christian community. She is not just a climate scientist attempting to persuade evangelical Christians of the dangers of climate change. She is an evangelical Christian herself, someone who is able to speak directly from her ethos ("we") about her faith in ways that reflect evangelical Christianity. Like Hayhoe's statement about science and faith, this preface reflects ideologics consistent with evangelical Christianity. Those ideologics exist among religious beliefs (e.g., God created the universe, the Bible is the Word of God) and between religious beliefs and politically conservative perspectives (e.g., government should not interfere in citizens' lives). Such ideologics comprise the densely articulated belief system held by many evangelicals, and it is through that belief system that Hayhoe and Farley invent the argument they forward in their preface.

That argument basically asks for a rearticulation of beliefs. Hayhoe and Farley want their audience of evangelical Christians to accommodate the idea that climate change is a problem and should be taken seriously. They make that argument not only by drawing on evangelical Christian premises, but also by accessing the tight braid of affect and judgment consonant with evangelical Christianity. The proliferation of short sentences—"We worship the Creator of the Universe. We believe that God spoke the world into existence and sustains it by His power. We believe that Jesus Christ is the way to eternal life"—aims to evoke in readers a shared sense of commitment. Hayhoe and Farley know who they are as evangelical Christians, and they foreground their affective connection to that tradition's belief system in the preface. In doing so, the passage takes on the feel of a creed, a statement of beliefs that for many Christians elicits a sense of devotion and belonging. The passage also prompts evangelical Christians to formulate what Gerard A. Hauser calls "practical syllogisms," enthymematic statements that elicit emotional responses (*Introduction* 169, 174-75). Because practical syllogisms provide a referent that prompts audiences to think, "I am the kind of person who believes x, therefore I should do y," Hayhoe and Farley tap into the tight braid of affect and judgment that comes from being an evangelical Christian. Reading this preface, an evangelical Christian audience might form the following practical syllogism:

- *Personal major premise*: I am an evangelical Christian, the kind of person who believes that God created the universe and that Jesus Christ is the way to eternal life.
- *Minor premise*: Hayhoe and Farley are evangelical Christians who believe that God created the universe and that Jesus Christ is the way to eternal life, but they also believe that climate change is a danger that should be taken seriously.
- *Conclusion*: Therefore, as an evangelical Christian, I should view climate change as a danger that should be taken seriously.

Certainly, this conclusion represents a partial realignment of the audience's values, but that's the point—Hayhoe and Farley want their audience to rearticulate their beliefs. They are not asking for a full restructuring, though. By arguing from a shared ethos, they hope that their audience feels comfortable hearing a perspective they might otherwise deem as alien. They also hope that their argument resonates with the audience's belief system, much of which Hayhoe and Farley share.

That rhetorical strategy emerges frequently throughout their book. Hayhoe and Farley ground their argument that evangelical Christians should be better stewards of the planet within the densely articulated belief system they share with their audience. In the introduction, for instance, they acknowledge that "As Christians, we're naturally suspicious of people who believe differently from us" (xv). They then note two evangelical Christian organizations that call for action on climate change. The first comes from the Evangelical Climate Initiative, "which state[s] that our moral convictions as evangelicals demand a response to the climate change problem" (xvi). Hayhoe and Farley write that a wide range of churches, denominations, and other organizations endorsed the initiative. The second call comes from the Southern Baptist Convention, a conservative evangelical Christian denomination. That call "declared that we as Christians should take responsibility for our contributions to environmental issues" (xvi). Toward the end of the book, Hayhoe and Farley ask for a "faith-based response": "Love God, love others, and remember the poor: this was the unwavering mandate of the early church more than two thousand years ago. And this is our solidly biblical motivation for caring about climate change today" (127). Through arguments grounded in their ethos as evangelical Christians, Hayhoe and Farley propose a rearticulation of beliefs wherein care for the planet can be linked to evangelical Christianity.

Other anecdotes reveal Hayhoe as an embodied, emplaced rhetor inventing arguments from within her ethos as an evangelical Christian. Hayhoe's narration in a YouTube video called "Secret: Climate Change Evangelist" begins with the following anecdote:

> One of the first times that we went to church in Texas, I met a couple and we were introducing ourselves. They asked, "What do you do?" I explained that I studied global warming. And they said, "Oh, that's wonderful! We need somebody like you to tell our children the right things. You would not believe the lies that they're being taught in school! They told us that the ice in the arctic is melting and it's threatening the polar bears." And I said, "Well, I'm afraid that that's true!" (Nova Science Now)

Viewers see Hayhoe initially claim authority as a churchgoer. "One of the first times we went to church" suggests that attending church is habitual, and Hayhoe alludes to a level of comfort by interacting casually with fellow churchgoers. Hayhoe's embodied presence within that sacred space offers an important opening for invention (Simonson 314). The physical space invites pleasantries between churchgoers who do not know each other, and Hayhoe's embodied presence announces that she inhabits or is interested in inhabiting the same dwelling place as regular attendees. By virtue of the fact that she is attending church, the couple reads Hayhoe as someone who shares their beliefs. And in many ways, she does, albeit with a difference: Hayhoe views climate change as a problem that evangelical Christians should take seriously. When the couple makes a statement to the effect that global warming is a hoax, Hayhoe sees the rhetorical opening and takes it (Crowley 52). She challenges the assumption that climate change is fake and invites a subtle but significant rearticulation of beliefs: evangelical Christians who attend church can and should view climate change as real. Hayhoe is able to do this rhetorical work because she is "equipped" to do so (Crowley 52). An evangelical Christian attending church interacting casually with other churchgoers, Hayhoe's embodied, emplaced positionality invites pleasantries from other churchgoers, which affords her Christian mind the opportunity to invent an argument that calls for a rearticulation of her interlocutor's belief system.

Still other anecdotes demonstrate the extent to which Hayhoe invents arguments from within the complex and "powerful web" of beliefs she inhabits as an evangelical Christian (Bizzell 32). Towards the end of the YouTube video, Hayhoe states the following:

> With climate change, much of our response to this issue is emotional. The fear of how our lives would be irrevocably changed if we uprooted our entire economy, and how our rights to enjoy the luxuries of energy and water might be ripped away from us.
>
> Well, as a Christian, we are told that God is not the author of fear. God is love. When we're acting out of fear, we're thinking about ourselves. When we act about love, we are not thinking about ourselves, we are thinking about others. Our global neighbors. The poor and the disadvantaged. The people who do not have the resources to adapt. And so I believe that we are called first of all to love each other, and second of all, to act. (Nova Science Now)

Within the space of a thirty second clip, Hayhoe weaves together a range of beliefs that function as powerful assumptions within evangelical Christian tradition. These assumptions include the beliefs that "God is not the author of fear," that "God is love," that

Christians are "called [...] to love each other," and that loving one's neighbors means caring for our "global neighbors."

Hayhoe's inventive work reflects the densely articulated evangelical Christian belief system she inhabits, and one way to reveal those articulations is by naming her biblical allusions:

- Mark 12:31-32: "'Love the Lord your God with all your heart and with all your soul and with all your mind and with all your strength.' The second is this: 'Love your neighbor as yourself.' No other commandment is greater than these."
- Luke 6:20: "Looking up at His disciples, Jesus said: 'Blessed are you who are poor, for yours is the kingdom of God.'"
- 1 Corinthians 14:33 (NKJV): "For God is not the author of confusion but of peace, as in all the churches of the saints."
- 2 Timothy 1:7: "For the Spirit God gave us does not make us timid, but gives us power, love and self-discipline."
- 1 John 3:1: "For this is the message you heard from the beginning: We should love one another."
- 1 John 4:8: "There is no fear in love. But perfect love drives out fear, because fear has to do with punishment."
- 1 John 4:16b: "God is love; whoever abides in love abides in God, and God in him."

Hayhoe's allusions to these passages would be familiar to an evangelical Christian audience and would resonate with an evangelical audience's belief systems (Cope and Ringer 119-20; Crowley 78-79). What's most striking, though, is the manner in which Hayhoe weaves together a wide range of beliefs in a brief argument about why climate change should matter to an evangelical Christian audience. Hayhoe demonstrates in this passage the extent to which her faith reflects the densely articulated evangelical Christian belief system, with the difference that climate change exists and should be taken seriously.

Notably, Hayhoe begins her argument by invoking a sentiment that would elicit an emotional response from an evangelical Christian audience. When Hayhoe states that "God is not the author of fear" but of "love," she connects her argument directly to the tight braid of affect and judgment shared by evangelical Christians who likely have had the experience of fearing a negative outcome but then finding comfort in God's promises. Worth noting here is the fact that by beginning with the personal premise—"When *we're* acting out of fear"—Hayhoe taps into the evangelical Christian belief that what matters most is personal salvation. Hayhoe later shifts from personal salvation to social concerns by listing the "others" who are affected by selfish thinking: "[o]ur global neighbors," the "poor and the disadvantaged," and so on. But beginning with her audience's personal sense of fear, comfort, and connection to the divine is a move that would resonate with an evangelical Christian audience. Finally, Hayhoe indirectly communicates an emotional subtext, one that again would be unavailable to a rhetor who has not inhabited an evangelical Christian ethos. The subtext of Hayhoe's message is that she understands the experiences of evangelical Christians because she has had similar experiences. As an evangelical Christian, she knows what it means to "act out of fear," and she knows what it means "to love each other" and "to act." Hayhoe's Christian mind allows her to invent arguments that resonate with her audience's densely articulated belief system.

Again, a rhetor who does not inhabit an evangelical Christian ethos would be able to invent arguments that draw on similar premises. Crowley, in fact, identifies love as a value that can be used in arguments supporting progressive agendas, and love is clearly featured among the biblical passages listed above (201). However, Crowley also acknowledges that the arguments most likely to resonate within densely articulated belief systems are those that already participate within that belief system. Because Hayhoe has inhabited evangelical Christian communities and thus formed the tight braids of affect and judgment consistent with that tradition, she can invent arguments and articulate openings that resonate within the belief system shared by many evangelical Christians. Hayhoe can draw on the full imaginative and emotional resources of evangelical Christianity in order to invent arguments about the consequences of climate change. Crowley viewed the densely articulated belief systems of evangelical and fundamentalist Christians as impediments to be overcome, but the inventive work of Hayhoe's evangelical Christian mind leverages those ideologics for deliberative ends.

One scene from *Years of Living Dangerously* illustrates the persuasive potential of Hayhoe's inventive work. Don Cheadle introduces viewers to Kevin Carter, a resident of Plainview, who is on his way to hear Hayhoe speak at a public forum. Carter tells Cheadle the following:

> You'd have to be a little bit crazy not to at least wanna know a little bit more about [what she has to say]. I mean, she certainly to me is somebody is more credible than somebody like Al Gore, if we're gonna pick on Al Gore, but she has, ah, the same beliefs as I do, as far as from a Christian, you know, base deal.

Carter knows Hayhoe shares his evangelical Christian faith, and her situated ethos predisposes him to listen to what Hayhoe has to say. Using Baumlin's terms, we might describe such ethos at work here as that which preexists rhetorical action (xvi). At the same time, Hayhoe's message demonstrates the inventive work of her Christian mind, as she again invents arguments from within the ethos she shares with her audience. Hayhoe tells an audience of Plainview residents the following:

> What's happening is we have this natural greenhouse effect here with this natural atmosphere, and we are adding an extra layer to it that was never intended to be there. When I look at the information that we get from the planet, I look at it as God's creation speaking to us. And in this case, there's no question that God's creation is telling us that it is running a fever.

Hayhoe describes earth as "God's creation" that is speaking back to "us," which includes Hayhoe and her audience, many of whom, like Carter, espouse some form of Christian faith. In doing so, Hayhoe links to the densely articulated evangelical Christian belief system the idea that care for the planet matters.

That act of articulation appears to work, at least for Carter. After Hayhoe's talk, Carter says the following: "You know, when you have somebody that believes the same way as you, and is from this part of the—or has lived here for quite awhile and is teaching at Texas Tech—you know, you see that conservative side of that, telling you the message, it sure makes a lot of difference." Certainly, what Carter references as persuasive is Hayhoe's situated ethos. But Carter also suggests that Hayhoe's "message" resonates with him. While it is not clear what Carter means by the "conservative side," it is possible he's referring to Hayhoe's inventive work of articulating arguments about climate change to the densely articulated evangelical Christian belief system he shares. If Carter is persuaded, it possibly results from who Hayhoe is—her "dynamic being-in-the-world" (Simonson 313)—as well as what and how she argues. What is ultimately noteworthy is the fact that Hayhoe's argument, grounded in her ethos as an evangelical Christian, resonates with Carter. Crowley theorized that densely articulated belief systems would be impervious to change, and that if they did change, then they might unravel. Neither seems to be the case for Carter. Granted, all we have is Carter's brief response to Hayhoe's talk, but the initial returns suggest that Hayhoe was able to rearticulate Carter's belief system in subtle but significant ways without undermining his identity as an evangelical Christian.

Hayhoe thus demonstrates the intellectual work that can best be accomplished by the evangelical Christian mind: inventing arguments from within one's ethos or dwelling place in ways that resonate with the densely articulated belief systems of other evangelical Christians. While arguments derived from such inventive work do reaffirm existing beliefs, they also ask for a reconsideration of others—in this case, the importance of care for the planet. And the context in which such inventive work takes place is that of ethos-as-dwelling place, the fact that, in this case, Carter and Hayhoe share a common faith and are located in the same geographic region. As such, Hayhoe is able to do what Crowley found elusive, namely open "paths of invention" for addressing the public divide between conservative religious and secular perspectives (201). Because Hayhoe is immersed within the densely articulated belief system of evangelical Christianity, she can speak from within its imaginative and emotional resources in ways that resonate with audiences that traditionally have rejected climate change.

Implications for Rhetorical Education

What implications does the inventive work of Hayhoe's evangelical Christian mind have for rhetorical education? Hayhoe's example prompts rhetorical educators to revisit core assumptions about rhetorical education. In recent decades, the purpose of rhetorical education has been to help students communicate effectively across difference (Carter; DePalma; Earle). That goal is a noble one, and I am not suggesting that rhetorical education abandon it. But Bizzell's question and Hayhoe's example prompt us to emphasize an aspect of rhetorical education that often goes overlooked, namely that of helping students argue from their own dwelling places to deliberate with likeminded audiences. Doing so would involve asking students to understand a different conception of ethos than that which rhetorical educators generally teach. Instead of promoting ethos as a form of method acting wherein students attempt to seem credible and authoritative about a topic they know little about, rhetorical educators can help students understand ethos in terms of the dwelling places they inhabit. Students developing arguments from within their dwelling places might be well-positioned to produce more compelling writing than they might otherwise produce. More importantly, they would be well-positioned to work productively within the contemporary constraints of in-group thinking that mark public discourse. Mike DePalma has argued that "rhetorical education must be adapted to address the exigencies of particular cultural and historical moments" (252-53). Given that our current historical moment is marked by in-group thinking that is deeply suspicious of perceived outsiders, it makes sense to equip students to recognize this constraint and leverage it for deliberative ends.

Rhetorical educators can achieve this goal by first introducing students to the two primary conceptions of ethos that Baumlin discusses. This theoretical instruction could focus on the difference between arguing to create an ethos versus arguing from within one's ethos. Using an example like Katharine Hayhoe, instructors could show how rhetors who make arguments for likeminded audiences invent from within their dwelling places. Instructors could also show how a rhetor like Hayhoe serves as an example of someone who espouses the views of a community, but with a difference. She is an evangelical Christian who believes in climate change, and that articulation affords her a line of argument unavailable to many other rhetors. The class could analyze Hayhoe's multimodal and print-based arguments to map her particular belief articulations in order to understand better how her perspectives align with and depart from traditional conceptions of evangelical Christian faith. Students could then be asked to identify a different rhetor who makes arguments for likeminded audiences, conduct their own analyses of that rhetor's work, and share their findings with the class. The object of such a unit would be to help students see whether rhetors who belong to a community hold novel beliefs that can be argued for on the basis of a shared ethos.

After completing those analyses, students could be asked to look inward at the communities to which they belong and the commitments they value. Here, students of faith should be encouraged to explore their faith communities, while students who do not subscribe to a faith could explore political, ideological, or other non-religious commitments. Students could conduct a kind of discourse community analysis wherein they define their community and explore its values. Instructors could then ask students to think about the perspectives they hold that differ from the community norm. To help them understand what these differences may look like, students could be introduced to the concept of vernacular religious creativity, which I define as the negotiations that religiously individuals make in relation to their pluralistic contexts (Ringer 20-35). I have taught this concept in undergraduate rhetoric and writing courses, and in my experience students have little difficulty grasping the concept. They can also readily name perspectives they hold that are not in lockstep with their communities (Ringer 31, 163-64; see also DePalma 256-60). Students could be asked to read Kimberly's case study (Ringer 83-113). While that case study demonstrates a missed opportunity, it also speaks to the possibilities implicit in arguing deliberatively within a community. It also serves as a model for helping students think about their own communities, the belief articulations they hold in common that would resonate with those communities, and the perspectives they hold that differ from what is commonly believed.

Students could then be asked to develop arguments grounded in the dwelling place they share with their community that argues in favor of the different perspective they hold. Like Hayhoe, students should not ignore their positionalities. Instead, they should speak from the places they inhabit and "'own' their arguments" (Perkins 75). Such ownership would entail writing from the "I" or "we" and locating their arguments clearly within the belief structures shared by the community. Students could develop their arguments using modes, media, and genres best suited to reaching their communities. At the end of *Vernacular*, I discuss a student named Kristen who wrote an open letter to her campus ministry and a personal letter to her pastor wherein she argued for a difference grounded in her ethos as an evangelical Christian. She called on members of her faith communities to rethink their approaches to the LGBTQ community, in part because her brother had just come out as gay. She chose the genres she did because she knew they would help her reach her intended audience, but other situations might call for students to produce social media campaigns, video PSAs, podcasts, infographics, or even sermons.

Certainly, there are risks to asking students to explore their own dwelling places in order to invent arguments. One risk is that the difference students argue for would represent perspectives that forestall rather than promote deliberative discourse. The difference students inhabit might align with positions many rhetorical educators would find repugnant, like white supremacy or anti-Semitism. This concern reflects one I have raised when I observe that vernacular religious creativity can function either to foster or hinder civil discourse, and that we always run the risk of students using what we teach them for purposes with which we disagree (Ringer 161-62). What I argue there pertains here as well: those risks are real, but they are risks we must take. Students can always choose to say or write something offensive or exclusionary, and sometimes instructors need to persuade students of the importance of arguing in ways that promote deliberative discourse. The larger risk as I see it, though, is that by ignoring the creative ways whereby religiously committed students adapt their faith in response to their social contexts, we miss out on the chance to help such students learn how to advocate for new perspectives within their communities. Kimberly was dissuaded from making an argument grounded in her faith, and as a result she was not trained to do the kind of inventive work her Christian mind has positioned her to do. We lost an argument we sorely need.

Another risk is that rhetorical education might become reduced to identity politics wherein evangelical Christians develop arguments for evangelical Christians, political liberals for other political liberals, and so on. This is a fair criticism, and one that the emphasis on in-group thinking within American politics prompts us to consider deeply (Daniell). It seems hard to imagine our democracy surviving if all we do is talk with those who share our beliefs. And yet if rhetoricians perceive the move towards in-group thinking as a constraint emerging from the current socio-political scene, then the question becomes not just how to change the scene, but also how to leverage its constraints for democratic ends. At the current political moment, when issues like climate change threaten our very existence, we would do well to explore every avenue for addressing such problems. While it is certainly not the only means available, one way to do so is by teaching students how to develop arguments from their own dwelling places that advocate for a just and sustainable future. If rhetorical educators can help students learn to argue deliberatively within likeminded communities like Hayhoe does, perhaps we can play a role in breaking down in-group thinking or at least opening lines of communication across groups. While it might be disturbing that Kevin Carter in *Years of Living*

Dangerously would be persuaded by Hayhoe but not by Al Gore when both make the same argument, the fact of the matter is that Hayhoe seems to have changed Carter's mind. Perhaps Carter would be less dismissive of other arguments regarding climate change by virtue of the fact that Hayhoe was able to reach him via shared ethos. And in that regard, Hayhoe seems to have achieved what Crowley seeks: the rearticulation of a densely articulated belief system that might represent a small but significant step toward a better world.

Works Cited

Baumlin, James S. "Introduction: Positioning *Ethos* in Historical and Contemporary Theory." Baumlin and Baumlin, pp. xi-xxxi.

—, and Tita French Baumlin, editors. *Ethos: New Essays in Rhetorical and Critical Theory.* Southern Methodist UP, 1994.

Bizzell, Patricia. "Faith-Based World Views as a Challenge to the Believing Game." *The Journal of the Assembly for Expanded Perspectives on Learning*, vol. 14, 2008-2009, pp. 29-35.

Carter, Shannon. "Living inside the Bible (Belt)." *College English*, vol. 69, no. 6, 2007, pp. 572-95.

Cheadle, Don, Harrison Ford, and Thomas L. Friedman. "Dry Season." *Years of Living Dangerously*, episode 1, Showtime, 13 April 2014. *Amazon Prime*, https://www.amazon.com/Years-Living-Dangerously-Showtime-Episode/dp/B00NDOZ92E/ref=sr_1_1?ie=UTF8&qid=1549462139&sr=8-1&keywords=years+of+living+dangerously+season+1.

Cope, Emily Murphy, and Jeffrey M. Ringer. "Coming to (Troubled) Terms: Methodology, Positionality, and the Problem of Defining 'Evangelical Christian.'" In *Mapping Christian Rhetorics: Connecting Conversations, Charting New Territories*, edited by Michael-John DePalma and Jeffrey M. Ringer, Routledge P, 2015, pp. 103-24.

Crowley, Sharon. *Toward a Civil Discourse: Rhetoric and Fundamentalism.* U of Pittsburgh P, 2006.

Daniell, Beth. "Whetstones Provided by the World: Trying to Deal with Difference in a Pluralistic Society." *College English*, vol. 70 no. 1, 2007, pp. 79-88.

DePalma, Michael-John. "Reimagining Rhetorical Education: Fostering Writers' Civic Capacities through Engagement with Religious Rhetorics." *College English* vol. 79, no. 3, 2017, pp. 251-75.

—, Jeffrey M. Ringer, and James D. Webber. "(Re)Charting the (Dis)Courses of Faith and Politics, or Rhetoric and Democracy in the Burkean Barnyard." *Rhetoric Society Quarterly*, vol. 38, no. 3, 2008, pp. 311-314.

Earle, Chris S. "Religion, Democracy, and Public Writing: Habermas on the Role of Religion in Public Life." *College English*, vol. 81, no. 2, 2019, pp. 133-54.

Elbow, Peter. "The Believing and Doubting Game—An Analysis of the Intellectual Enterprise." *Writing Without Teachers*, 2nd ed., Oxford UP, 1998, pp. 147-91.

Hauser, Gerard A. *Introduction to Rhetorical Theory.* 2nd ed., Waveland P, 2002.

Hayhoe, Katharine, and Andrew Farley. *A Climate for Change: Global Warming Facts for Faith-Based Decisions.* Faith Words, 2009.

Holiday, Judy. "In[ter]vention: Locating Rhetoric's *Ethos*." *Rhetoric Review*, vol. 28, no. 4, 2009, pp. 388-405.

Hyde, Michael, editor. *The Ethos of Rhetoric*. U of South Carolina P, 2004.

Jarratt, Susan, and Nedra Reynolds. "The Splitting Image: Contemporary Feminisms and the Ethics of êthos." Baumlin and Baumlin, pp. 37-64.

Lauer, Janice M. *Invention in Rhetoric and Composition*. Parlor P, 2004.

LeFevre, Karen Burke. *Invention as a Social Act*. Southern Illinois UP, 1987.

Lessl, Thomas M. "Civic Engagement from Religious Grounds." *Journal of Communication and Religion* vol. 32, Nov. 2009, pp. 195-98.

Medhurst, Martin J. "Filled with the Spirit: Rhetorical Invention and the Pentecostal Tradition." *Rhetoric and Public Affairs*, vol. 7, no. 4, 2004, pp. 555–572. *JSTOR*, www.jstor.org/stable/41939953.

—. "Religious Belief and Scholarship: A Complex Relationship. *Journal of Communication and Religion*, vol. 27, March 2004, pp. 40-47.

The NIV Study Bible. Grand Rapids, MI: Zondervan, 1985.

Nova Science Now. "Secret: Climate Change Evangelist, with Katharine Hayhoe." *YouTube*, 2 May 2014, www.youtube.com/watch?v=T1eGJLqxxKQ.

Perkins, Priscilla. "'Attentive, Intelligent, Reasonable, and Responsible:' Teaching Composition with Bernard Lonergan." *Renovating Rhetoric in Christian Tradition*, edited by Elizabeth Vander Lei, et al., U of Pittsburgh P, 2014, pp. 73-88.

Pollard, William G. *Physicist and Christian: A Dialogue between the Communities*. Seabury, 1961.

Ringer, Jeffrey M. *Vernacular Christian Rhetoric and Civil Discourse: The Religious Creativity of Evangelical Student Writers*. Routledge, 2016.

Simonson, Peter. "Reinventing Invention, Again." *Rhetoric Society Quarterly*, vol. 44, no. 4, 2014, pp. 299-322.

Steiner, Mark Allan. "Reconceptualizing Christian Public Engagement: 'Faithful Witness' and the American Evangelical Tradition." *Journal of Communication and Religion*, vol. 32, Nov. 2009, pp. 289-318.

Swearingen, C. Jan. "Rhetoric and Religion: Recent Revivals and Revisions." *Rhetoric Society Quarterly*, vol. 32, no. 2, 2002, pp. 119-37.

Zulick, Margaret D. "The *Ethos* of Invention: The Dialogue of Ethics and Aesthetics in Kenneth Burke and Mikhail Bakhtin." Hyde, pp. 20-33.

Contemplative WAC: Testing a Mindfulness-based Reflective Writing Assignment Across Courses

Jared Featherstone

Abstract: *This qualitative study examines the effects of the Mindfulness Journal Assignment (MJA), a semester-long integration implemented in five different university courses, to understand its potential for teaching and learning. Of particular interest were the patterns found in the reflective writing of students engaging in the MJA and the connection of those patterns to both classroom and Writing Across the Curriculum learning objectives. The most frequent themes occurring in the 111,906-word dataset were metacognitive awareness and self-regulation, both of which are significant for learning transfer and WAC. The findings of this study are promising in that the inclusion of a contemplative writing assignment is associated with positive habits of mind, such as metacognition and openness, which are prerequisites for common university course objectives such as critical thinking, problem-solving, and transfer. The development of these fundamental, domain-general skills makes this type of assignment an appropriate intervention for the emerging Contemplative Writing Across the Curriculum movement.*

After using iterations of the same mindfulness-based reflective writing assignment in different university courses and noticing its holistic impact, as evidenced in student writing, I began to see potential for this intervention in the emerging Contemplative Writing Across the Curriculum movement. The basic components of the assignment are listening to a 12-minute guided mindfulness meditation and then freewriting for at least five minutes about the meditation experience once a week for the duration of the semester, followed by a final reflective essay that reconsiders their entries collectively. Among the wide range of themes to emerge in the data and analysis is the interconnected nature of mindfulness, metacognition, transfer, and Writing Across the Curriculum. This exportable, content-neutral Mindfulness Journal Assignment (MJA) is worthy of further study in that it shows potential for use by other faculty to meet learning objectives, enabling more educators to integrate contemplative pedagogy into their courses. The current study examines the effects of the MJA, a semester-long integration implemented in five different university courses, to understand its potential for contemplative writing across the curriculum. Specifically, the current research addresses the following questions:

1. What patterns and themes can be seen in the reflective writing of students engaging in the MJA?
2. How do these themes connect with common learning objectives and Writing Across the Curriculum?

In addition to well-known benefits of potentially reducing stress and anxiety in college students (Bamber and Schneider 29), mindfulness interventions have also been found to strengthen fundamental learning faculties such as working memory and attention (Jha). Related, essential skills that correlate with success in most academic disciplines are those associated with metacognition (Nilson; Schraw; Zimmerman and Bandura). Metacognition is commonly understood to have two basic aspects, awareness and the self-regulation enabled by awareness (Schraw 115-116). Mindfulness has been associated with both aspects of metacognition in both empirical and theoretical scholarship. Tomasz Jankowski and Pawel Holas, through analysis of existing neuropsychological data and theoretical views of mindfulness, define the processes and skills of mindfulness using a framework of metacognition (76-77). In considering a specific metacognitive application of mindfulness, Ravi S. Kudesia, Markus Baer, and Hillary Anger Elfenbein studied the effects of "mindful metacognition" on the ability of undergraduate college students to solve problems. In two studies, the researchers confirmed that these skills enhance students' ability to move beyond initial, derivative solutions to more insightful or creative solutions (6-7).

Though she does not emphasize meditation as a means of training, Harvard psychologist Ellen Langer, in studying the role of mindfulness in teaching and learning for decades, has identified numerous educational benefits resulting from mindfulness, including the potential enhancement of problem-solving ability (Langer, "Mindfulness"; Langer and Moldoveanu). She encourages instructors to facilitate mindfulness to increase student awareness of and responsiveness to variation and perspective, a shift that would move students beyond mindless rote methods that limit learning and enable students to overcome self-limiting mindsets ("Mindful Education"; "Mindful Learning"). Both increased awareness and problem-solving abilities have application in the development of students' writing.

Barry J. Zimmerman and Albert Bandura's study concluded that self-regulation had a positive influence on student performance in a writing class and that such practices that develop self-regulation should be taught in the classroom (855-859). Connections between metacognition and writing were also demonstrated in Douglass J. Hacker, Matt C. Keener, and John C. Kircher's pilot study that used eye-tracking technology to monitor student writers and concluded that "writing is applied metacognition" (170). More recently, Raffaella Negretti studied the relationship of metacognition, writing, and learning in college students through qualitative analysis of student journal entries produced over the course of a semester. She found that metacognitive awareness changes students' understanding of writing tasks and enables them to self-regulate (170-173).

The field of writing studies, after some decades moving in other directions, has renewed attention to the cognitive factors that underlie writing. The 2011 Framework for Success in Postsecondary Writing, for example, developed by the Council of Writing Program Administrators, the National Council of Teachers of English, and the National Writing Project, focuses on cultivating certain "habits of mind" in college students. Among those habits are "metacognition," "flexibility," "openness," and "engagement." Patrick Sullivan argues that the development of these habits should be at "the center of our teaching practice" (149). In addition, research has explored the effects of many of the same qualities in terms of the "dispositions" of student writers (Bromley, Northway, and Schonberg; Driscoll and Wells).

Along with student dispositions that are effective across learning contexts, research has also identified important fundamental concepts, termed threshold concepts, that, when learned, can enable students to both engage in a particular discipline of study, as in Writing in the Disciplines, and also to apply knowledge in new contexts, as in Writing Across the Curriculum. Linda Adler-Kassner, Irene Clark, Liane Robertson, Kara Taczak, and Kathleen Blake Yancey describe five threshold concepts, four of which hinge upon mindfulness, though the connection is not explicitly acknowledged in their work (20-40). The relevant concepts are "writing always occurs in context, and no two contexts are alike," "reflection is critical for writers' development," "genre awareness contributes to successful transfer," and "prior knowledge, experience, attitudes, and beliefs set the stage for writing and shape new writing experiences" (21-40). Underlying each of these threshold concepts, critical to learning and academic performance, are metacognitive awareness and self-regulation, echoing the findings of Zimmerman and Bandura, Susan Nilson, and Langer ("Mindful Education"). As noted earlier in this article, metacognition and self-regulation are closely associated with mindfulness practice (Jankowski and Holas).

Both metacognition and mindfulness have also been studied in connection to another phenomenon relevant to both the field of writing studies and Writing Across the Curriculum programs: transfer. Significantly, Gregory Schraw's influential research concludes that metacognition is "domain general," meaning that it can be developed and applied across a variety of contexts, such as different academic disciplines (113). More recently, work by both Rebecca S. Nowacek and Elizabeth Wardle identifies metacognition as a habit of mind necessary for successful transfer of writing skills from one context to another. Building on this connection, Gwen Gorzelsky, Dana Lynn Driscoll, Joe Paszek, Ed Jones, and Carol Hayes interviewed and analyzed the writing of 123 students from four universities to identify the specific subcomponents of metacognition. Based on their findings, they suggest that instructors explicitly teach these subcomponents to scaffold students toward "construction metacognition," a skillset that enables them to employ metacognitive skills effectively across a variety of writing tasks and contexts (233-236). These learning outcomes are consistent with the International Network of WAC Programs (INWAC) Statement of WAC Principles and Practices that encourages instructors to develop both rhetorical awareness and genre awareness in students, both of which require metacognition. Another intersection of metacognition and WAC can be seen in the WAC Clearinghouse's emphasis on writing to learn, with reflective response papers and journaling identified as common writing to learn assignments, in which the use of writing is not simply a transactional means of communication but "a tool for discovering, for shaping meaning, and for reaching understanding," as a core approach in WAC pedagogy (Kiefer, Palmquist, Carbone, Cox, and Melzer).

Reflective writing, such as journaling, is also identified as a natural and effective part of contemplative pedagogy (Barbezat and Bush 104, 125-132), a modern movement featuring first-person, subjective, experiential work that trains real-time awareness and enables personal insight (Barbezat and Bush 6) and often includes the explicit integration of contemplative practices such as mindfulness meditation. In recent years, the systematic integration of contemplative pedagogies into writing instruction has become a distinct subfield of writing studies, as discussed by Alexandria Peary (7-9). Peary specifically emphasizes the use of mindfulness to develop real-time, present moment rhetorical awareness and awareness of the "intrapersonal rhetoric" that underlies writing and thinking (35-39). Mindfulness builds metacognition and can result in "a detachment that readies the learner for critical thinking" (5). Part of Peary's rationale for mindfulness as a natural fit for composition pedagogy, one that aligns with INWAC's "writing as rhetorical" principle, is that "First-year composition pedagogy is replete with different goals of awareness: our students regularly practice rhetorical awareness, genre awareness, audience awareness, disciplinary awareness, and process awareness" (13).

Christy Wenger also argues for a contemplative writing pedagogy integrating mindfulness and yoga, emphasizing present moment awareness of the body to fully engage with the writing context, and countering the oppressive disembodiment characteristic of academic writing (*Yoga* 44). Wenger also emphasizes the role of "attention literacy" ("Teaching Attention" 55), developed through mindfulness practices, as a productive addition to writing curricula because it is "a literacy necessary for student success" ("Teaching Attention" 58). Both Marlowe Miller and Karolyn Kinane, explaining the distinction between contemplative writing practices and traditional journaling or reflective writing, note that it is the combination of reflective writing or journaling with a contemplative practice, such as mindfulness, that distinguishes this pedagogy. Kate Chaterdon acknowledges the link between these contemplative writing pedagogies and transfer: "If the implementation of contemplative writing practice can help students develop a greater metacognitive awareness, then it stands to reason that it can help students to transfer their writing knowledge" (52).

Despite the emergence of contemplative writing pedagogy and the strong link across mindfulness, metacognition, and transfer (Gorzelsky, Driscoll, Paszek, Jones, and Hayes; Jankowski and Holas), few empirical studies have been conducted on contemplative writing. No empirical studies have been published on the contemplative writing assignments and their potential as a WAC initiative. The current study addresses this research deficit by offering findings and methods to build upon in the Contemplative WAC movement.

Research Design

Context, Courses, and Participants

The study analyzes the reflective writing of 54 students, ages 18-24, enrolled in five different courses at a large, state university. Participants varied in terms of major, writing ability, ethnicity, and gender. The courses included in the study were first-year composition (15 students), contemplative literature (15 students), writing tutor education (19 students), contemplative writing (two students), and a project-planning workshop for students in the honors program (four students). Common learning objectives across the courses included critical thinking about the course content, personal reflection and application of course content, writing process awareness, genre awareness, and clarity of written communication. While writing was a feature of each course, the approach varied. The first-year writing course focused on the production of texts in various genres; the contemplative literature focused on responding to a range of contemplative texts; the writing tutor education course prepared students to be effective writing tutors through immersion in theory and practice; the contemplative writing course involved students reading the writing of contemplatives and writing about first-hand experiences with contemplative practice; and the project-planning course focused on the process awareness and production of research papers. The courses also varied in delivery with three face-to-face, one hybrid, and one online. I was the researcher and instructor of record for four out of the five courses in the study. I am a professor in the writing department and director of the university writing center and also an experienced practitioner and trained teacher of mindfulness meditation.

Given these features, the study aligns with the practices of action research, specifically the "practitioner as researcher" model developed by Estela Mara Bensimon, Donald E. Polkinghorne, Georgia L. Bauman and Edlyn Vallejo to establish an approach that not only involves participation in the intervention but also the ultimate goal of fostering institutional change. In the current study, I am the researcher who is a professor and meditation instructor examining the effects of my own interventions on students for the purpose of improving the quality of learning in my courses and, potentially, across courses in a variety of disciplines. The rationale for the practitioner-researcher approach is twofold. First, the combination of writing, teaching, and meditation expertise in one researcher is not common. Second, outsourcing any one of these interventions would disrupt the continuity of the course and the consistency of data interpretation. Lastly, as Negretti argues, only the course instructor could know whether the student journal entries were authentic responses or simply attempts to recapitulate course content (in this case, the meditation instructions or exchanges from class discussion). Aligning with this reasoning, the student writing under examination in the current study was produced to meet the requirements of the researcher-practitioner's semester-long contemplative writing assignments in various courses.

Although these courses all have a significant writing component, the subjects of study are quite different. The idea was to test the potential of the Mindfulness Journal Assignment in these courses for export across a wider variety of courses in the curriculum. In my role of researcher-practitioner, I was able to identify and analyze the pedagogical implications of the findings because of my particular dual training in both writing and meditation instruction. After this initial phase, the MJA can be shared and, if need be, adapted for use more widely across the curriculum.

Mindfulness Journal Assignment

The Mindfulness Journal Assignment (MJA) was developed and refined over five years as it was implemented in a variety of courses. Each iteration of the assignment included mindfulness meditation instruction, journal entries, and a cumulative reflective essay spread over a semester. The meditation instruction was given through real-time classroom interaction, through pre-recorded online guided meditations, or through both classroom and online delivery. Both the online and face-to-face meditations followed the standardized instructions used in both Mindfulness-based Stress Reduction and Koru Mindfulness, which train a non-judging awareness using sensory anchors. The classroom mindfulness practice took place at the beginning of each class with the researcher both leading and taking part in the meditation. The in-class meditation sessions were timed using the Insight Timer app. The online guided meditations, both 12 and 24-minute versions, were pre-recorded and hosted on Soundcloud for students to stream or download. These online meditations also followed standard mindfulness meditation protocol.

The journal entries were submitted periodically over the semester, and feedback was given to students through the course management system. The journal entries were free-write exercises taking place immediately following a mindfulness meditation practice. In some classes, students were asked to do additional entries focusing on connections to course content. The cumulative reflective writing pieces were assigned as a final journal entry toward the end of the semester or as part of the final exam for the course. Grades for the assignment were based on completion and depth of thought, and not on specific content criteria, in order to minimize leading or influencing the content.

While there were some variations of the assignment language and scope, according to the course context, the essence of the assignment remained the same over the courses. The following language was used for the majority of students in the dataset:

> You will keep a journal of your experiences with mindfulness meditation. Each weekly practice session should have a corresponding journal entry. So, at a minimum, your first Meditation Practice Journal will contain seven reflections (1-3 paragraphs each).
> Here's the process for each session.
> 1. Find a place in which you are unlikely to be interrupted or distracted (bedroom, forest, backyard, etc.) for the duration of the practice. Silence phones, tablets, laptops, TVs, or other devices.
> 2. Sit in a way that allows you to be relaxed but alert. Meditation is not sleep. You can sit in a chair or on the floor with a cushion. Follow the instructions. (Please let me know if you are confused by any of the instructions).
> 3. Listen to the guided meditation (about 12 minutes) and follow the instructions.[1]
> 4. When the session is over, freewrite for 1-3 paragraphs (or more if you are inspired) about your meditation experience. Try not to overthink or edit your natural pattern of thought. (We'll have time for that later). You can write about how you felt, what was difficult, what you noticed about the way your mind works, the particular patterns of thought you experienced, emotional content, moods, any insights that arose for you during the session. Record the time and date of this entry.

Data Collection and Analysis

All student writing for the MJA was submitted through the university's online learning management system. Once IRB approval for the study and student permission for use of their work was secured, the data was exported and uploaded to NVivo, a software

---

1. The guided meditation can be found at https://soundcloud.com/zentones/12-minute-guided-meditation

system for coding and analyzing qualitative data. In total, the data set consisted of over 670 journal entries and 37 final papers, totaling 111,906 words of student writing.

After reading the entire data set without coding, I then read the data set a second time, coding for emergent themes. During this stage of the project, I had not yet narrowed my research questions, so I employed an open coding, more recently described as initial coding (Charmaz), which seeks to "remain open to all possible theoretical directions suggested by your interpretations of the data" (qtd. in Saldana 115). During the coding process, categories were created, revised, and combined as more examples made the distinctions clear. In addition, it was clear that a single passage might embody several codes, so I decided to allow for overlapping codes. For instance, the "body awareness" code may be evident in the same passage for which "increased focus" and "self-regulation" are present. In this way, the codes show both large umbrellas, such as "metacognition" and "self-regulation," along with subcategories, such as "suspension of judgement," which might overlap with both of the larger categories.

These emergent themes were refined based on patterns noticed in my initial reading, my experience of teaching the courses, and my experience as a certified mindfulness meditation teacher. In this stage I was moving through one of the "second cycle coding methods" identified by Johnny Saldana as "pattern coding" which organizes but also begins to "attribute meaning to that organization" (235). In order to determine whether a passage should be coded with a particular theme, I had to consider the context of the passage and interpret the student's intended meaning. Being the teacher of most of these courses who interacted with these students in the classroom proved useful in helping me understand more abstract or obscure writing. My perspective was also relevant in that the informal and introspective nature of the writing might not be as readily understood by someone who has not engaged in the practice and teaching of mindfulness for many years. As noted in the Research Design section, my background and role motivated the "practitioner as researcher" (Bensimon, Polkinghorne, Bauman, and Vallejo) approach to the project.

Results and Discussion

The coding process revealed a number of consistent, emergent themes in the data set. Themes are mostly self-explanatory, though the two common components of metacognition, "metacognitive awareness" and "self-regulation," were decoupled in the coding process because they did not always emerge simultaneously.

Table 1 summarizes the appearances of themes from the most frequent to the least frequent.

Table 1
Emergent themes found in student journal entries and self-reflections

Emergent Themes	Number of Appearances
Metacognitive awareness	602
Self-regulation	389
Body awareness	347
Stress reduction	316
Personal Insight	221
Awareness of environment	194
Noticeable increase in mindfulness	176
Difficulty with practice	175
Distracted by thoughts of future tasks	165
Applied outside meditation context	114
Increased focus	108
Suspension of judgement	66
Judging self or practice	65
Tolerance of discomfort	49
Improved work habits	45
Goal setting	37
Focusing on past	33
Connection to coursework	31
Awareness of technology	13

Metacognition and Learning

As Table 1 shows, the two most frequently occurring themes to emerge from the 111,906 words of student text analyzed are "metacognitive awareness" and "self-regulation," the two central aspects of metacognition. This frequency is significant in that it points to the fundamental quality of metacognition, a skill closely associated with mindfulness (Jankowski and Holas), transfer (Nowacek; Gorzelsky, Driscoll, Paszek, Jones, and Hayes), and the habits of mind identified as key to effective writing ("Framework"). Also, it is worth noting that many passages coded for metacognition were also coded for other themes in the data set, reinforcing the fundamental and generative quality of metacognition. Metacognition, which takes many forms in this data set for both learning and stress reduction, does appear to be "domain general," as Shraw's research indicates (113). Here is an example of a passage coded for "metacognitive awareness" and "distracted by thoughts of future tasks."

> *I found myself thinking a lot- making a list of final assignments I need to do, planning my day, thinking about finals, thinking about how I have to call my parents. It was like complete chaos. One thought led to another thought which led into another thought.*

In the following passage, the student has recognized a mind pattern and how this recurring thought pattern affects daily life, a realization that shows ways the assignment might fit well into contemplative pedagogy's goal of creating first-person, experiential learning that moves students toward personal insight (Barbezat and Bush).

> *...it led me to think about how often I plan what I'm going to say in my life. I do it before many, many conversations. I order my thoughts before I say them, and spend much of my life acting out a script I've composed for myself.*

In an excerpt from a late-semester entry, a student is able to notice a change in thinking after engaging with the MJA, showing the way that mindfulness can help students transcend "self-limiting mindsets," as described by Langer ("Mindful Learning"; "Mindfulness").

> *I considered how I thought at the beginning of this year and discovered that it is much different than my current thinking process. I used to be prone to stress and to micro-analyzing situations that didn't deserve that type of analysis. Now, I am able to take a step back from stressful situations and look at them in a grand context. Assignments that I am worried about...I can now put on the shelf of priorities in my mind.*

In this passage, we can see the interplay between real-time awareness of thinking and a reflective awareness that looks back at prior mental activity. The MJA, unlike traditional journaling or reflective essays, seems to enhance both immediate, real-time awareness and distant, reflective awareness, and to put those two shades of metacognition in conversation. As Peary notes, one of the most powerful benefits of a mindfulness-based writing pedagogy is that it grants more access to real-time rhetorical awareness. As Miller and Kinane separately note, this real-time awareness, as opposed to the more common past-tense reflection, is one of the distinguishing features of contemplative writing pedagogy.

The fact that metacognition features so prominently in the text from the MJA could be support for the complementary nature of mindfulness and writing in enhancing student learning. In using an assignment that includes both mindfulness and reflective writing, we are reinforcing the development of metacognition, establishing the ground for development and learning.

The frequent appearance of the "self-regulation" theme is also significant, considering the research on its influence on learning and academic achievement (Nilson; Zimmerman and Bandura). Once students are aware of habits of mind, learning processes, and hindrances, they can take steps to change or improve. This benefit of mindfulness has wide potential application in disciplines that rely on problem-solving skills, a link shown in studies by Kudesia, Baer, and Elfenbein, and Langer and Moldoveanu. The following student journal excerpts show the reported effects of the practices on academic self-regulation.

> *When I am in conversation with others, or am sitting in class and realize I am no longer focused on the professor's lecture, I take a moment. Deep breath in, deep breath out, deep breath in again, releasing the thoughts, I bring myself back to focus. ...this new ability is spilling over into other parts of my life...when I am trying to study, I realize when I am just reading over material and not actually learning.*

The following passage shows overlapping themes of "self-regulation," "improved work habits," and "suspension of judgement" as they specifically apply to writing. The suspension of judgement shown here is an example of the productive detachment noted by Peary and evidence that mindfulness-based writing assignments may help cultivate the habits of "openness" and "flexibility" called for in the 2011 Framework for Postsecondary Success in Writing.

> *I have noticed since completing the mindfulness training I am open to allowing my thoughts to completely fill a page before moving on to assessing and proofreading my work. This change in my outlook enabled me to more easily read my own writing, as well as the writing of others, without being immediately judgmental.*
>
> *I think that I've learned to not judge myself as much, which is something that I can apply to tutoring sessions. By not judging myself I can also learn to not judge others. It is important to keep an open mind while tutoring, meaning there can be no judgments going on in my brain.*

Importantly, the second excerpt explicitly describes the transfer of non-judgement, a habit cultivated in the MJA, to the separate context of tutoring sessions at the writing center.

In addition to the central role of writing to learn featured in the MJA, the connection between mindfulness and the common learning objective of increased critical thinking, a link noted by Peary (5), might be of particular interest to writing across the curriculum programs. In order to think critically, one must first be aware of one's current thinking on the subject, for, as Schraw and Rayne Sperling Dennison found, there is a significant relationship between awareness and self-regulation. For any university course attempting to get students to move beyond inherited or unexamined notions about the subject matter or the world, the MJA's two-level approach to metacognition, real-time awareness during meditation and long-term reflection in the journals, might be applicable. The following journal excerpt shows the potential growth in critical thinking that might result from the MJA.

> *When confronted with an idea I initially disagree with, I take a step back and think if it's strong despite my own views. This mentality makes conversations more productive, makes me more tolerant to different ideas, and allows me see what areas I need improvement on without it being the end of the world.*

Again, this data excerpt shows the power of contemplative writing pedagogy in that the student's personal insight and increased ability to think critically about their own cognitive patterns has significant applicability toward a learning objective of critical thinking. In addition to being personally relevant and applicable to course learning objectives, the insight captured in such entries is domain general in that it is not bound up with particular course content, leaving the possibility of transfer to other contexts.

Focus and the Management of Distraction

Another high-ranking theme in the MJA data set was "increased focus." The common pattern was for students to become aware of the state of being unfocused early in the semester and then, later in the semester, after more meditation and reflection, experience a noticeable increase in their ability to focus, a trend that reinforces Wenger's argument for the inclusion of attention training in writing courses ("Teaching Attention").

> *However, I've been noticing that I'm more concentrated in our in class meditations. I find my wandering less and less and I can realize that I'm thinking more quickly.*
>
> *In meditation practice the other day I noticed I improved on being able to focus and stay alert while also being calm and less tense.*

In the following passage, we see the overlapping themes of "increased focus," "self-regulation," and "improved work habits," but, most importantly, we see the attention skills developed in the MJA being transferred to the context of another course. The student's newfound attention literacy is a noticeable change that occurred within a single semester.

> *I always had to make an excuse to get up because I was mentally agitated in anticipation for the whole three hours. However, I found that by the end of the semester I was able to sit through the entire three hours with only the ten minute class break in the middle. I didn't fully notice this effect until the end of the semester, but when I did it felt like a revelation.*

Again, these are far-reaching skills that could apply in any academic discipline. In addition to prioritizing commitments, students are also faced with the difficulty of managing the pervasive distraction of smartphones and social media (Turkle; Twenge). "Awareness of technology distraction," often emerging with a form of "self-regulation" reveals another domain-general skill that would benefit both students and faculty in university courses.

> *Near the beginning of the session, I felt my phone vibrating somewhere on my bed. It took some willpower to resist the urge to check who was calling me but I managed to do it.*
>
> *One other difficulty that I faced was not using my cellphone… My mind kept jumping to what I might be missing. I was getting the occasional vibrating notification but did not check to see what it was.*
>
> *My biggest distraction has always been my phone. Although I still reach for it when I'm doing my work, I am able to notice when I'm doing it, and stop myself.*

Significantly, the last excerpt above indicates that the student has transferred new habits, the ability to self-regulate technology use and maintain focus, from the context of the MJA to a separate study context.

Personal Insight

The code of "personal insight" was used to capture expressions of insight that resulted from mindfulness and/or reflection components of the MJA. The appearance of this theme resonates with the more traditional name for mindfulness meditation, *vipassana*, or insight meditation. Interestingly, these insights were present even in courses that had no explicit contemplative theme or discussion of realization.

> I had never felt so aware of my presence outside of thought. ... I was able to have an outside perspective of the fight without being overly subjective...While focused on my breathing, I realized that I got overly defensive about something and was too prideful to admit it...it made me realize that a majority of fights/arguments I've gotten into in my life are almost entirely because of my pride or how easy it for me to get defensive and accusatory. This revelation will most likely stick with me for the rest of my life and make me reconsider the way I conduct myself in moments of disagreements.
>
> I also learned that I place my worth in academic "success." I believe that if I do not complete my homework every night, I will fall behind, and then I will receive poor grades. I allow myself no grace or relaxation because I am too determined to finish what I had started. Meditation, though, has taught me that taking a physical and mental break is healthy, rewarding, and ironically increases my productivity throughout the rest of my day.

Again, the passages show the potential of personal insights cultivated in the MJA being transferred to other personal and academic contexts. The personal and academic are not separated as traditional university learning contexts might encourage (Wenger, "Yoga Minds" 44-45), but they are integrated, the goal which contemplative pedagogy seeks to achieve (Barbezat and Bush).

Applications to Contemplative WAC

One of the motivations for designing the MJA and conducting qualitative research on student submissions was to explore the possibility of the MJA as an exportable, customizable WAC assignment that could be used in a variety of disciplines to deepen learning and facilitate transfer. In several ways, the study results indicate that the assignment has this potential. First, the learning-related themes appear across all five courses. Second, both the existing literature and the results of the current study point to a productive overlap among the concepts of mindfulness, writing, metacognition, and transfer. By including both mindfulness training and ongoing reflective writing, the MJA pushes students to think more critically about themselves, the course subject matter, their daily life experience and to integrate these artificially separated spheres. They are able to notice and move beyond unexamined writing and thinking habits. They are able to access ideas and insights outside of their previous range.

The MJA data also shows promise for meeting common learning objectives in university courses, such as critical thinking, process focus, problem-solving, and transfer. The enhanced metacognitive skills and personal insights lead students to think more critically about themselves, the subject matter, and their surroundings. By increasing awareness of their thinking, environment, and academic habits, students become aware of the thinking, reading, and writing processes they engage in, many of which were previously unexamined. As the data indicates, this increase in awareness is often paired with a newfound ability to make positive changes through self-regulation and to transfer skills to new contexts.

Limitations and Directions for Future Research

The current study was designed to be a starting point for a more systematic study of contemplative writing pedagogy and its potential for developing important, transferrable skills and habits that meet core learning objectives of university courses. Future research might strengthen claims made here by testing such an assignment in disciplinary courses not related to writing studies to see if the results are similar. In addition, future research might gather data related to course content, such as test answers or essays, to see if an increase of metacognitive skills trained in the MJA show up in other work for the class and if a more course-specific transfer can be discerned.

More broadly, future research should corroborate the qualitative findings with direct measures of relevant outcomes, such as metacognition, through student work, interviews, or surveys. A validated scale such as Schraw and Dennison's Metacognitive Awareness Scale or Kirk Brown and Richard Ryan's Mindful Attention Awareness Scale could be used as a pre- and post- measure to assess the results of the MJA more objectively.

In order to gain a clearer sense of the correlations between the assignment and the qualities or skills evident in the emergent themes, future research could further standardize the components and delivery of the assignment. Because the assignment and its role in the courses was under development when the data was being generated (the courses took place over four years), there was some variation in application, like the amount of meditation time required of students and the number of journal entries collected. Along with this standardization would be the need to have a control group of students in the same courses who did not receive the MJA intervention, enabling a comparison of effects.

Lastly, the MJA itself could have, by design, influenced the content of the journal entries. Although the writing prompts did not provide any specific language that was replicated in the journal entries, some direction had to be given in order to help students understand broadly what they might address in their entries. In the following passage from the instruction, one could argue that themes of metacognitive awareness, personal insight, difficulty with practice, and suspension of judgement could, to some degree, be the result of the prompt and not the mindfulness practice: "You can write about how you felt, what was difficult, what you noticed about the way your mind works, the particular patterns of thought you experienced, emotional content, moods, any insights that arose for you during the session." Though this study examines the assignment as a whole, which includes the practice and writing prompt, it could be useful to look for ways to trace the effects of the component parts in order to understand exactly what led to the results found.

Despite the limitations, the findings of this study are promising in that the inclusion of a contemplative writing assignment is associated with positive habits of mind, such as metacognition and openness, that are prerequisites for common university course objectives such as critical thinking, problem-solving, and transfer. The development of these fundamental, domain-general skills makes this type of assignment an appropriate intervention for the emerging Contemplative Writing Across the Curriculum movement.

Works Cited

Adler-Kassner, Linda, Irene Clark, Liane Robertson, Kara Taczak, and Kathleen Blake Yancey . "Assembling Knowledge: The Role of Threshold Concepts in Facilitating Transfer." *Critical Transitions: Writing and the Question of Transfer*, edited by Chris Anson and Jessie Moore, The WAC Clearinghouse and University Press of Colorado, 2016, pp 17-48. https://wac.colostate.edu/books/perspectives/ansonmoore/.

Bamber, Mandy, and Joanne Schneider. "Mindfulness-Based Meditation to Decrease Stress and Anxiety in College Students: A Narrative Synthesis of the Research." *Educational Research Review*, vol. 18, 2015. *ResearchGate*, doi:10.1016/j.edurev.2015.12.004.

Barbezat, Daniel P., and Mirabai Bush. *Contemplative Practices in Higher Education: Powerful Methods to Transform Teaching and Learning*. 1st ed., Jossey-Bass, 2013.

Bensimon, Estela Mara, Donald E. Polkinghorne, Georgia L. Bauman and Edlyn Vallejo. "Doing Research That Makes a Difference." *Journal of Higher Education*, vol. 75, no. 1, 2004, p. 104-26.

Bromley, Pam, Kara Northway, and Eliana Schonberg. "Transfer and Dispositions in Writing Centers: A Cross-Institutional, Mixed-Methods Study." *Across the Disciplines*, vol. 13, no. 1, 2016, https://wac.colostate.edu/atd/articles/bromleyetal2016.cfm.

Brown, Kirk Warren, and Richard M. Ryan. "The Benefits of Being Present: Mindfulness and Its Role in Psychological Well-Being." *Journal of Personality and Social Psychology*, vol. 84, no. 4, 2003, pp. 822–48, doi:10.1037/0022-3514.84.4.822.

Charmaz, Kathy. *Constructing Grounded Theory*. 2nd ed., SAGE Publications Ltd, 2014.

Chaterdon, Kate. "Writing Into Awareness: How Metacognitive Awareness Can Be Encouraged Through Contemplative Teaching Practices." *Across the Disciplines*, vol. 16, no. 1, 2019, pp. 50-65.

Driscoll, Dana, and Jennifer Wells. "Beyond Knowledge and Skills: Writing Transfer and the Role of Student Dispositions." *Composition Forum*, vol. 26, 2012, http://compositionforum.com/issue/26/beyond-knowledge-skills.php.

Gorzelsky, Gwen, Dana Driscoll, Joe Paszek, Ed Jones, Carol Hayes, Chris Anson, and Jessie Moore. "Cultivating Constructive Metacognition: A New Taxonomy for Writing Studies." *Critical Transitions: Writing and the Question of Transfer*, edited by Chris Anson and Jessie Moore, The WAC Clearinghouse and University Press of Colorado, 2016, pp. 215–46, https://wac.colostate.edu/docs/books/ansonmoore/chapter8.pdf.

Hacker, Douglas, Matt C. Keener, and John C. Kircher . "Writing Is Applied Metacognition." *Handbook of Metacognition in Education*, Routledge, 2009, pp. 154–72.

INWAC. *Statement of WAC Principles and Practices*. WAC Clearinghouse, 2014, https://wac.colostate.edu/principles/.

Jankowski, Tomasz, and Pawel Holas. "Metacognitive Model of Mindfulness." *Consciousness and Cognition*, vol. 28, Supplement C, 2014, pp. 64–80. *ScienceDirect*, doi:10.1016/j.concog.2014.06.005.

Jha, Amishi. *Improving Attention and Working Memory Through Mindfulness Training*. Mindfulness in Education Network, Bryn Mawr College. https://vimeo.com/39906585.

Kiefer, Kate, Mike Palmquist, Nick Carbone, Michelle Cox, and Dan Melzer. *An Introduction to Writing Across the Curriculum - The WAC Clearinghouse*, 2000-2018. https://wac.colostate.edu/resources/wac/intro/.

Kinane, Karolyn. "The Place of Practice in Contemplative Pedagogy and Writing." *Across the Disciplines*, vol. 16, no. 1, https://wac.colostate.edu/atd/special/contemplative/.

Kudesia, Ravi S., Markus Baer, and Hillary Anger Elfenbein. "A Wandering Mind Does Not Stray Far from Home: The Value of Metacognition in Distant Search." *PloS One*, vol. 10, no. 5, 2015.

Langer, Ellen J. "A Mindful Education." *Educational Psychologist*, vol. 28, no. 1, Winter 1993, pp. 43-50. *EBSCOhost*, doi:10.1207/s15326985ep2801_4.

—. "Mindful Learning." *Current Directions in Psychological Science*, vol. 9, no. 6, Dec. 2000, pp. 220–23. *EBSCOhost*, doi:10.1111/1467-8721.00099.

Langer, Ellen J., and Mihnea Moldoveanu. "The Construct of Mindfulness." *Journal of Social Issues*, vol. 56, no. 1, Spring 2000, pp. 1-9. *EBSCOhost*, doi:10.1111/0022-4537.00148.

Miller, Marlowe. "Contemplative Writing Across the Disciplines." *Across the Disciplines*, vol. 16, no. 1, 2019, pp. 1-5.

Negretti, Raffaella. "Metacognition in Student Academic Writing: A Longitudinal Study of Metacognitive Awareness and Its Relation to Task Perception, Self-Regulation, and Evaluation of Performance." *Written Communication*, vol. 29, no. 2, 2012, pp. 142–79. *CrossRef*, doi:10.1177/0741088312438529.

Nilson, Susan. *Creating Self-Regulated Learners: Strategies to Strengthen Students' Self-Awareness and Learning Skills*. Stylus, 2013.

Nowacek, Rebecca S. *Agents of Integration: Understanding Transfer as a Rhetorical Act*. Southern Illinois University Press, 2011.

Peary, Alexandria. *Prolific Moment: Theory and Practice of Mindfulness for Writing*. Routledge, 2018.

Saldana, Johnny. *The Coding Manual for Qualitative Researchers Third Edition*. 3rd edition, SAGE Publications Ltd, 2015.

Schraw, Gregory. "Promoting General Metacognitive Awareness." *Instructional Science*, vol. 26, no. 1–2, 1998, pp. 113–25. *link.springer.com*, doi:10.1023/A:1003044231033.

Schraw, Gregory, and Rayne Sperling Dennison. "Assessing Metacognitive Awareness." *Contemporary Educational Psychology*, vol. 19, no. 4, 1994, pp. 460–75. *ScienceDirect*, doi:10.1006/ceps.1994.1033.

Sullivan, Patrick. *A New Writing Classroom: Listening, Motivation, and Habits of Mind*. University Press of Colorado, 2014. *JSTOR*, http://www.jstor.org/stable/j.ctt9qhkqz.

Turkle, Sherry. *Alone Together: Why We Expect More from Technology and Less from Each Other*. Basic Books, 2012.

Twenge, Jean M. *IGen: Why Today's Super-Connected Kids Are Growing Up Less Rebellious, More Tolerant, Less Happy—and Completely Unprepared for Adulthood—and What That Means for the Rest of Us*. Atria Books, 2017.

Wardle, Elizabeth. "Understanding 'Transfer' from FYC: Preliminary Results of a Longitudinal Study." *WPA: Writing Program Administration - Journal of the Council of Writing Program Administrators*, vol. 31, no. 1/2, Fall/Winter 2007, pp. 65-85.

Wenger, Christy I. "Teaching Attention Literacy." *Pedagogy*, vol. 19, no. 1, Jan. 2019, pp. 53–78. *Crossref*, doi:10.1215/15314200-7173752.

—. *Yoga Minds, Writing Bodies: Contemplative Writing Pedagogy*. The WAC Clearinghouse and Parlor Press, 2015, https://wac.colostate.edu/books/perspectives/wenger/.

Zimmerman, Barry J., and Albert Bandura. "Impact of Self-Regulatory Influences on Writing Course Attainment." *American Educational Research Journal*, vol. 31, no. 4, 1994, pp. 845–62. *JSTOR*, doi:10.2307/1163397.

STEMM-Humanities Co-Teaching and the Humusities Turn

Hella Bloom Cohen

Abstract: *Donna Haraway calls for a new Humanities that attends to the role of this traditionally anthropocentric field on a damaged planet. The Humusities, she offers, empower us to teach at the intersections of observation, speculation, and affective reasoning. This article considers co-teaching and interdisciplinary teaching structures as part of the Humusities model. Drawing from interviews and pedagogical materials of professors who have co-taught STEMM-Humanities classes, student feedback from these sections, and current research on interdisciplinary education, I theorize the possibilities and limitations of the interdisciplinary Humusities at the undergraduate level. The article explores how we translate the tenets of Haraway into a co-taught curriculum, while considering the objectives, benefits, and drawbacks of doing so. Several pedagogical and procedural issues are discussed: "norming" student performance in courses where two or more instructors are likely using different assessment modalities; navigating STEMM-Humanities co-teaching within current university budget structures; considering how university size and collegial climate affects implementation; and revealing roadblocks that exist relating to Registrar policy, enrollments, student majors, and hiring practices. I also speculate how the Humusities turn can redistribute university wealth and mitigate educational threats at the state and federal levels. Like science fiction in Haraway's Staying with the Trouble, co-teaching across the Humusities engages in "storytelling and fact telling; it is the patterning of possible worlds and possible times, material-semiotic worlds, gone, here, and yet to come" (31). With this sentiment in mind, I explore what is entailed in the process of humanizing STEMM and composting the humanities.*

The Humusities—Donna Haraway's neologism for ecoconscious Humanities in the post-Anthropocene—empower us to teach at the intersections of observation, speculation, and affective reasoning. The term invokes the muck and the mud within the etymology of "humus," and invites a return to the soil for those of us in a field that has historically looked up rather than down. After Haraway, the silos of the laboratory and library stand poised to disassemble. Stringed course content and interdisciplinary teaching structures can prepare students to disprivilege their Enlightenment 'I's—to slow decay and to sow growth. Humusities courses can look like: hermaphroditic snail behavior and gender nonconforming literature; urban gardening and black theological ecologies; actuarial modeling and critical studies of race and ethnicity; zoological planning and animal narrators; global fashion marketing and Silk Road history; applied nuclear physics and Daoist peace philosophy; graph theory and Haraway's "tentacular thinking." These are examples of themes—some imagined, some realized—in courses within a STEMM-Humanities co-teaching model, and this article will consider that model as a method of implementing "the Humusities for a Habitable Multispecies Muddle."[1] I explore what is entailed in the process of humanizing STEMM and composting the humanities.

Drawing from interviews and pedagogical materials of professors who have co-taught STEMM-Humanities classes, student feedback from these sections, and current research on interdisciplinary education, I theorize the possibilities and limitations of the interdisciplinary Humusities at the undergraduate level. I also advance a materialist critique of Haraway as a warning for those of us doing the work of remaking the liberal arts to avoid what I see as her class-blindness as we deploy co-teaching and multidisciplinary programming. Guiding pedagogical questions include: How do we translate the tenets of Haraway into a co-taught curriculum? What are the abstract and measurable objectives, benefits, and drawbacks of doing so, and on what philosophical assumptions are we operating? How do we "norm" student performance in courses where two (or more) instructors are likely using different assessment modalities? Guiding procedural questions include: How does STEMM-Humanities co-teaching work within current university budget structures, and how does university size and collegial climate affect its implementation? What roadblocks exist relating to Registrar policy, enrollments, and student majors? How does co-teaching impact hiring practices? How does the Humusities turn redistribute university wealth, and/or encroach upon disciplinary turf? Lastly, but not exhaustively, how do the Humusities talk back to educational threats at the state and federal levels? Like science fiction in Haraway's *Staying with the Trouble*, co-teaching across the Humusities engages in "storytelling and fact telling; it is the patterning of possible worlds and possible times, material-semiotic worlds, gone, here, and yet to come" (31). By softening the hard sciences and hardening the soft sciences, hopefully we might open up the curiosity cabinets of both to ont(ec)ological questioning.

Haraway offers a mantra that I suggest we embrace to re-create the liberal arts: "becoming with." She announces the multidisciplinary genealogies of her heuristics—loudly and often—while refusing to submit to the defeatism or sentimentalizing entailed as we watch our departments erode or in some cases die (12). This furious commitment to hope she labels "becoming with," and the entire work is a vignette-like collection of "becoming with" examples. For Haraway, these models look like using string theory, game theory, and calculus (iterated integrals) to theorize "terrapolis"—companion species terraforming in infinite permutations. This also looks like STEMM-Humanities community alliances such as a Southern California human-Racing Pigeon relationship building initiative, sponsored by a collaborative arts and ornithology program, whose platform is the online community PigeonBlog. Through PigeonBlog, Haraway explores the politics surrounding community-based human-animal work that does not have the stamp of academically sanctioned STEMM research, commenting that "perhaps it is precisely in the realm of play, outside the dictates of teleology, settled categories, and function, that serious worldliness and recuperation become possible," and adds, "That is surely the premise of SF" (23-24). Haraway's definition of SF is "a sign for science fiction, speculative feminism, science fantasy, speculative fabulation, science fact, and also,

---

1. The title of the 2018 Modern Language Association panel that facilitated an earlier version of this article; it plays off of Haraway's phraseology in *Staying with the Trouble*.

string figures" (10), and adds that *play* is essential to her vision of SF as the site of recuperation of our damaged planet. "Playing games of string figures," she writes, "is about giving and receiving patterns, dropping threads and failing but sometimes finding something that works, something consequential and maybe even beautiful, that wasn't there before, of relaying connections that matter, of telling stories in hand upon hand, digit upon digit, attachment site upon attachment site, to craft conditions for finite flourishing on terra, on earth" (10).

I want to suggest that as pedagogues we take from Haraway what she finds at the center of multidisciplinary storytelling: joy and play. (As we are busy lamenting the neoliberal institution's instrumentalization of knowledge production, is it possible to remember fun?) With play at the center, she is able to critique the process by which human-animal projects are given sanction, for instance. Under the umbrella of Serious Research, she wryly mentions, projects that look and smell like pigeon fancy but masquerade as humorless are often not subjected to the same objections regarding animal consent as the Southern California racing pigeon collective has been, but she identifies amusing human-animal projects as equal or even better examples of generative worlding, or world-recovery. Serious Research, devoid of fun and story-telling, yet the kind that gets grants, assumes a mythic human/nature divide. As curriculum designers, program directors, and stewards of the new academy, we ought to be more intentional about collapsing that divide. The result, Haraway suggests, are more generative and responsible companion species interactions, and I argue this progressive thinking also generates a methodological and institutional upshot: more and more purchase in the premise that the STEMM/Humanities dichotomy is itself mythological. Moreover, we seem to have reached an impasse, where that divide is no longer even possible, both for practical and ethical reasons. The budget crisis in the Humanities, first ushered in by corporate neoliberalism, now affects the sciences, too, in the current reactionary and anti-intellectual Trumpian era.

Lest we get lost in the optimism that *Staying With the Trouble* exudes, Haraway's notion of play is far from utopic. There is no universalizing law for how to treat—how to "be-with"—animals; likewise, the very ethic of interdisciplinarity—that boon that will help multispecies organisms tell our stories to each other—falls short of implementation given the deep class barriers that scaffold Higher Ed, and the corporate institution's exacerbation of these barriers despite its promise to correct them. How exactly the distinctions between different types of companion species interactions are arranged, what produces these differences, and how to secure funding to study and play with these formations could be located in a Marxist or materialist investigation, but Haraway avoids this avenue of evaluation. While a sustained class analysis is all but absent in Haraway, she does seem to gesture to it anecdotally, as in the comment, "if only we could all be so lucky as to have a savvy artist design our lofts, our homes, our messaging packs" to be more sustainable (29). Since capitalism's excesses form the basis of ecocritical thought, perhaps it goes without saying that social class distinctions produce, in part, distinct sets of companion species interactions. I am thinking, for example, of the intersectional ethics relating to the role poverty plays when decisions are made to support or resist big agribusiness and industrial farming. As we remake the Humanities into the Humusities, we need to be more intentional and proactive about leveling these distinctions. Equity must

37

form the basis of STEMM-Humanities co-teaching and interdisciplinary programming, rather than serving as an afterthought.

Then there is the potential recklessness of prematurely declaring the death of the Human. In the Introduction to *The Posthuman*, Rosi Braidotti underscores the hypocrisy of, on the one hand, the West's ubiquitous privileging of the human category, and on the other hand, its inextricable assemblage to "rights," when so many humans have so little of the latter. Moreover, "not all of us," she points out, "can say, with any degree of certainty, that we have always been human, or that we are only that. Some of us are not even considered fully human now, let alone at previous moments of Western social, political and scientific history" (1). In her final pages, Braidotti circles back around to challenge the prefix "post," in turn: "Not all of us can say, with even a modicum of certainty, that we have actually become posthuman, or that we are only that" (186). Both Braidotti and Haraway are materialists, and both are affirmative in their politics and in their solutions to the environmental crisis caused by anthroprocentrism, but, in tone, Braidotti proceeds with caution where Haraway trudges forth in an almost euphoric celebration of the postindustrial muck and the possibilities therein. Let Braidotti co-guide us in our co-teaching methodologies.

A capitalist critique in *Staying with the Trouble* is relegated to questions about the life of the university, rather than individualized, lived experiences of capital; true, we can only work within the confines of our own power communities. Since readers of this venue likely are uniquely poised to effect change within university structures, Academia is my focus here. Anna Tsing, the feminist anthropologist and cultural critic who chronicles the diverse lives of fungi, prefers academic work that declines "either to look away [from the garbage produced by capitalism's excess] or to reduce the earth's urgency to an abstract system of causative destruction" (Haraway, *Staying* 37). This work excites Haraway as it "characterizes the lives and deaths of all terran critters in these times" (38). Where does worrying about turf in academia fall into this preferred paradigm? Haraway would just as soon do away with siloed academic disciplines. We might extrapolate this from her utopic yet cheeky call to "Imagine a conference not on the Future of the Humanities in the Capitalist Restructuring University, but instead on the Power of the Humusities for a Habitable Multispecies Muddle!"

Multidisciplinary panels, conferences, programs, and even departments are cropping up across industries, while Academia—a body that historically has been the safeguard of non-instrumentalized knowledge—guardedly follows suit, as it tries to balance relevancy with integrity. It can be hard to determine which motivating factors are entirely market-driven and which are holistic, soul feeding, and brainy. If our metric is environmental health and our compass is the survival of nonhuman and human life, I think we just might avoid a wrong turn. The stakes are high for us to imagine our intellectual labor as prescriptive, as predictive of better possible futures, rather than just carnival in an otherwise generic disciplinary order!

In all seriousness, how very small worrying about disciplinary boundaries feels in a neofascist era, in light of the greater threat to thought at every level—both microbiologic and institutional. My next signal in this essay is to probe how we might mitigate this threat at the institutional level, even if just in our tiny corner of the Capitalosphere. Implicit in Haraway's work is a challenge to the *not*-Humanities to see themselves as complicit in storytelling, to decompose the notion that "hardness" is real and the only sensory space that "matters." Humusities work represents a twofold challenge aimed at the STEMM-Humanities divide on both ends: the challenge is not just to the hard sciences to see themselves as soft, as engaged in the art of mythmaking just as much as the Humanities albeit through different methodologies, but also to the Humanities to admit that storytelling is not owned by humans. There exist practical applications of decentering the human story even in the most unlikely of places. Most Humanities academics are aware of underlying neoliberal motivations to diminish the arts in the pursuit of professional programs, motivations that share a timeline with the move to value science over stories, but are monomaniacally market-driven in a way that the first phase of Humanities erosion was not. Hence, it is no wonder that Humanities scholars might be wary of being team players during our current shift.

Perhaps, though, we have not considered how this shifting emphasis actually exposes the instability of the very category "professional," and how that might ultimately be beneficial for us. For instance, many universities—usually with external grant incentives—have shored up new funding initiatives around bridging the arts and sciences and healthcare. The crisis within the latter clearly drives the funding swell, especially given its centrality as a talking point in recent national politics. The multibillion-dollar industry has a lot of concerned players: Big Pharma, the employees who work for the biggest employer in the U.S. (Thompson), and the roughly 80 million uninsured or underinsured Americans for whom the system is not working ("32 Million Underinsured"), to cite a few. While this funding is unfairly instrumentalized and academically restrictive, especially to scholars for whom adding a health initiative to their field is a stretch, it is often more broadly construed than one imagines; additionally, it is folded within larger machinery already in place to support interdisciplinary programs, curricula, and research that bridge the hard and soft sciences generally. One finds a glut of funding of the sort in institutionally hosted grant matchmaking repositories like Pivot. I argue that this represents an unintended consequence of the market-driven transferal: ever-expanding bounds of what constitutes the "professional" and/or the "hard" sciences and an eagerness of funders and their university partners to consider offbeat ideas and projects that reach into the liberal arts. This can only eventually fold back in on itself, collapse back into the (post)human, the liberal, the storytelling, the foundations. For some, to expand one's field may hurt a bit in the interim, and it may feel like one is giving in to a utilitarian value system, but if the eventual effect is fewer siloes and more cosmic thinking, it just might be worth it. The cautionary tale, however, would be told in retrospect from a dystopia of total privatization, and that will be the most difficult byproduct to avoid. Although, I am not entirely convinced such privatization will not happen irrespective of the integrity of our siloes; in which case, our social fabric is already on fire, and we will have to rise from the ashes regardless.

An announcement on the latest report from the National Academy of Sciences on the merits of STEMM-Humanities initiatives conveys "an important trend in higher education: programs that intentionally seek to bridge the knowledge and types of inquiry from multiple disciplines—the humanities, arts, sciences, engineering, technology, mathematics, and medicine—within a single course or program of study. Professors in these programs help students make connections among these disciplines in an effort to enrich and improve learning" ("News"). When The National Academies reviewed data culled from more than 200 integrated programs and curricula nationally on the outcomes relating to integrative approaches to learning at the graduate and baccalaureate levels, they found "limited but promising evidence that a variety of positive learning outcomes are associated with some integrative approaches—including improved written and oral communication skills, content mastery, problem solving, teamwork skills, ethical decision-making, empathy, and the ability to apply knowledge in real-world settings.... Surveys show that these skills are valued both by employers and by higher education institutions" ("News").

Many of us have already done this kind of work tangentially in our interdisciplinary curricula and scholarship, and perhaps in co-taught courses; I would urge expanding the model to be more intentional about STEMM-Humanities pairings in particular, as well as to expand it beyond upper-level coursework, highbrow scholarly communities, and Honors programs. My current research on "aspirant" schools that include course pairings generally shows that the model saves the institution money. It is a cost-saver for several reasons: through a package deal, students save money on home credits by opting not to take the course in the "opposite" field elsewhere, as they often do; further; the model attracts revenue-generating grants for the institution.

Several U.S. universities and colleges are already catching on, deploying curricula that deemphasize humans as sole storytellers. Having examined course information and reflections from five Humanities pedagogues at varying stages in their careers from public and private institutions of different sizes and rankings, my general sense is that this model is successful, generative, and transformative for both student and instructor(s), with little-to-no negative impact on the institution's bottom line. In cases where co-taught or team-taught STEMM-Humanities courses satisfy two or more requirements for graduation and/or are available for banded tuition rates, this model represents money-saving opportunities for students, while at the same time opens up prospects for interdepartmental grants and external funding, bringing prestige and extra budgetary income to the institution.

One of my interviewees, AB,[2] a Philosophy doctoral candidate at a large public, R1 institution with medium-tier ranking[3] and lower-tier endowment (309 million for a university of 40,000), co-taught a STEMM pedagogy course designated as a Philosophy course with a Master Teacher from the Education Department. It was part of a pilot education program for prospective regional math and science teachers, whose headquarters are another large public R1 university with higher prestige and funding. The course satisfied the upper-level Scientific Perspectives requirement, as well as a university Core requirement, and its aim was to study the methods of math and science within the broader historical and philosophical context of these methods. AB reports that the most rewarding element of the course was:

> watching students' judgment about what they do transform. At first, they expressed nervousness about philosophy; about studying a subject that, in their perception, "doesn't have any real answers." They agreed that they like

---

2. To protect interviewees' identities, initials used are pseudonymous.

3. Overall institution rankings based on *U.S. News and World Report*

studying math and science because there are certainties. Over the course of the semester, those certainties, placed into historical and philosophical context, began to look less and less so! I loved watching them find ways to transform their nervousness about uncertainty into excitement about new possibilities for joy, wonder, and discovery in what they study, and excitement about opening up a new generation to those possibilities.

For AB, teaching this course was an expression of her "philosophical/political conviction that a humanities education is necessary for a healthy, functioning democracy." Aligning herself with Martha Nussbaum's position in *Not for Profit*, she writes,

> I am convinced that a humanities education is just what keeps democratic skills alive—imagining other lives through literature and art, asking critical and imaginative questions through philosophy, and realizing the historical and political contingencies at work in one's worldview. As STEMM disciplines are often touted as those most profitable in terms of career trajectories and economic "development" goals, I think STEMM majors are more vulnerable to the gradual effacement of democratic values in the course of their education.

Another professor from a large, R1, top-tier public institution (3.6 billion endowment) reported success with three single-instructor STEMM-Humanities courses: a history of biology course, a course that interrogated the disconnect between popular and academic historical records, and a biographies of physicists class. This History professor, CD, discovered that his students experienced an attitudinal shift, from initial skepticism of this required class for those in the math and science education program, to surprise and joy. In CD's words: "not all of them are as willing to believe that History is something that will be of value to them, especially the math majors. Still, most of those initial skeptics eventually change their mind, and it's rewarding to see it happen."

Feedback from an English professor at a well-endowed (4.1 billion), medium-sized private, top-tier liberal arts university reiterates the experiences of my public school interviewees. For four years, EF has co-taught an undergraduate honors seminar with the Chair of the Physics department on "Science/Fiction." A full professor and former Chair, EF reports it as "the most rewarding undergraduate teaching experience of my career." The course explores the relationship between science and science fiction by examining canonical scientific writing and SF. The course aims, according to EF, to scrutinize "the distinctive modes of imagination and style in the two activities, as well as their social and cultural influences." In the past, EF also taught several iterations of a First Year Writing Seminar with the head of Information Technology on the topic of "Online Gaming." In EF's words, "We mixed game theory with the history and social implications of information technology while surveying some of the landmark video games from *Myst* to *Lord of the Rings Online*. This seminar came to a close when I put the whole thing online as a MOOC for Coursera, where 85,000 students have taken the class so far." The multidisciplinary—though largely engineering and history—students receive elective credits for the course depending on their major. EF's favorite thing about co-teaching in this model is that it broadens our understanding of the Humanities.

EF's model reminds me of potential teaching points from Haraway's collection *Simions, Cyborgs, and Women: The Reinvention of Nature*. In her chapter "Biopolitics of

Postmodern Bodies," she praises researchers Terry Winograd and Fernando Flores for challenging the "rationalist paradigm for understanding embodied (or 'structure-determined') perceptual and language systems and for designing computers that can function as prostheses in human projects" (213). Haraway draws inspiration from their work to theorize "postmodern cyborgs that do not rely on impermeable boundaries between the organic, technical, and textual" (215). She endorses these cyborgs as they are "directly oppositional to the AI cyborgs of an 'information society', with its exterminist pathologies of final abstraction from vulnerability, and so from embodiment" (215). It seems to me that IT-Humanities hybrid courses work to position ethical reasoning at the center of an industry that is alarmingly powerful and increasingly deregulated.

An English professor, GH, from a small private, regional liberal arts university ($74.8 million endowment) was similarly enthusiastic about an Honors Seminar she co-taught twice called "Writing Environmental Wrongs." The curriculum included Environmental literature with Biology, centered on "The Prairie." In her words, most fulfilling was

> the expansion of knowledge I experienced, while watching the students experience a similar growth. It had been a long time since I'd had science, and the way we approached scientific thinking in that course was really complementary to the way we studied poetry and essays. The days when we were in the field, taking samples, watching bison, then lounging in the tall grass reading passages out loud were The Best!

Her enthusiasm was tempered by some sincere challenges, however, including "integrating the interdisciplinary content enough so that the students achieved both biology and lit learning goals. It was a lot of work for them and somewhat frustrating for each of us, at times. It definitely required thinking more broadly about our disciplines and how they intersect in the context of a liberal arts education."

Overall, these STEMM-Humanities classes proved successful despite significant differences among the bureaucratic structures of the universities, and faculty were able to teach within normal budget allocations and constraints of their contracts. I asked each professor whether assessment presented additional challenges in courses where two (or more) instructors were using different assessment modalities. All generally hand-waved the issue of "norming" student performance and confirmed that collegiality and transparency seemed to dissuade conflicts organically. Drawbacks emerged, however, regarding pressures relative to achieving tenure; from the perspective of one of the senior professors and former Chairs at a prestigious, research-driven institution, early-career faculty tenure files were perceived to be at risk if faculty taught too many courses not wholly and rigorously within their disciplines in their first five years. This suggests that while interdisciplinary training is an attractive aspect of an early-career faculty member's curriculum vitae upon hire, in practice co-teaching is still devalued as one builds their professional profile toward tenure.

This may have something to do with the fact that many undergraduate institutions consign co-teaching and interdisciplinary collaboration to First-Year Core curricula, which may have the unintended consequence of demoting co-teaching in perceived rigor. These frameworks are easier to norm, which satisfies university assessment initiatives and accreditation rubrics, regardless of how comfortable individual faculty are with leaving grades to be worked out organically. Universities do not like engaging in risk and tend to look toward aspirant programming to make broad or deep curricular changes. Numbers on the outcomes of interdisciplinary teaching in Core requirements often look favorable, as shown in a recent study on the effect of an Interdisciplinary First-Year Experience Program for Technology majors at Purdue University, which yielded measurable progress on students' "perceived learning transfer, and sense of academic engagement" (Chesley, Kardgar, Knapp, Laux, Mentzer, Parupudi). The report examined over 500 first-year students over a two-year span (AY 2015-2016 and AY 2016-2017) who took courses co-taught by Technology, English, and Communication instructors with the aim of producing better synthesis among all three fields through collaborative learning, lecture, and facilitation. Purdue's study cites ten previous records of improved undergraduate learning outcomes and retention among STEMM vocational majors (nine engineering samples, one accounting) who took integrated STEMM-Humanities courses in their first-year installment of the Core at their respective institutions.

University size and collegial climate does not seem to persuade or dissuade co-teaching, in the general sense. Where there is a will there is a way. STEMM-Humanities co-teaching works within current university budget structures if it is placed in the first-year Core, and continues to measurably improve retention rates; although, I should mention that this model is under fire at my home institution as university budget cuts have increased the need for faculty to take fuller loads in their home departments. The model can also work in special programs like Honors or, at bigger institutions, high school-to-college feeder programs with public STEMM initiatives like AB's, as long as these retain their own funding streams. Wealthy, private, medium-sized institutions such as my interviewee EF's have achieved integrated co-taught sections that allow students to "double-dip" within regular course structures, but as of now, these courses only count as electives. It would seem we are still a far cry from a fundamental interdisciplinary overhaul, which could in part be due to logistical difficulties in the Registrar, but is probably much more likely a symptom of enrollment-based economics.

Of course, this could all be assuaged with legislation that drastically reduces the privatization of Higher Ed, an improbable scenario in the U.S., especially given recent political trajectories. In the interim, I argue that the ideological shift of a Humusities turn, combined with the uptick in grant opportunities for STEMM-Humanities couplings, has the potential to redistribute university wealth. Not only could this shift arrogate more external funding to the Humanities, thus reducing the dependence on enrollment, but it could also better address the gender and race disparities that persist within both STEMM and Higher Ed at large. If colleges and universities enable true interdisciplinarity, taking risks by expanding co-teaching and integrative learning beyond the Core and special programs, the nature of the degree will start to matter less than the degree itself, and the forgotten values of a liberal arts education might be realized again—hopefully this time more inclusively.

My impression is that there exist class barriers to realizing this vision that none of the professors I interviewed mentioned explicitly. In my research so far, I find that while the STEMM-Humanities co-teaching model at public universities seems to be relegated to specific programming (the model is more freely integrated across curricula at private schools), there is an inverse relationship between the wealth of the university and the model's availability to all students. EF and his colleagues are free to dream up innovative curricular pairings as electives, ostensibly available to all students who can afford the school's pricey tuition, while GH's school reserves funding for interdisciplinary pedagogies for Honors students, or, in other words, the already upwardly mobile. She reported that she and her colleague "both got credit for teaching the seminar, even though it was low-enrolled and we did it together. Honors. That's where the money for innovation and interdisciplinarity is at [Institution]." GH's observation returns me to my grievance with *Staying with the Trouble*: we are in need of a Marxist critique of the systemic barriers to realizing the Chthulucene that Haraway envisions.

Still, Haraway writes with an urgency to breaking down the STEMM-Humanities divide. The oft-lamented crisis ascribed to the Humanities is suddenly a shared symptom of the instrumentalist university in the neofascist state. My colleagues are worried about saving the humanities. We talk a lot about that. We talk less about saving our planet. What if interdisciplinary education saves both? Since the myth of the unemployable and underpaid Humanities major has been debunked (see Anders; Grasgreen), we might consider a less self-referential and less internal crisis-driven argument for saving them. Several recent peer-reviewed articles and online listacles catalogue the reasons and ways to save the Humanities—some more obvious than others in their agendas[4]—whose premises now appear flawed and self-interested. But the enemy of my enemy is my friend.

If the human is at stake, the process of saving the human relies on relinquishing the exceptionalism that in the first phase inspired us to save ourselves. The romance of nature no longer abides, or in Haraway's words, "None of the parties in crisis can call upon Providence, History, Science, Progress, or any other god trick outside the common fray to resolve the troubles" (*Staying* 40). There will be no hero; "But still, we are in the story of the hero and the first beautiful words and weapons, not in the story of the carrier bag" (42). Haraway partially disavows Bruno Latour here, who proposes a way out of the destructive arc of history through the motif of war, a battle against absolutist concepts such as those itemized above. For Haraway, any war requires a binary enemy-hero story, of which there can be none; our troubles cannot be solved in the Anthropocene (43).

Nor can they be solved in the Capitalocene. Blaming capital for the earth's destruction still privileges man. Yet, "the infectious industrial revolution of England mattered hugely, but it is only one player in planet-transforming, historically-situated, new-enough, worlding relations. The relocation of peoples, plants, and animals; the leveling of vast forests; and the violent mining of metals preceded the steam engine; but that is not a warrant for wringing one's hands about the perfidy of the Anthropos, or of Species Man, or of Man the Hunter" (48). Man still executed the earth's destruction, but it is less about his inventions and more about the accoutrements of capital and globalization that treaded and turned over the earth. She proposes a less binaristic, less self-flagellatory (and hence, less self-congratulatory) awareness of earth's symbiosis. The Chthulucene is a space "neither sacred nor secular" (55), wherein we can allow for the reality that crit-

---

4. I am thinking, for instance, of Craig Klugman's "How Health Humanities Will Save the Life of the Humanities," in which Klugman cites the misleading statistic that Humanities majors make less money than their non-Humanities peers.

ters are "relentlessly opportunistic and contingent," which in turn ushers in a kind of hope and then generative, innovative thinking about how we can start thinking-and being-with even the most single-celled among us. It is an impoverishment of thought to diminish the world to a vision of actor/human versus reactor/animal. She does not imagine the Capitalocene as our last chapter, or our last "biodiverse geological epoch" (49).

Clearly invoking Deleuze and Guattari, she illustrates Power/Capital as *not* a singular event with a single author/actor. Perhaps it is this new collaborative framework for thinking futurity that entails a new STEMM-Humanities think-tank infrastructure—at every level of educational institutions. Some might contend that Haraway's methodology is so expansive as to be meaningless. She draws from assorted indigenous mythologies, pigeon behavior, microbiomes, coral, SF, and more. To what extent are her examples—ideas to "think-with"—diminished or even defamed in the process of modeling her vision? What would an indigenous scholar in Critical Race Studies think? A microbiologist, who has spent years carefully collating the actual stories microbes tell rather than the ones humans tell of them? Do the ends justify the means, if the lesson we internalize is that the human story must be deemphasized if we are to survive in the muck?

She calls us to make like squid and bacteria and work together across disciplines and methodologies (she seems especially keen on biology-Humanities pairings) and disparages "worried colleagues at conferences" (67), implying tenure requirements unnecessarily squelch innovative thinking toward the Humusities, which my field research supports. Quirkily, she in turn flaunts the venues that published the very paper in which she presents her argument, seemingly uninterested in the way her privilege as a white, Ivy, prolific, senior scholar heading an academic center that is expressly broad in scope intersects with her ability to do this kind of work. Let us as Humusities scholars supplement *Staying with the Trouble* with an interdisciplinary co-teaching program in pursuit of equity, and one that is ultimately in pursuit of a healthy public sphere.

Works Cited

"32 Million Underinsured in U.S., Report Finds." *Time*, 24 Mar 2014.
AB. Email Interview. 4 December 2017.
Anders, George. "Good News Liberal-Arts Majors: Your Peers Probably Won't Outearn You Forever." *The Wall Street Journal*, 11 Sep 2016.
Braidotti, Rosi. *The Posthuman*. Polity, 2013.
CD. Email Interview. 4 December 2017.
Chesley, Amelia, Asefeh Kardgar, Sarah Knapp, Dawn Laux, Nathan Mentzer, Tejasvi Parupudi. "Assessing the Impact of an Interdisciplinary First-Year Experience Program." *Proceedings of the ASEE Annual Conference & Exposition*, Jan. 2017, pp. 2620-2631.
EF. Phone Interview. 20 November 2017.
GH. Email Interview. 15 December 2017.
Grasgreen, Allie. "Liberal Arts Grads Win Long-Term." *Inside Higher Ed*, 22 Jan 2014.
Haraway, Donna. "Biopolitics of Postmodern Bodies." *Simions, Cyborgs, and Women: The Reinvention of Nature*. Free Association Books, 1991, 203-30.
--. Staying with the Trouble: Making Kin in the Chthulucene. Duke, 2016.

Klugman, Craig. "How Health Humanities Will Save the Life of the Humanities." *Journal of Medical Humanities*, 38.4, 2017, pp. 419-430.

"Report Urges Development and Evaluation of Approaches that Integrate STEMM Fields with Arts and Humanities in Higher Education." National Academies of Sciences, Engineering, Medicine. Nationalacademies.org. 7 May 2018. http://www8.nationalacademies.org/onpinews/newsitem.aspx?RecordID=24988&_ga=237129952.1902651955.1525701361-2134768044.1458052166

Thompson, Derek. "Health Care Just Became the U.S.'s Largest Employer." *Atlantic*, 9 Jan 2018.

Seeing Writing Whole: The Revolution We Really Need

Keith Rhodes

Abstract: *Composition classes have difficulty achieving the aims of the CCCC position statement entitled Students' Right to Their Own Language, for reasons related to why we have difficulty integrating calls for building rhetorical listening more fully into our curricula. A fundamental assumption that writers alone are responsible for the success of written communication leads to results that sustain privileged discourse and upset any sense that readers, too, have an obligation in any written transaction. A field of Writing, properly constituted, needs to challenge that assumption of readerly privilege overtly so that we can shift toward teaching students better ways to manage that entire transaction; meanwhile, we should emphasize practices that weaken the grip of readerly privilege, such as Elbow's integration of the vernacular into writing and expanded efforts to use Young's code-meshing approaches with broader audiences of students.*

The Need for a Writing Revolution

I wish to propose a true revolution: a way of thinking about writing that has little continuity with how the field of rhetoric and composition has traditionally presented it. While I build this call out of existing scholarship, I mean to urge a further step, openly declaring that composition and writing classes are simply no longer what we have traditionally said they are. We need a revolution that radically re-positions the scholarship that we do, the courses that we teach, and even how we identify ourselves. Above all, I propose that an identified profession of Writing should focus on the entire transaction of writing, focusing at least as strongly on how writing is read. And by this I don't mean reading in the traditional sense of closely reading fine literature and difficult texts; I mean developing the ability to read a diverse range of texts written by everyday writers, listening to a diverse range of voices with enhanced interpretive ability. No longer should we put the entire burden of successful writing on writers. Instead, a discipline of Writing should treat readers and writers as equally responsible partners in forming meaning by means of written words.

As a small example of the difference that could make, we might turn toward addressing the possible reading deficiencies of those who complain about "bad writing." For a teasing example, we might worry about the intellectual deficiencies of anyone who genuinely cannot interpret a series of terms unless it contains an Oxford comma. That is, the changes that matter have much less to do with trying to teach students how to please powerful audiences and much more to do with linguistic diversity, with what Krista Ratcliffe has called rhetorical listening, with what Patrick Sullivan more plainly calls listening and reading, with what Peter Elbow has called vernacular eloquence. And this change seeks, at last, to build structural support for students' genuine rights to their own language. So as revolutions go, it rather conservatively draws on a great deal of current knowledge and theory; but it rather radically proposes that we cannot hope to use that theory effectively within the current paradigm of writer-focused writing classes—classes that make writers and their assumed deficiencies the entire focus, thereby giving currently empowered readers mastery over writing.

It might sound odd to say that the current paradigm gives readers mastery over writing, but that's a natural outgrowth of a rhetorical focus on audience, and it is perhaps the most critical problem with the current paradigm. True, in composition classes we sometimes position writers as textual heroes, boldly going forth to change the world with their assertions. But notice what we ask of students in doing so: study your rhetorical situation and fit into it as well as possible, attending carefully to audience and genre. In terms of any transferable skill, audience looms overwhelmingly over the entire transaction. The lesson sent by this focus on audience is to please those in power—the normal audiences for which students expect to write (and write for in school, too, to please their graders).

Further, scholars—in our field and beyond—internalize and model the submissive rhetorical stance that comes with that paradigm. It's not mysterious why IMRaD format has become increasingly dominant, nor why scholarship seems increasingly required to have literature reviews and to "create a research space," in John Swales' oft-repeated phrase. In Bakhtin's term, we've made scholarly writing, too, increasingly "monologic," focused on having authors prove that they partake of the "conversation in the field," fluent in all the latest genre conventions, jargon, and (ahem) affordances. It's almost as if the most successful writer will be one who surprises us the least, conforming most expertly to the model we already imagine, constructing readers as masters to be served in precise, settled ways. (By the way, I fully intend the sexist connotations of "master," believing patriarchy to be a significant part of the current paradigm, even if I will leave that particular argument to more expert voices.) This readerly hegemony drives most of the need for revolution. Pedagogical gains within such a submissive construct rarely tend toward the risky—and highly productive—dangers of open-ended problem-solving. Instead, an attitude of writerly submission inculcated in composition classes bleeds out into the larger culture, generating a good portion of the complaint that "Students/graduates can't write." That is, if a vast and varied multitude of readers feel entitled to read exactly what they expect, it's not surprising that they rarely get it from novices in writing such things. But I argue that there's more wrong with that attitude than with our writers, and that it creates more problems than it solves—for writers, readers, and for the culture writ large. Thus, in this article I will also defy that submissive convention to some extent—no doubt to the displeasure of those whose reading of this text might be most deeply constructed by it.

The revolution we need must upset this paradigm and dash that mythic dream of solving all problems of written communication at the site of production. Instead, a post-revolutionary discipline would explore the full transaction of writing—its production and its uses, what goes right and wrong with both, and why. Scholarship in the field similarly would lose its grounding in the concerns surrounding the artificially constructed situation of first-year Composition and move more fully into exploring more often what goes right and wrong in writing activities that occur naturally elsewhere. Above all, it would pay rich attention to the issues of style and genre, in all their social complexity, examining how we might expand both writers' *palettes* and readers *palates*—how we might improve both production and consumption of varied language and forms, unified into a study of inventive interpretation. That work entails moving outward and examining such things in writings generated for direct purposes in workplaces, social media, civic forums, and personal exchanges. Many scholars already do this work, but in a way that focuses mostly on what writers might do better rather than on how the entire transaction might work better. As Sullivan explains well (85-94) in his own call to revolution, research into how people read would need extensive expansion, building upon scholarship currently focused largely on K12 language arts. But a field of Writing would then need to upset the normally submissive power relations of school reading, too, focusing less on interpreting and instrumentalizing the meanings being expressed by more empowered writers and focusing more on learning to interpret and use the expressions of all writers—including especially the less empowered voices and dialects that everyday readers encounter constantly in life and at work.

That is, the move into valuing and studying a full range of writing calls us to study and value a full range of reading as a necessary, complementary piece. Put most simply, the revolution we need brings reading into play as part of the problem with writing. And to the extent that something is not working, the abilities of both writers and readers in the scene would merit examination and critique. Ultimately, in our classes we'd then want to teach students about this entire transaction, developing transformable practices of both writing and reading that can help writing transactions fulfill these needs, broadly imagined.

But first, we need a revolution. And one strong priority should be making "Students' Right to Their Own Language" a genuine goal, a goal that is crucial to any sense that we have generated a "successful" profession. The current profession of rhetoric and composition/writing studies has not done that; it has not yet really even tried. By saying that, I do not mean to diminish the enormous importance and quality of the position statement adopted by the Conference on College Composition and Communication in 1974, entitled "Students' Right to Their Own Language" (hereinafter often referred to as the "Statement"). Indeed, the true disciplinary centrality of that Statement to a more complete field of writing drives my entire interest in this argument. We would all be better off if that thoroughly researched and well-established position became an ordinary part of the social order, not just of writing as a profession and area of study, but of America, the West, the World.

The problem with the Statement, ultimately, is one of genre. The Statement falls into the category of "thoughts and prayers," a ceremonial plea and lament, when it needs to be a plan for strategic action. We know this by its effects. The Statement has had meager impact on how writing is taught and evaluated. Teaching under its direction remains a dubious practice in potentially leading lambs to slaughter (and, most likely, tossing any such aberrant sheepdogs in with them). Despite the themes of the most current CCCCs, even in light of Asao Inoue's call for antiracist assessment and Vershawn Ashanti Young, Rusty Barrett, Y'Shanda Young-Rivera, and Kim Brian Lovejoy's ambitious advocacy of codemeshing, responsible teachers still have great cause to fear implementing the Statement. That fear persists even though our current profession still has no proven, viable means for preparing students to acquire the valued languages of power if they have not been raised to them already. Progressive yearnings to offer students this "right" crash and recede like waves washing against the rocky cliffs of things like the stated course goals of our composition programs, the most popular textbooks for composition, and even aspirational documents like the Association of American Colleges & Universities' "Written Communication VALUE Rubric" and the "WPA Outcomes Statement." In many years, we might pry away a few rocks of resistance by incremental means like those we've used so far.

Even my plea cannot yet escape that paradigm—and neither does the "Statement on Students' Right to Their Own Language" itself, by the way. Like most if not all of my readers here, I am privileged under this current paradigm, thoroughly habituated to use something like the language of power. A few stylistic twists to the contrary, I rarely venture outside disciplinary language conventions, ones which Elbow reminds us construct nobody's true home language (4). Thus, both intentionally and habitually, I conform, as our students understand they must do as well; and as they also fear in our classes, I may well be "disciplined" for my failure to do so more fully. The current profession has established a rhetorical situation in which contending for a right to home language would contradict the most essential socially constructed purpose of the current paradigm: preparing all writers to bear the entire burden of submissively serving up to their reading masters whatever those reading masters might want. Within such a paradigm, to talk of a writer's "right" to anything—not just home language, but anything at all—is a plain absurdity. Our current professional organizations, and all our work, and all our students, are "servile" not as a matter of choice, an option among many others, but as a necessary outcome of the current paradigm. And so long as the system with which we are identified consists only of production, addresses only what the writer might do to improve the communicative transaction, the Statement cannot be anything other than ceremonial and wishful. One might as well talk of the right to ignore gravity.

Similarly, any attempt by current professional organizations in the field to implement the Statement would yield to that same gravitational pull. Certainly, all our outlets welcome and support the most fervent advocates of such a thing. But even the most expert advocacy becomes accepted somewhat like a species of wishful faith healing; when the "patients" need urgent care, we turn to more orthodox methods—even when, at the present stage of pedagogical development, those methods are about as effective in "curing" home language as bloodletting and trepanation were at curing disease.

The Problem with Evolution Rather Than Revolution

We can imagine solving this limited problem of "correctness" eliding the right to home language with a mere shift of framing, but the current paradigm of readerly hegemony will not permit it. A profession of Writing would need to follow up that argument for the priority of home language over correctness with concerted disciplinary action showing that it believes its own case—something that, judging by its actions, the current profession seems unable to do. Most likely, we need a true revolution, and that revolution must be one of practice, not just of talk.

But what practice? We have some contenders. Most famously in our scholarship, Krista Ratcliffe's method of "rhetorical listening" fits extraordinarily well with the post-revolutionary agenda that I have sought to sketch out. Attending to the entire writing transaction necessarily works in the ways Ratcliffe explains. Right now, culturally dominant parties assume they can simply stand back as empowered audiences and expect others to cater to their whims, greatly interfering with both the efficiency and equity of communication. A more efficient, thorough, and effective rhetorical method would entail engaging dominant parties in rhetorical listening—in meeting speakers and writers closer to the source of the communication, in more fully shared language. In fact, I think of Ratcliffe as providing a very large portion of the particulars for a post-revolution discipline of Writing, such that I can save much time simply by saying, "Read Ratcliffe!"

Yet we must also attend carefully to why Ratcliffe's own work has not yet had such an effect, and why more unorthodox efforts make sense. In sum, Ratcliffe presents elegant, refined arguments to narrow audiences. To be unfair and listen badly for a moment, it is as if Ratcliffe imagines that, to stage the revolution, we need only persuade a narrow band of well-published scholars within our own field, and the rest would unfold from on high. But the first problem with such a view, even in a more generous form, is that the hierarchies of privilege within this profession itself have been built within the old paradigm. Appealing to that privileged internal elite so expertly will deservedly—and so also problematically—earn great praise within those ranks. But it also produces texts that prove uninviting, to say the least, to the larger external audiences we also need to persuade.

To be more fair, certainly it is enough to ask of anyone to write such brilliantly insightful and profound work as Ratcliffe's; now it falls to her readers to translate it and apply it and spread the word. Ratcliffe has attended carefully to the practical work that she seeks to foster, providing useful examples from her own teaching and very specific pedagogical frameworks for using them. Even so, I can't help but wonder at the degree to which Ratcliffe's own rhetorical choices seem unnecessarily limiting. At bottom, Ratcliffe's work seems far more promising for use after the revolution than as its means—a plan for what experts need to build within a new field rather than a means to get there.

By contrast, Patrick Sullivan has clearly aimed at broader audiences in writing his own argument for a stronger focus on the reception of texts. His style reaches out in various ways—using plain and familiar language, translating any necessary specialized language, attending to readerly "flow" with techniques like highly indicative subtitles, and using methods like repetition and narrative to help readers settle into his arguments more comfortably. He then provides extensive, clearly explained teaching materials capable of being lifted and used nearly "as is" to accomplish the goals for which he advocates. Clearly, Sullivan has written to be read and understood by a broader audience, and he shows great attention to that complementary responsibility of speaking to be heard. Meanwhile, he shares with Ratcliffe a distinctly practical orientation, similarly seeking very particular changes in teaching and going a good distance toward explaining and enabling them. Further, he directly states his revolutionary intent. He has a chapter entitled "Revolution" (98). His closing paragraph consists of this one sentence, repeated from earlier use: "The time for revolution is now" (184).

Like Ratcliffe, Sullivan urges "a pedagogy of listening" (2). In brief summary, he urges eschewing simplistic "essay" formats and even argumentation itself, asking students instead to pursue exploratory, reflective writing that engages fully with what they are reading and hearing, seeing the flow of that engagement as the main goal. Like Ratcliffe, Sullivan extends "listening" to reading, in fact urging that writing teachers spend a great deal more time and thoughtful effort building students' abilities to read as good listeners (85-90). In pursuit of getting us to join his revolution, Sullivan provides copious and detailed practical advice.

So again, there is an extent to which I can shorten much of this argument into simply "Read Sullivan!" And to be fair, five or six years is not a lot of time to give for a scholarly book to achieve any kind of far-reaching revolutionary impact. Yet I suspect that Sullivan's use of a different sort of rhetorical tactic may hinder its genuinely revolutionary impact. That is, for a revolutionary, Sullivan seems curiously eager to show that everything he urges already fits well within a broad *status quo ante*. The text makes frequent resort to long quotations from existing, well-regarded texts, showing how extensively his main ideas have already been thought out by others. I imagine him in the guise of the Wizard of Oz, telling us that we already have everything we seek, needing only to acknowledge it in some ceremonial way. But without the magical ruby slippers, Dorothy wasn't getting home to Kansas. Actually getting somewhere is a horse of a different color.

When I think of the work left largely aside in Sullivan's agenda, I am pointed back to Ratcliffe. That is, the revolution that will create a pedagogy of listening will necessarily require challenging well-entrenched cultural power dynamics. It's not a revolution that we can successfully prosecute in our classrooms alone, with a change of lesson plans. At every level above classroom teachers, powerful figures will disagree, and strongly, with what such teachers would be doing. The revolution that Sullivan imagines won't fit departmental course goals, expressed institutional general education goals, or the idea of "writing" in the minds of authorities beyond the Composition program (or even, often enough, within it). Most teachers can't afford to storm these particular barricades. Despite all its rhetorical generosity in surface matters, Sullivan's argument may well have a very small and limited real audience: writing teachers already empowered to teach as they wish, or at least to teach consistently with this particular vision. In a different sort of way, Sullivan again provides a teleological vision, but not yet the means, for revolution.

And all that should seem normal and expected. Anyone working within the current paradigm ultimately either sustains it or simply runs up against its constraints and can go no farther. The composition teacher's tools will not tear down and rebuild the composition teacher's course goals—well, at least not without some transitional work.

Speculative Steps Toward the Revolution

I openly confess to have no final set answer; but the kinds of directions we could explore seem clear enough to offer as speculative instruments, at least. Some who have read earlier versions of this argument have been dismayed (to use an understated casting of the reaction) that I have no more exact direction or manifesto to offer. But I think the reality here is that the shift in direction that I propose is at once so simple and so disruptive that only a fool would seek to claim exactly how it would go and how it might end up. And so for other readers this argument has seemed profoundly frightening, a leap into the void that could disrupt professional structures and career paths in this already fragile and often threatened profession. My sense, then, is that my greatest responsibility is to propose next steps—things to do now from within current structures that could have revolutionary consequences without simply burning down the house.

I suggest that code-meshing steps most ably into this breach, so long as we extend the concept by means that could make it a more universal approach—and I will suggest that approaching code-meshing by means of imitation offers those means. That's potentially a revolutionary step that we could take in our classrooms very soon, under the plausible and genuine guise of teaching better rhetoric, and particularly better attention to style and genre.

I'll also now confess to believing that teaching writing very strongly entails teaching style—especially in Kate Ronald's sense of producing writing that sounds as if someone is at home in the text, an intuitive much more than a formalistic endeavor. I could go on and on about that, having researched it as my main area of professional focus for many years (see, e.g., Rhodes). My brutally concise summary of that work is that students benefit greatly from experimenting with a broad range of styles, especially if that work is grounded in social and rhetorical considerations. On closer study, it turns out that they benefit little, in the long run, from being offered "codes of power," such as Joseph Williams's admittedly astute formulae for clarity; such formalistic instruction simply doesn't "take." Thus, above all, students need to build a kind of intuitive, creative intelligence to work well with what Ann Berthoff so aptly called the "allatonceness" of writing.

"Code-meshing," in Young, Barrett, Young-Rivera, and Lovejoy's meaning of the term, helps students to "mesh" their home languages with languages of power. It's intentionally opposed to "code-switching"—asking those who speak and write disfavored dialects to learn the languages of power, and to use those empowered dialects exclusively when conversing with those in power. Its central feature—"meshing" rather than switching codes, producing texts that blend features of home and privileged dialects—helps students view, as the authors say, "Standard English as expansive and inclusive, as being able to accommodate and include their culture and dialect" (3). By far the main importance of that pedagogical method for students remains its noted ability to avoid the negative "emotional and racial effects" of code-switching (that is, of essentially segregating home and privileged language, entirely switching codes to use each in its own setting) (5). Perhaps the strongest argument in favor of code-meshing remains that simple racism has much greater effects on students' prospects than whatever dialect they learn to use (5). In terms of the argument here, we can say that code-switching not only puts all the burden of communication on less empowered writers and speakers but also—and perhaps partly for those reasons—causes significant personal and social harm. So we can start with a practice of code-meshing as a helpful way to work with speakers and writers of disfavored dialects. But while code-meshing can clearly help such students, perhaps it can do a great deal more for a broader range of students. Teachers just have to find a way past the problem that most students, and by far most teachers, have no immediately obvious alternate codes of their own to mesh.

A. Suresh Canagarajah's Introduction to *Literacy as Translingual Practice* illustrates (among a great many other useful things) why teachers might be able to start working with more varied and translingual styles and voices even before having generated a perfected body of theory and practice for crosscultural codemeshing. As Canagarajah explains, schools have been complicit so far in artificially sustaining monolingual practices, doing much to create and sustain an atmosphere in which such practices become artificially disempowering. Yet in the rest of our lives (think, for example, of television advertisements), our larger culture willingly negotiates diverse cultural and linguistic practices. Normal school writing is actually the source and chief instance of the problem of monolingual power. It makes sense to shift that perspective in ways that code-meshing permits in part because classrooms aimed at producing Standard Written English genuinely create the problem that they have no ready means to solve. So, at the very least, we can apply the first rule of filling holes: first, stop digging them; stop insisting on Standard Written English. Canagarajah's collection as a whole offers bountiful examples of responsible alternatives.

Even teachers ready for that first step will rightly have other anxieties in going any farther with translingual practices, of course. What do teachers do about students whose "home" languages seem to correspond closely with privileged dialects? First, as Elbow explains, that concern partly ignores the important "vernacular" dimension of spoken language, something that writers have always drawn upon for effective style. As Elbow declares, "In short, *'correct writing' is no one's mother tongue*" (4). Or, as he later puts it in what he calls its "negative form," "[O]ur culture of literacy functions as though it were a plot against the spoken voice, the human body, vernacular language, and those without privilege" (6-7). As he ultimately concludes "it takes strong force (usually political, sometimes military) to squash the inevitable human linguistic tendency toward divergence" (372). As a result, it becomes entirely possible to position all students as having suppressed voices to explore—either their own, internalized ones or ones that they hear around them. Furthermore, we can and should work with a broad range of dialects for practical reasons with widespread benefits. Such work should help all students improve stylistic flexibility and control, and so the perceived value of their writing. And everybody has at least some variation from the imagined norm available as a starting place for that exploration.

Meanwhile, if less privileged students are ever to have true rights to their home languages, we will first have to expose a broader range of students to reading, working with, and understanding a broader range of Englishes and dialects. And in turn, helping more students become comfortable with writing and reading a wider range of home languages should enhance communication generally. Thus, it should be that writing teachers could work out how to make aggressive use of code-meshing and vernacular writing to expand the range of students' writing and reading style.

Such approaches raise great risks, of course—naïve cultural appropriation, or a simplistic essentializing of other voices, among others. Nevertheless, there could be much to gain from widespread use of code-meshing in writing classes, for all students. After all, as Young writes in the "Coda" to *Other People's English*, "[W]e also hope this book will serve as a framework for understanding language in ways that can help anyone reduce language prejudice and promote the power of language as opposed to the codes of power" (156). The most basic method for expanding code-meshing into a broader practice would entail having all students identify the ways in which, as Elbow contends, all of us have at least some differences to negotiate with some mythic, idealized standard form of English. I can also imagine that it serves the larger purposes of code-meshing well if we mess up the power relations among codes, finding ways to ask students with more privileged voices to engage seriously with less privileged dialects, and holding them (and ourselves) accountable for understanding that work responsibly. Again, that is a kind of work that could pay large cultural and economic benefits, generating more skilled reading of less privileged dialects by larger audiences, in turn breaking down the artificial cultural dominance of privileged dialects. Meanwhile, it may also be effective and valuable style work for all students who engage with it.

Thus, writing teachers from more privileged backgrounds (that is, for related structural reasons, by far most college writing teachers) might best start with modified imitation exercises, where the quality of the result could be referenced to a specific example. That method could avoid the dangerous problem of invoking thinly imagined stereotypes. And it might well be prudent in our early going to focus on voices from far corners of English dialect rather than from across the street, for related reasons. One might easily extend Elbow's own approach to helping students "mesh" their own vernacular into languages of power with playful imitation of dialects near and far, simply to get a sense of how other styles feel and what difference they make. Elbow suggests using Dohra Ahmed's anthology *Rotten English*, a collection of culturally disfavored (but clearly powerful) voices, for other purposes; but it would also seem like a natural source for useful imitation exercises of this kind. And since that collection brings in a variety of English dialects from around the world, the language would be unfamiliar and broadening for most of our students across class lines.

My own experience with this approach has not risen to the point of producing reliable evidence, but it offers grounds to hope that this approach has prospects worth further and broader exploration. In much earlier, much more poorly grounded attempts at cross-cultural stylistic imitation, I found that privileged students erred too often in the direction of seeing dialect as deficiency, focusing their attempts at imitation on exaggerating errors and limited, stereotypical "moves." But lately I have been asking students to start by imitating dialects with which they had no familiarity, and to base imitations closely on model texts. I have found an interesting contrary tendency when students err: they now mainly "correct" error, regularizing the dialect in more of a true meshing with their own vision of a standardized language. Their efforts thus open up interesting conversations about the nature of code-meshing, as well as the actual variety of their different interpretations of how that standardized language works. But even more encouraging has been the extent to which students more often fully engage with an unfamiliar dialect in their imitations once we have explored its nature together a bit. Meanwhile, translative imitation—seeking to discuss some incident or idea that has genuine (even if often playful) connections with the content and ideas in the original—deepens students' understanding of the text itself with which they are engaging. I have been encouraged to do more of this work—and will.

But perhaps most significantly, these experiences have alerted me to my own deficiencies in preparation for this kind of work—deficiencies born of a career spent focusing on other matters of more concern within the current paradigm of writing. Looking to the future, the linguistic skills and cultural sensitivity needed to manage code-meshing from all directions probably should become more prominently demanded of those who claim to have expert preparation as writing teachers. That is, ultimately any revolution must be disruptive, must entail some destructive energy, must leave some current experts behind. But a large-scale turn toward the practices of rhetorical listening and code-meshing, already in swing, would seem to have great potential for helping writing teachers re-tool on the fly, becoming also the right kind of people to develop the new paradigm. I say this well aware of the phenomenon that Thomas Kuhn documents—the ways in which revolutions tend ultimately to entirely supplant old paradigms, with adherents to the old ways never changing their minds but simply dying off. I have higher hopes for people who study all these matters of cultural change so assiduously; but if that's the way it must be here as well, better to get started at it sooner, so that at least we can stop generating further generations of those devoted to the old paradigm.

Epilogue: The Author's Pragmatic Ideology

I add here one final point that I wish were not necessary, but that probably is. And I add it last not as a "gotcha" for those who might have read this entire argument differently, but because it really should, structurally, be nothing more than an afterthought. The fundamental intention of this argument is to improve the means by which writing accomplishes its ends—defining those ends broadly only to include every human motivation for writing. I do not start with any assumption that linguistic diversity is good in and of itself, or that being inclusive is good in and of itself, or even that patriarchy is bad in and of itself. I simply find it self-evident that broadening the range of writing most people can read is a surer, quicker, cheaper, more efficient, and more productive path to better communication compared to attempting to regularize all language use in narrowly constricted ways. Popular culture offers abundant evidence that people generally agree. Indeed, the prevalence of varied discourse in most of life should serve to put the burden of proof on those who contend otherwise. Writing classes have labored for too long under an absurd assumption that regularization is the better approach, even despite the prominent evidence that grammar instruction—the most obvious and general outcome of that assumption—has had such dismal record of performance. We should, of course, welcome any genuine evidence to the contrary; but as in the grammar debates, it would be wise not to hold our breath while we wait.

For now, I will rest my case on a simple thought experiment. Let us posit two parties to a communication. The first is fluent in a non-standard dialect but has not yet learned Standard Written English. The second knows Standard Written English well, but has not yet learned the other dialect. What do we suppose would be the most efficient means by which we could ensure that these two parties understand each other very fully? As soon as we put aside any thought of privileging Standard Written English, the answer clearly appears: help them read each other effectively. That pragmatic end is my only agenda in this argument. The rest simply serves that end and, of course, many others.

Works Cited

Ahmed, Dohra, editor. *Rotten English: A Literary Anthology*. Norton, 2007.

Canagarajah, A. Suresh, editor. *Literacy as Translingual Practice: Between Communities and Classrooms*. Routledge, 2013.

—. Introduction. Canagarajah, pp. 1-10.
Elbow, Peter. *Vernacular Eloquence: What Speech Can Bring to Writing.* Oxford UP, 2012.
Inoue, Asao B. *Antiracist Writing Assessment Ecologies: Teaching and Assessing Writing for a Socially Just Future.* Parlor Press, 2015.
Kuhn, Thomas. *The Structure of Scientific Revolutions.* 1962. 4th ed., University of Chicago P, 2012.
Ratcliffe, Krista. *Rhetorical Listening: Identification, Gender, Whiteness.* Southern Illinois UP, 2005.
Rhodes, Keith. "Feeling It: Toward Style as Culturally Structured Intuition." *College Composition and Communication*, vol. 71, no. 2, 2019, pp. 241-267.
Ronald, Kate. "Style: The Hidden Agenda in Composition Classes, or One Reader's Confession." *The Subject is Writing*, edited by Wendy Bishop, 2nd ed., Heinemann, 1999, pp. 169-182.
"Students' Right to Their Own Language." *Conference on College Composition and Communication*, cccc.ncte.org/cccc/resources/positions/srtolsummary.
Sullivan, Patrick. *A New Writing Classroom: Listening, Motivation, and Habits of Mind.* Utah State UP, 2014.
Swales, John. *Genre Analysis: English in Academic and Research Settings.* Cambridge UP, 1990.
The Wizard of Oz. Metro-Goldwyn-Mayer, 1939.
"WPA Outcomes Statement for First-Year Composition (3.0)." *Council of Writing Program Administrators*, 17 July 2017, http://wpacouncil.org/aws/CWPA/pt/sd/news_article/243055/_PARENT/layout_details/false.
"Written Communication VALUE Rubric." *Association of American Colleges & Universities*, https://www.aacu.org/sites/default/files/files/VALUE/WrittenCommunication.pdf
Young, Vershawn Ashanti. "Coda: The Power of Language." Young, Barrett, Young-Rivera, and Lovejoy, pp. 153-156.
Young, Vershawn Ashanti, Rusty Barrett, Y'Shanda Young-Rivera, and Kim Brian Lovejoy. *Other People's English: Code-Meshing, Code-Switching, and African American Literacy.* Teachers College Press, 2014.

SPECIAL SECTION: THE TOIL OF FEELING: EDUCATION AS EMOTIONAL LABOR

Teaching at the End of Empire

Wendy Ryden

To say we are living in difficult times is both a truism and an understatement. Authoritarianism is on the rise as the neoliberal order deteriorates into something unpredictable and uncontrollable. Inequality gaps and oppression—economic, gender, racial and ethnic—widen and persist. Environmental and climate damage run rampant, unabated. Wars and domestic violence, the threats of nuclear weapons, multiply and intensify. And yet it seems we are expected to carry on with our professional and personal lives as though they are not thoroughly imbricated in this maelstrom. Of course that is not possible—nor desirable. So how do we proceed in the face of this enormity we confront?

When the call for "The Toil of Feeling: Education as Emotional Labor" was put out in 2019, we did not yet know what 2020 would bring, how it would starkly reveal our deep dysfunction. But perhaps we sensed a crisis was impending, a culmination of not just the last four years but the last forty. We have been teaching in a time of crumbling facades, when the anemic bracketing of so-called "politics" from ordinary lives has been hopelessly shorn of its illusion. Let's not pretend anymore, even the meekest among us, that we can have conversations about education without speaking about the society in which we live and its myriad deficiencies and disasters. Education can no longer fiddle while the country, the world, burns in so many ways. It is evident that professionalization and corporatization must not be the moral imperatives of higher education, that we must renew our commitment to educating whole human beings, to caring for them and for ourselves, and to educating for change.

In 2019 in the *New Republic*, Matt Ford writes, "The constant exposure to Trump's rhetoric and governance carries its own measurable toll," and compares this to "a tax ... on the national psyche—one that can never be repaid." The least powerful of us, "the younger and less affluent ... women ... black and Hispanic Americans" feel the stressful effects disproportionately. Before 2020 this emotional and material "tax" of being whipsawed through the devastation of the Trump fiasco was already well in evidence, making it abundantly clear to educational practitioners how much emotional labor is at stake in teaching and learning, how much more beyond the usual considerable investment has been required of us. We have been confronted with outrage after outrage. Our blood boils; our hearts break. Perhaps it has never been so apparent that feeling is work.

As this issue goes to press, we contemplate our autumn returns to campuses in a climate of literal lethality and an educational culture, indeed a world, likely forever changed by this year's failures. Perhaps it's fair to say that teaching and learning have always been occurring in crises; the world has never been perfect. But that commonplace does not do justice to the current moment. While many in our ranks are among the more fortunate, we are, so many of us, feeling the wear and tear of the work we must find a way to continue to do if we are lucky enough to (still) be employed. May we all find the courage and resources, the pleasures and rewards we need to carry on. Perhaps recognizing and trying to understand the central way in which our feelings are indeed part of the toil we perform, as the contributors to this special section do, is a place to begin.

Work Cited

Ford, Matt. "Trump's Tax on the National Psyche." *New Republic*, 21 August 2019. https://newrepublic.com/article/154818/trumps-tax-national-psyche .

FYC Students' Emotional Labor in the Feedback Cycle

Kelly Blewett

Abstract: *This essay explores the emotions first-year composition students experience when receiving feedback on their writing. Culling data from 32 hours of interviews with students, as well as two different data streams students provided regarding their emotional reactions to feedback, I argue that students undergo what Arlie Hochschild calls transmutation as they process feedback on their writing. Two implications are suggested: first, that future studies should utilize non-alphabetic tools for capturing emotion; second, that teachers wishing to assist student reception of feedback should be attentive to building rapport in the classroom. Finally, the essay calls for additional study of the impact of positionality on rapport-building and, in turn, the feedback cycle.*

In his contribution to the book *Encountering Student Texts*, Charles Bazerman indicates that a first draft of his essay presented a picture of "the teacher in control of a complex set of relationships" (140). The subsequent revision, however, which emphasized the changeableness of the teacher's self-presentation, reminds Bazerman of the mythic hero Menelaus's attempt to capture the sea king Proteus in order to gain passage across the water. In the myth, Menelaus's task is difficult because Proteus is unstable, constantly shifting shapes. Menelaus eventually imitates Proteus's guises. He successfully grabs Proteus's hands, and then, as Bazerman concludes, "the god assume[s] a stable shape and reveal[s] the way home across the sea" (146). Both figures in the myth are involved in an act of transmutation, or changing from one form to another. Bazerman suggests the same is true of teachers as they read and respond to student writing.

But feedback in the writing classroom is a recurring situation that can cast students and teachers into rigid roles and arouse a range of emotions. Lisa Ede notes that she dreads her students' responses to her feedback before she even writes it (152). Nancy Sommers refers to the day of handing back papers to be "the loneliest" she experiences as a teacher, fraught with uncertainty about what her students will do with the comments she's painstakingly produced (x). Nonetheless, she seeks to find pleasure in responding to student work.

Sommers' attempt to find pleasure when reading student writing while keeping what we might deem inappropriate emotions (boredom, disgust, exhaustion, anger) at bay also suggests transmutation, as Arlie Russel Hochschild has used the word in her discussions of emotional labor. For Hochschild, transmutation means "the link between a private act, such as attempting to enjoy a party, and a public act, such as summoning up good feeling for a customer" (19). Understanding how such labor takes place—and its attendant affects—is difficult. Scholars of affect such as Kathleen Stewart use words like "slides" and "snaps into place" and "becomes a something" to describe the "surges" of affect that that make up the texture of daily life (6, 15, 9).

As these words suggest, and as Bazerman's essay demonstrates, considering feedback and emotion at the same time entails a commitment to studying inferred dynamics, vibes, relational perception, and the essential changeableness that underlies these phenomena. This article will share how I attempted to uncover these aspects of feedback through a qualitative study at a large Midwestern university that prioritized student/teacher relationships and feelings.[1] My study is instructive for those of us committed to understanding the flows of emotion through which students and teachers inhabit their expected roles and through which student writing is mediated. I'll ultimately argue that studying the kind of emotional labor inherent in receiving feedback requires methods that move beyond particular vocabularies of emotion—even words informed by emotion studies—and should include nonalphabetic modes for students to communicate their emotional reactions to teacher feedback.

In the following paragraphs, then, I will first make the case that studying students' emotions as they read teacher feedback is a worthwhile pursuit, one that responds to longstanding calls within response literature, and takes us into the very heart of the communicative interchange of teaching writing. Next, I'll present the methods I used to try to access students' affective responses to feedback, which included 32 hours of one-on-one interviews with students and a collection of written data that featured two ways of tracking emotion—one by words (which were gathered after the student had processed the feedback), and one by images (which were gathered as the student was receiving the feedback for the first time). Disparate streams within the data set will be traced to suggest that how and when we ask students to comment on their emotions have a strong governing effect on the types of emotions they report, which I interpret as evidence of transmutation in action. An examination of one first-year student, Joseph, vividly illustrates the movement from the internal protean swirl to the stable, public face which students have been schooled to perform. Ultimately, I demonstrate that students undergo a process of transmutation that mirrors what Bazerman and others (Sommers; Ede; Murray) have discussed from the teacher perspective. Periodically, I will offer snapshots from the data—glimpses of particular students using nonalphabetic or metaphoric modes for discussing feedback—to show what a reliance on vocabulary alone misses: an emphasis on intensities and surges, a stronger and more ambivalent mix of positive and negative emotions, and a desire to use language that feels more accessible, vibrant and personal.

Literature Review: Emotion and Feedback

Those familiar with response literature in composition know the long history of examining the written comments outside of a classroom context, either by having many teachers look at and respond to a single student paper (Batt; Daiker; Connors and Lunsford; Smith; Straub and Lunsford) or by having students respond to decontextualized feedback on a sample student paper (Bowden; Straub, "Exploratory"). Such studies do little to tell us how students receive and interpret specific feedback. Richard Straub has argued that this is not actually the point of work like *Twelve Readers Reading*: "the goal is not to determine how . . . the student would likely understand it. The proposed analysis

---

1. Following Laura Micciche, I do not distinguish among the words feelings, emotions, and affects. See "Staying."

is concerned with the way the teacher creates himself in his comments, his persona as it may be construed from the words on the page" (*Practice* 84). His remark leaves a reader wanting to see students grappling with particular feedback from particular teachers.[2]

The unsatisfactory nature of these studies led Jane Fife and Peggy O'Neill to argue that on the topic of response our theories and methodologies need to do much more to acknowledge the complexity of the classroom scene. When conducted, such studies have upset established notions of how feedback works. For example, Carol Rutz studied the classroom of Luke, an experienced writing teacher. In addition to collecting samples of his commentary, she attended his class and took notes, interviewed Luke, and interviewed two students in his class. After the term was over, she gave student drafts from his class to a team of three raters.

> The graph of Luke's responses yields a graph similar to the reader profiles obtained by Richard Straub and Ronald Lunsford. . . It displays important information about Luke as a responder, to be sure, and the patterns are revealing—in part. However, this stark, two-dimensional assessment of Luke's work as a reader of student texts lacks the context, including the dimensions of space and time, that better and more completely inform the relationship that Luke and his students developed during the fall of 1996. (126)

She contrasted the "two-dimensional" impressions of the assessors with the impressions of Luke's students, who interpreted feedback from Luke in light of a lot more data about Luke—how he spoke in the classroom, how he framed and explained assignments, the feedback he offered to class as a whole. In short, they regarded his feedback through his classroom persona. The incorporation of their perception of Luke as a teacher made a significant improvement in their ability to interpret Luke's comments. In Luke's words, which Rutz borrowed to title her chapter, students became "marvelous cartographers," adept at mapping the connections between the classroom and the paper's margins. Studies like Rutz's reveal the impoverished nature of feedback scholarship. I reported a similar finding in my own study, which followed the feedback cycles of two teachers, including Elise, who at the time had eighteen years of experience. Elise made a comment on a student paper that I perceived as ambiguous, even potentially aggressive ("It's not that your introduction is 'bad,' it's just that it needs work"). As I considered the comment over time, my interpretation hardened, especially as outside sources confirmed my impression.[3] The teacher's actual student, Kaari, however, was unperturbed by the comment, because, she told me in an interview, she "imagined my teacher saying it in her voice." The teacher's voice, in Kaari's mind, was kind. Thus, Kaari rightly concluded "[The professor] didn't mean any harm by [the comment]." Data beyond the decontextualized comment made up a gap in a way that worked for the student and sustained a productive feedback cycle. Codes are insufficient. Language cannot be understood in a vacuum.

These research stories suggest that emotion is an important dimension of the "marvelous cartography" of Luke's students, though Rutz doesn't explore emotion much.

---

2. See Knoblauch and Brannon, who make similar points in "Emperor."

3. See Garber on the rhetorical effect of scare quotes.

The emotions students have when they receive feedback seems to be tied to the way they perceive their teachers and to what kind of relationship they have with their teachers. A long history of scholarship in K-12 emphasizes that students who have stronger relationships with teachers tend to do better in school, to like it more, and to go farther in their education (see Raider-Roth). Relationships and emotions are less often studied at the college level. Yet they are central to the writing classroom, and it is impossible to properly understand how feedback works without attending to them. In her introduction to *Composition Forum*'s special issue on emotion, Laura Micciche writes, "emotion remains viable for investigating relationships writ large—what I take to be the general province of emotion studies." Far from an extra feature of communication, emotion is central in getting things done. If emotion studies can help us understand how feelings mediate the psychic and the social, the individual and the collective (Ahmed 119), then these acts of transmutation merit our attention.

As I've already suggested, existing work highlights the emotional transmutation teachers enact (consciously or subconsciously) when responding to student writing. Lad Tobin also explores teacher/student relationships, laying bare his own efforts to maintain the tone of a supportive coach in his comments, while also suppressing emotions and reactions that would undermine that performance. He writes: "I find it an almost constant challenge . . . *to perform the role* of an infinitely curious reader, even when I might be feeling bored or disapproving. Fortunately, while being and performing may not be exactly the same thing, I've always found that each naturally follows the other" ("Strategic" 203, emphasis added). His emphasis on "performing" his way to having the right feelings echoes Hochschild's point that when we "manage feeling we contribute to the creation of it" (18). Managing emotions is exactly what Piper Murray argues that teachers do when responding to student work:

> I would be willing to bet that the more we may be feeling like lodging accusations in our students' margins (cliché! overgeneralization! awk!), the harder we work to prevent those accusations from actually making their way anywhere near our students' writing—the more careful we are, for example, to carefully *transform* such impulses into expressions of interest rather than frustration . . . (99, emphasis added)

For Murray, emotional labor of transmutation is required when outlaw emotions—blame and anger, in this case—threaten to bubble to the surface. While Murray and Tobin relied on their own experience to direct their investigations, Jacob Babb and Stephen Corbett have investigated, via surveys, the emotions professors experience when they issue a grade of F to a student. One of the most common sets of feelings was disappointment and self-doubt; the teachers sensed that they had not supported the students enough. This might be another way of articulating concern that they didn't properly fulfill their role. Less scholarship has examined transmutation from the student point of view, although some work points in that direction.

For example, Chris Anson, Deanna Dannels, Johanne Laboy, and Larissa Carneiro's "Student Perceptions of Oral Screencast Responses to Their Writing: Exploring Digitally Mediated Identities" surfaces the concept of facework, borrowed from Erving Goffman. This term explains what is at stake for students during an evaluative situation such as receiving critical feedback. Students need to protect themselves from face threat by focusing on aspects of the response that are affirmative—for instance, on the fact that the teacher likes them as a person, likes their writing generally, or is motivated to help them. Thus, the student may receive the criticism with openness. Thomas Newkirk similarly focuses on how students' feelings—specifically, embarrassment and shame—influence their educational experiences. He writes, "the emotional underlife of teaching and learning deserves as much attention as technique or procedure" (13). When students' egos are threatened, learning may slow or students may shut down.

Likewise, Dana Driscoll and Roger Powell examine the role of emotion in writing development in college. Through a qualitative, longitudinal study of thirteen writers, Driscoll and Powell argue that students' emotional states, traits, and dispositions have great impact on their ability to transfer lessons about writing from one context to another. Ultimately, they argue that teachers should work to foster positive environments in their classroom in order to purposefully circulate positive emotions, which can then facilitate student learning. They zoom in on response as one such intervention point: "Faculty, in our study, often gave good feedback from the perspective of improving the draft but not necessarily from the perspective of managing a delicate writer; the effect of this feedback did not always result in generative emotional states."

I build on this work and connect the personalized accounts of transmutation reported by teachers when reading and responding to student writing with a study designed to explore how emotional labor works for students receiving teacher feedback. Such work is long overdue in feedback studies and connects contemporary conversations around emotion and learning to the feedback cycle in the writing classroom. The questions I approach through this study are as follows:

1. What emotions do students experience when they receive feedback?
2. Do students transmute the emotions they experience when receiving feedback?
3. What research methods might shed light on the emotional transmutation of students in composition classroom?
4. What can teachers do to make it more likely that students will stick with the writing process in the midst of difficult feedback?

Study Overview and Methods

This study took place at an urban university in the Midwest in the fall of 2016. In order to understand the interplay of relationality and feedback in first-year writing, I pursued a purposeful sampling of writing teachers and first-year students. Teachers were selected based on their course evaluations; previous classes had "strongly agreed" with the following statement from their course evaluations: "My teacher provided effective feedback in this course." As I will explore in the discussion section, I came to question the role that bias played not only in the course evaluations of the teachers I selected, both of whom were cis-gendered, able-bodied white women, but also in impacting the way students perceived these teachers, starting on the first days of the class. Students were invited to participate in the study based on how they scored on a Motivated Strategies for Learning Questionnaire, an instrument designed by educational researchers at the

University of Michigan to measure student motivation in relation to particular academic classes (see Duncan and McKeachie). In each class, two students who scored in the top quartile of respondents and two students who scored in the bottom quartile were chosen to enroll in the study. In addition to difference in degree of writing motivation, the eight students were also diverse in terms of race, gender, and intended career path. The goal in pursuing such a sample was not to make study results generalizable, but rather to increase the likelihood that I would study information-rich examples of the feedback cycle in action. Data collected consisted of 32 hours of student interviewing in accordance with Irving Seidman's guidelines in *Interviewing as Qualitative Research* (four interviews per participant, spread out over the course of the semester), all graded writing from the course, and sixteen prewriting activities, which primed students to discuss their emotional reaction to teacher feedback.

The goal of the interviews was to understand the feedback cycle from the students' perspective. I was drawn to phenomenological interviewing because it prioritizes the subjects' meaning-making, regarding them as the experts on the phenomenon at hand. The first interview (around week three of a fifteen-week term) attempted to understand the students' history of receiving feedback on their writing, as well as their initial impressions of their composition class. The second and third interviews took place after students had received professor feedback on two different assignments. I had copies of their graded work on hand when the students came in, and we conducted a detailed interview that asked the students to reflect on how they received the feedback, what they thought about particular moments in the feedback, and what they would do next. The purpose of these interviews was to gather information about students' reception of feedback in action, as close to the moment it happened, and to give them tools to unpack their reactions in ways that would make the interviews comparable to each other. While I wanted the interviews to be semi-structured, mainly around a discussion of the marked-up paper, I also wanted to give the students room to reflect on the feedback before they arrived at the interview. For this reason, I asked the students to complete a prewriting exercise before the second and third interview. Through the process of analyzing my data, I came to regard the prewriting exercises as useful sources in themselves, particularly because they offered seemingly incongruent data on the emotions students experienced.

Prewriting Activities: Word Banks and Emoji Stickers

Before the second and third interviews, students completed a required prewriting exercise. From a word bank the students were asked to choose a word representing the dominant, strongest reaction they had to the feedback they received on their writing. The words in the bank were informed by scholarship regarding the range and relationship between various emotional states (McLeod, Parrott, Plutchik, Raider-Roth, Shaver, and Tobin), as well as words already used by the students in the first interview to describe reactions they had to feedback they'd received in the past. In its approach, the compilation of this word bank is not dissimilar from other studies that have attempted to use words to stand in or represent affective states. Babb and Corbett write of designing their own survey:

We offered nine options for emotional responses: disappointment, sadness, frustration, anger, joy, vindication, concern, surprise, and confusion. In an attempt to provide an element of cross-research comparison, these options are the same as those Nicole I. Caswell used in her 2011 study (like ours, including a WPA listserv survey) of teachers' expressed negative emotions while responding to their students' writing assignments (with the exception that we included "vindication" and "frustration" and omitted "disgust").

Comparing the list of emotional states offered in my word bank to Babb and Corbett, as well as Driscoll and Powell, I find myself wondering why I didn't include disappointed or confused. Nonetheless, variations of those words—frustrated, disgusted, angry, annoyed—did make the list. In all, students chose fourteen dominant words from the word bank. The word bank included the following emotions: angry, accepting, amused, annoyed, bored, disgusted, distracted, frustrated, interested, happy, peaceful, proud, sad, satisfied, surprised, and trusting.

As I looked at the fourteen completed word bank selections, I immediately saw patterns emerging: many students chose the same words after reading their feedback (trusting, accepting, satisfied). This similarity across high-and-low motivated students and across two classrooms raised interesting questions about what kinds of emotions "stick" (a term I borrow from Ahmed) to productive working relationships in first-year composition and how students seek to manage their emotions to perform the expected student role. The exchange might be plastic, easily fungible, and managed by the kind of politics of politeness Wendy Ryden highlights in her study of kitsch in the writing classroom. The writing teacher, perhaps, becomes a "simplistic symbol for ready and pre-digested consumption," or, in other words, a teacher from whom the student can easily receive feedback (Lugg qtd. in Ryden 84).

However, the easy representation of a static interchange, in which teachers and students inhabit easily recognizable roles, is undercut through the second prewriting activity: the application of emoji stickers next to specific marginal comments to reflect student reactions to each comment. According to Merriam-Webster, emojis are "any of various small images, symbols, or icons used in text fields in electronic communication (as in text messages, e-mail, and social media) to express the emotional attitude of the writer, convey information succinctly, communicate a message playfully without using words, etc." At the request of one of the student participants, emoji stickers were purchased and made available to all students to use during the second and third interviews. During the second interview, seven of the eight focal students opted to use the stickers to tag their emotional reactions to particular teacher comments. During the third interview, however, the number went down to four. I emphasized in my communication with students that using the emoji stickers was optional, while the word bank was required. It was after the study concluded, when I examined the emotions expressed by the stickers and the emotions expressed by the word bank, that I noticed a difference in the two data sets. I argue these differences suggest a stickered trail of transmutation.

Results: Disparate Streams of Data

In her study about the emotions that sorority sisters experience when they move from pledges to full membership, Faith Kurtkya suggests coding emotional language in three ways: positive, negative, or mixed. She found that coders could agree on these categories, while other attempts to break down and analyze emotions were more difficult to validate. (These three categories seem to overlap with those used by Powell and Driscoll: generative, negative, and mixed.) In my study, when we apply those three categories to the emotions students listed in response to the prompt, we see that all dominant emotions identified by students were positive, with the exception of one.

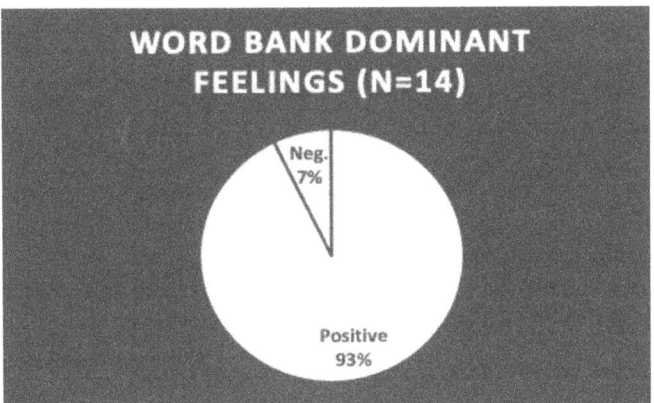

Figure 1: Positive (n=13) and Negative (n=1) Dominant Emotions from Word Bank.

Overwhelmingly students' reactions—as reported and reflected on during the interview—were positive. The most often used words included "accepting" and "trusting." Of course, this is exactly how students are indoctrinated to perceive their teachers. As Lynn Worsham has written, "all education is sentimental, [and] all education is an education of sentiment" (163). The students themselves talked about the generic nature of the trust they have for their teachers. Here are some representative comments on this point:

- "I trust almost all the professors I have and the feedback they give us. I feel like they're professionals at it. It's really hard not to believe them or to say they're wrong instead of you're wrong."
- "I wouldn't want to think negatively about a teacher's comment because I know it's their job to help me improve, not to make me feel like I'm not doing good."
- "Whether or not you were one of their best students, they all care about their students, as long as you're showing up and trying. You haven't given up, they haven't given up."
- "I don't know if I've ever not trusted a teacher."
- "I'm usually very trusting . . . I don't distrust. The acceptance is pretty much the same all around."

These comments suggest that trust is a relational state that most students enter with all teachers, or at least they seek to enter that state. They also hint at something more: for trust to be established and maintained, the students remind themselves of the teacher's authoritative role, which is to provide expert feedback geared toward improvement. They see the teacher's role as essential to the transaction of the classroom: "you haven't given up, they haven't given up." These students are essentially articulating how they stay, as Sommers puts it in "Across the Drafts," "open and receptive" to teacher feedback (253).

Trusting a generalized teacher—following this emotion rule—is key to maintaining the expected student role, which Sommers has argued is one of the most important indicators of whether a student will be successful in college. The students are talking about the student responsibility to accept what the teacher says. This is the inverse of the teacher responsibility Bazerman describes: "we as teachers have a responsibility to accept that piece of [student] writing according to our best lights" (142). For the student, "accepting" feedback on their writing "according to [their] best lights" may involve believing that the teachers are there to support them and to help them improve. They must embrace the role of the novice, at least initially.

While trust emerges as a key, if generic and plastic, and, as Wendy Ryden might say, "kitschy," affect that circulates between students and teachers, the word bank responses alone do not sufficiently reflect the transmutation process students went through as they prepared to inhabit this role. As we move to the emoji responses, more negative emotions appear with nearly half being negative (see figure three).

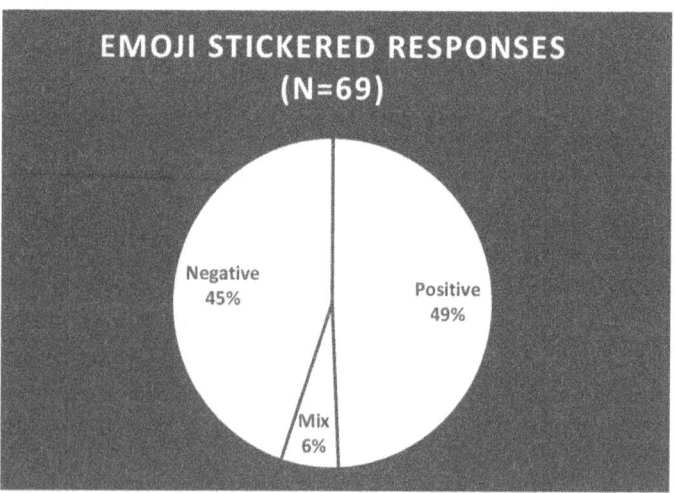

Figure 2: Positive (n=34), Mixed (n=4) and Negative (n=31) Emojis

As figure 3 shows, there is a much more ambivalent mix of positive and negative emotions reported in the emoji prewriting than in the word bank prewriting. Admittedly, the sample size for this data set is small. Of the eight students, only half completed the emoji sticker prewriting prior to the second and third interviews. Nonetheless, I find the gaps between the data sets compelling, particularly when supplemented through the interview data. Examining the case study of Joseph, a student who used the emoji stickers to express his reactions to unexpected critical feedback while still arriving at a positive word bank emotion, provides more insight into the relationship between figures two and three.

Case Study: Joseph's Strategic Forgetfulness

Joseph, a second-year student who intended to enter the medical field, was selected as a high-motivation student. I noticed early on in our interactions that Joseph relied heavily on his peers for affirmation of his writing. At his friends' recommendation, for instance, he took Honors writing in high school. As a first-year college student, Joseph enrolled in his particular section of FYC because his high school friend was also in the course. He and his friend sat near each other, discussed the class over lunch, and wrote papers at side-by-side computer stations in the library. He also sent every paper he wrote to his girlfriend, as his quote below elaborates:

> I wrote the paper and then I sent it to her. Well, first I sent it to [my friend] to check and he corrected the grammar and stuff, like if a word was wrong or it needed a comma or something like that. He fixed that stuff and sent it back and told me what I needed to work on. Then I sent it to her to see what she said. We were on a GoogleDoc and she made comments. We spent like five hours on it. I trust her in English.

Joseph's reliance on his peers for assistance is an important component of what Bazerman calls "the history and personality" of the student and sets the stage for the negative surprise he would shortly receive. After Joseph resolved each of his girlfriend's concerns, he anticipated getting an A on the paper, or maybe a B at worst. But his paper got a C. He said:

> I was honestly very shocked. It was bad. I was on BlackBoard. I saw my grade, it went from an A to a B, and it was a low B. Yeah, I saw my overall grade and I was like, "Oh no, what went in?" Then I scrolled down and I see the research essay and it's a C. Then my heart dropped. I got angry at myself. Not at [the professor], but more at myself because I thought I did a lot better. I was shocked because I didn't think that was going to be the outcome. I was expecting at least a B or an A. I just thought I put enough work in to be a B or an A.

As Joseph read through the comments, he began applying emoji stickers to make a trail of his reactions. Figure four offers an overview of the images that Joseph stickered to his draft. The images can be read from right to left, like a row of text.

Figure 3: Joseph's Emoji Responses to Marginal Comments on his Paper

While applying words to emojis is an interpretive act, I see here a range of negative feelings, including shock and dismay, disgusted sighing, woundedness, speechlessness, and hysterical laughter. As I reviewed these stickers during the interview, Joseph and I had the following exchange:

Kelly: Gosh, a lot of tears.

Joseph: Yeah.

Kelly: You get hysterical right at the end.

Joseph: It honestly was hysterical. By the time I checked through all the comments, I was like, "Oh my god, there's so much to do." It just got funny, I guess.

Joseph's emotions, as articulated during the prewriting activity, however, were not hysterical, tearful, or negative. Instead, Joseph's dominant word was accepting. Joseph's freewrite immediately following these selections was as follows:

> Accepting is the dominant emotional response. I say this because I know the feedback [the professor] gave is solely to make my essay better. She stated, "Joseph, good focus in this draft. In revision, work on the writing itself." The reason this captured my attention is because it let me know the focus or ideas of the essay were good. . . . Moving forward, I plan to start to revise the essay this weekend. I believe that since I see the revisions/comments she made as constructive, I am able to forget the "negative" emotions I feel and focus on making the essay better.

Joseph's narrative illustrates Hochschild's point that "[t]his emotion system works privately, often free of observation . . . It is a way of describing how we intervene in feelings in order to shape them" (57).

To accept his professor Elise's evaluation of his writing, Joseph must also accept that his self-assessment was incorrect—and that the assessments of his girlfriend and friend were also incorrect. The double-edged—almost self-cutting—element of this reversal was articulated by another student, Kaari, a low-motivation student who commented that for each positive emotion she wrote on her prewriting activity, she also felt the opposite emotion toward herself. Thus even as she wrote that she was "informed" by her teachers comments, she also acknowledged that she had previously been—and would, without her teacher's intervention, continue to be—"ignorant." Moving from the swirl of receiving critical feedback to accepting it is not automatic, even for a highly-motivated student such as Joseph. Kaari's discussion of the emotions that faced the teacher and the emotions that faced herself as a student are mirrored in Joseph's interview transcript, where he makes the point of saying that the emoji faces are not looking towards his teacher but instead towards himself. He was experiencing what Anson and his colleagues call face threat, "those communications which challenge a person's desired self-image" and are "typically met with defensiveness" (384). In these instances where the ego is threatened, write Bruce Ballenger and Kelly Myers about revision and emotion, the student may "seek to reduce or eliminate [the cognitive dissonance], particularly if it threatens their self-concept" (592).

Why was Joseph able to see Elise's comments as useful and persist? Part of the answer is that he knew he had to see them as constructive in order to hold up his end of the social bargain of the classroom. Again, Bazerman gets at the essence of the deal: "the interaction that occurs between student and teacher across the student's paper is framed and driven by the reason we have come together in such a contrived dyad: for the students to learn to write better" (143).

By reflecting on the situation of the communication and the role of his teacher, Joseph managed to discipline himself into the position of, as James Gee would put it, saying/doing/believing the right combination to inhabit the student role. As he said in the interview: "I'm going to work hard on this revision, I'm going to get it done early, and I'm going to meet with my teacher to confirm I'm on the right track." While Driscoll and Powell suggest that students' ability to handle negative circumstantial emotions has to do with their emotional disposition, I see a nuance here: it has to do with his perception of the teacher's ability to fulfill her end of the classroom bargain. The fact that all eight of the focal students overwhelmingly managed to arrive at a similar small subset of dominant emotions in the word bank suggests Joseph's process of transmutation is not unique. We might extrapolate that his management of his emotions is as mundane as the self-regulation of the airline stewardesses studied by Hochschild in the early eighties—and that his emotional management is just as key to his successful completion of his work as their "managed heart" was to theirs.

Discussion

To the research questions I posed at the beginning of this study, I now offer the following answers. Yes, students experience outlaw emotions when reading feedback. And, yes, emojis seem to unlock more ambivalence regarding the feedback cycle than words alone. Timing also seems critical. When students are asked to reflect on emotions after reading the feedback, they report more positive emotions than when asked to reflect on emotions while reading the feedback. When receiving critical feedback, students seem to focus on generic student/teacher roles to mediate their reactions. In all, this study thus suggests that those of us invested in the role of emotion in the writing classroom should pay attention to the modalities we use when researching emotion and to ways that professors can offer cues that they are fulfilling the expected role of professor. I will elaborate on each of these points briefly below.

Emojis and Non-Alphabetic Modalities

Joseph's use of emojis led to a more nuanced understanding of his emotional reaction as he read particular teacher comments. In this essay, I've put these emojis together and suggested that they offer a more compelling portrait of the reading than the word bank counterparts. This, in turn, points to something broader: visual tools like emojis more accurately capture the waves and surges of emotion than words alone. They are better equipped to represent the changeableness of emotion states. As Joseph transitions from sad crying to funny crying, we see a shift in his emotional state that a single word would efface. And capturing these shifts, that changeable quality, is central to those of us who are interested in what Newkirk calls the "emotional underlife" of learning (4).

Secondly, emojis are better suited for capturing the intensity of emotional responses. This intensity might seem overblown or hyperbolic, but that's part of the semiotic system of emojis. Although hyperbolic, these images are representing resonances that feel true to the student and unlock new directions to explore through research. Bazerman writes, "How the student perceives the teacher as an audience will influence what the student will write, with what attitude, and with what level of intensity" (142). Emojis offer a way of finding "hot spots" in student reaction to professor feedback that are promising. They need not merely be negative, as was the case in Joseph's emoji reaction. Consider Cailey, the student who initiated using the emojis because she felt that they "flew with the times." Cailey's use of the emoji below prompted an interesting discussion of her reaction to her professor's reaction to her paper.

Figure 4: Heart Eyes

Cailey used this particular emoji to symbolically represent her affective response to a comment. Sarah, Cailey's teacher, made (a checkmark) during a conference. Cailey explained: "She got super excited about [the conclusion] . . . . I was going with her. She made me pumped up. Like, 'Yeah.' She kept checking, and I was like, 'You keep checking it. I like that.'" She later referred to this moment as "sparking." For Cailey, "sparking" with Sarah over her paper—as documented by the heart-eye emoji—was a (relatively) intense emotional exchange. Dictionary definitions of "Heart Eyes" on Emojipedia and EmojiDictionary emphasize the erotic undertones of this emoji: "crush, lovestruck, adored, heartthrob." While I don't think that Cailey felt exactly these emotions toward Sarah, there was something charged in her response. Cailey's use of the word "sparking" also implies the kind of relational fire-making that is more often used to describe romantic love or attraction than teacher/student connection. She's hinting at the important role libidinal affect might play in one's experience of composing. Without the emoji, this underlying intensity to the exchange would have been lost. Emojis capture more than words alone.

Finally, emojis are appealing for their playfulness and their relevance to the ways that students communicate today. Emojis are immediately available on most student phones and are closer to the emotional vocabulary of students' everyday lives. Studies of the use of emoticons in personal communication offer similar findings. After analyzing 92 surveys that provided "open-ended accounts of their reasons for using emoticons across virtual platforms," researchers found that the top reasons that these emoticons were used was to "aid personal expression." Sub-themes included "establishing emotional tone" and to "lighten the mood" (Kaye, Wall, and Malone 463). Such topics are also explored in the recent book *Because, Internet* by Gretchen McCulloch, which examines for a lay audience what Geoff Nunberg calls the "ironic, informal, and expressive" uses of language that have developed online. Considering the vocabularies students generally employ is vital for those of us interested in tracking the flows of emotion in the classroom. While Bazerman's Greek myth captured, for him and for some readers, the intensity of the struggle to determine the ideal way to engage a student writer, other semiotic systems, beyond literary allusion or a list of emotional states in a word bank, can accomplish something similar. We open ourselves to our students' perception by switching semiotic systems because, as Hochschild writes, "to name a feeling is to name our way of seeing something" (223). We need to see beyond the vocabularies we've used in the past.

Performing the Teacher Role by Consciously Building Rapport

The study suggests a generic trust between the teacher and the student greased the wheels of the affective exchange and made it possible for students receiving critical feedback to transmute negative emotions to outward displays of acceptance. This finding raises the question about what teachers can do to present themselves in ways that support student emotional labor. A study by Nathan G. Webb and Laura O. Barrett provides an instructive complement to the findings presented here. Analyzing the first-year communications classroom space, Webb and Barrett sought to understand which teacher behaviors were perceived as building rapport.

While rapport building has received attention as a component of productive relationships in scholarship of teaching and learning contexts, it hasn't received as much attention within composition studies. To understand students' perceptions of rapport, Webb and Barrett coded open-form student responses on a survey. They found that student responses were easily coded using a system previously established by scholars who had studied "consumerist settings" (Gremler and Gwinner). Their categories for rapport building behaviors included: attentive behaviors, common grounding behaviors, courteous behaviors, connecting behaviors, and information-sharing behavior. Table 1 offers a brief overview of each of these components.

Table 1: Rapport-building Behaviors

Uncommonly attentive behaviors	Personal interest and recognition to students—calling students by name, demonstrating excitement, prompt responses, getting all students involved in class
Connecting behaviors	References to humor, pleasant conversation, friendly interaction
Information sharing behaviors	Give advice, impart knowledge, communicate clear expectations
Courteous behaviors	Honesty, empathy, respect
Grounding behaviors	Speaks on the students level and finds similarity with the student

Consciously building rapport in the classroom using these kinds of behaviors seems to communicate to students that the professor is inhabiting the expected teacher role. In my analysis of students' comments between receiving feedback and reporting acceptance, I saw many references to the rapport-building behaviors Webb and Barrett described. A few brief examples are below:

- "She goes into great detail when explaining things." (information-sharing)
- "Listening to her read the syllabus, I was watching her as a person." (information-sharing)
- "She always goes over the rubric." (information-sharing)
- "She's young and easy to relate to." (grounding)
- "She radiates calm." (courteous)
- "When she asks questions, everyone is pretty involved." (attentive)
- "She gets excited and incorporates the whole class with it." (attentive)

Although it might seem that building rapport has little to do with feedback, the data suggests a link between these areas that merits further consideration. And, in light of Hochschild's work, such a link makes sense: as the airline stewardesses in her book displayed the proper face and felt the right feelings, they also paved the way for the customer to inhabit the right frame of mind (and heart). Hochschild writes, "the social bottom usually looks for guidance to the social top. Authority carries with it a certain mandate over feeling rules" (75). The rapport-aiding behaviors uncover similar emotional rules as apply to teaching; students perceive the performance of these rules as cues to perform their own student role, which involves engaging in the expected work of the class, doing the emotional work required to be open to critical feedback, and responding to critical feedback through revision

Conclusion

Like Charles Bazerman, I find myself a bit unnerved as I conclude this essay. In both instances, a simple answer was discarded for a messier one. Bazerman had to admit that the relationships he develops with students are protean rather than predictable, and that his reading and responding practices are more "ramshackle and ad hoc" than he previously imagined (140). In the case of my study, complications also emerged. While the data demonstrates that students are managing their emotions to accept critical feedback and while I do believe that purposefully establishing rapport may assist students in that process, it is also imperative to consider how a teacher's identity presentation impacts their ability to establish rapport with students—and, in turn, the delicate emotional ecosystem students inhabit as they receive critical feedback.

The two teachers featured in this study who excelled at establishing rapport were selected due to students' course evaluations. Yet, of course, such evaluations are subject to bias. Evidence suggests course evaluations are higher for those perceived as men than those perceived as women (MacNell et al.) and for those perceived as white than for teachers perceived as other (Lazos). What this means for my study is that perhaps two white-women focal teachers conform to student bias regarding the appropriate teacher for a composition class. Many of the student comments quoted above regarding rapport-building behavior are overtly gendered and appearance-based, with students commenting on a teacher's age ("she's young") and emotional disposition ("she radiates calm"). When a female-identified student says she was "watching [the professor] as a person," it's hard to know if she would comment similarly about a teacher perceived as male.

The idea that women are particularly suited to teaching writing plays into the mother-teacher trope that is prevalent in composition (see Schell), in which nurturing women help students "clean up" their writing and adjust to college life. Students perhaps have internalized these stereotypes of the composition teacher, and therefore are more likely to see feedback more favorably from presumed female, presumed straight, and presumed white teachers. Lisa Martin describes this kind of bias as the base of role congruity theory (Voeten), a point expanded by Sylvia Lazos in "Are Teaching Evaluations Hurting Women and Minority Teachers?" Lazos writes: "Unconscious bias, stereotypes, and assumptions about role appropriateness are the subject parameters that students unconsciously carry in their heads and use to shape the way they perceive their women and minority professors . . . In sum, women and minority professors' performance in the classroom is fraught with potential land mines" (166). Hochschild's study, while not using the language of role congruity theory, also emphasized that preconceived notions of identity were in play for the airline stewardesses she studied. "[T]hey are not simply women in the biological sense," she explained. "They are also a highly visible distillation of middle-class American notions of femininity. They symbolize Woman" (175). We already have substantive evidence that teaching evaluations are biased, but it's harder to pinpoint how bias impacts invisible classroom procedures, even those as mundane as receiving feedback on an essay.

These concerns offer very real pressure to classroom conditions and interactions, especially in required writing courses where labor is so often contingent and student evaluations are important for teachers who wish to maintain employment. At the same time, this study, and others like it, make me hopeful. So much of the scholarship on response has neglected to probe the dynamics that underlie the process. Approaches that examine this exchange through the lenses of emotional labor and relational perception seem to bring us closer to understanding how classroom dynamics inform the writing process and the feedback cycle. The challenge lies in how to explore this phenomenon without re-inscribing disempowering tropes or falling into transactionalism. We need work that examines explicitly how positionality impacts relational perception and affective exchanges in the classroom, and how this, in turn, impacts the feedback cycle. In all, it is important to understand that transmutation is unfolding in writing classrooms today, and that both teachers and students engage in this process in order to stay with the project—the writing itself—that brings them together.

Works Cited

Ahmed, Sara. *Cultural Politics of Emotion*. Routledge, 2004.

Anson, Chris M., Deanna P. Dannels, Johanne I. Laboy, and Larissa Carneiro. "Students' Perceptions of Oral Screencast Responses to Their Writing: Exploring Digitally Mediated Identities." *Journal of Business and Technical Communication*, vol. 30, no. 3, 2016, pp. 378-41.

Babb, Jacob and Stephen Corbett. "From Zero to Sixty: A Survey of College Writing Teachers' Grading Practices and the Affect of Failed Performance." *Composition Forum*, vol. 34, 2016, np.

Ballenger, Bruce and Kelly Myers. "The Emotional Work of Revision." *College Composition and Communication*, vol. 70, no. 4, 2019, pp. 590-614.

Batt, Thomas A. "The Rhetoric of the End Comment." *Rhetoric Review*, vol. 24, no. 2, 2005, pp. 207-23.

Bazerman, Charles. "Reading Student Texts: Proteus Grabbing Proteus." *Encountering Student Texts*, edited by Bruce Lawson, Susan Starr Ryan, and R. Ross Winterowd. NCTE, 1989. 139-146.

Bowden, Darsie. "Comments on Student Papers: Student Perspectives." *Journal of Writing Assessment*, vol. 11, no. 1, 2018, np.

Caswell, Nicole I. "Dynamic Patterns: Emotional Episodes Within Teachers' Response Practices." *Journal of Writing Assessment*, vol. 7, no. 1, 2014, np.

Connors, Robert and Andrea Lunsford. "Teachers' Rhetorical Comments on Student Papers." *College Composition and Communication*, vol. 44, 1993, pp. 200-223.

Daiker, Donald A. "Learning to Praise." *Writing and Response: Theory, Practice, and Research*, edited by Chris M. Anson, NCTE, 1989, pp. 101-13.

Driscoll, Dana and Robert Powell. "States, Traits, and Dispositions: The Impact of Emotion on Writing Development and Writing Transfer Across College Courses and Beyond." *Composition Forum*, vol. 34, 2016, np.

Duncan, Teresa Garcia and Wilbert J. McKeachie. "The Making of the Motivated Strategies for Learning Questionnaire." *Educational Psychologist*, vol. 40, no. 2, 2005, pp. 117-28.

Ede, Lisa. "On Writing Reading and Reading Writing." *Encountering Student Texts*, edited by Bruce Lawson, Susan Starr Ryan, and W. Ross Winterowd, NCTE, 1989, pp. 147-159.

Fife, Jane Mathison and Peggy O'Neill. "Moving Beyond the Written Comment: Narrowing the Gap between Response Practice and Research." *College Composition and Communication*, vol. 53, no. 2, 2001, pp. 300-21.

Garber, Megan. "The Scare Quote: 2016 in a Punctuation Mark." *The Atlantic*, 23 December 2016. Web.

Gee, James. *Sociolinguistics and Literacies: Ideology in Education*. Routledge, 1990.

Gremler, Dwayne D., and Kevin Gwinner. "Rapport-building Behaviors Used by Retail Employees." *Journal of Retailing*, vol. 84, no. 3, 2008, pp. 308-324.

Hochschild, Arlie Russell. *The Managed Heart*. U of California P, 1983. Kaye, Linda K., Helen J. Wall and Stephanie A. Malone. "'Turn that Frown Upside-Down': A Contextual Account of Emoticon Usage on Different Virtual Platforms." *Computers in Human Behavior*, vol. 60, 2016, pp. 463-67.

Kurtyka, Faith. "Learning How to Feel." *Composition Studies*, vol. 45, no. 1, 2017.

Knoblauch, Cy and Lil Brannon. "Introduction: The Emperor (Still) Has No Clothes—Revisiting the Myth of Improvement." *Key Works on Teacher Response: An Anthology*, edited by Richard Straub, Boynton-Cook, 2000, pp. 1-16.

Lazos, Sylvia R. "Are Student Teaching Evaluations Holding Back Women and Minorities?" *Presumed Incompetent: The Intersections of Race and Class for Women in Academia*, edited by Gabriella Gutierrez y Muhs, Yolanda Flores Niemann, and Carmen G. Conzalez, Utah State UP, 2012. 164-85.

Martin, Lisa. "Gender, Teaching Evaluations, and Professional Success in Political Science." *Political Science & Politics*, vol. 29, no. 2, 2016, pp. 313-19.

MacNell, Lillian, Adam Driscoll, and Andrea N. Hunt. "What's in a Name: Exposing Gender Bias in Student Ratings of Teaching." *Innovative Higher Education*, vol. 40, no. 4, 2015, pp. 291-303.

McCulloch, Gretchen. *Because Internet: Understanding New Rules of Language*. Riverhead, 2019.

McLeod, Susan H. *Notes on the Heart: Affective Issues in the Writing Classroom*. SIUP, 1997.

Micciche, Laura R. *Doing Emotion: Rhetoric, Writing, and Teaching*. Heinemann, 2007.

—. "Staying with Emotion." *Composition Forum*, vol. 34, 2016, np.

Murray, Piper. "'Containing Creatures We Barely Imagine': Responding to 'Bad' Students' Writing." *A Way to Move: Rhetorics of Emotion & Composition Studies*, edited by Dale Jacobs and Laura R. Micciche, Heinemann, 2003, pp. 92-100.

Newkirk, Thomas. *Embarrassment and the Emotional Underlife of Learning*. Boynton-Cook, 2017.

Nunberg, Geoff. "Ironic, Informal And Expressive, 'New Rules Of Language' Evolve Online." National Public Radio, 20 August 2019, https://www.npr.org/2019/08/20/749946265/opinion-ironic-informal-and-expressive-new-rules-of-language-evolve-online.

Parrott, W Gerrod, ed. "Volume Overview." *Key Readings in Social Psychology: Emotions in Social Psychology.* Taylor & Francis, 2001, pp. 1-21.

Plutchik, Robert. "A General Psychoevolutionary Theory of Emotion." *Emotion: Theory, Research, and Experience,* edited by Robert Plutchik and Henry Kellerman. Academic Press, 1980, pp. 3-35.

Raider-Roth, Miriam. *Trusting What You Know: The High-Stakes of Classroom Relationships.* Jossey-Bass, 2005.

Rutz, Carol. "Marvelous Cartographers." *Classroom Spaces and Writing Instruction,* edited by Ed Nagelhout and Carol Rutz, Hampton Press, 2004, pp. 117-32.

Ryden, Wendy. "Conflict and Kitsch: The Politics of Politeness in the Writing Classroom." *A Way to Move: Rhetorics of Emotion & Composition Studies,* edited by Dale Jacobs and Laura R. Micciche, Heinemann, 2003, pp. 80-92.

Schell, Eileen E. *Gypsy Academics and Mother-Teachers.* Boynton/Cook, 1998.

Seidman, Irving. *Interviewing as Qualitative Research.* 4th ed. Columbia Teacher's College Press, 2013.

Shaver, P. and J. Schwartz, D. Kirson, C. O'connor. "Emotion Knowledge: Further Exploration of a Prototype Approach." *Journal of Personality and Social Psychology,* vol. 52, no. 6, 1987, pp. 1061.

Smith, Summer. "The Genre of the End Comment: Conventions in Teacher Responses to Student Writing." *College Composition and Communication,* vol 48, no. 2, 1997, pp. 249-68.

Sommers, Nancy. "Across the Drafts." *College Composition and Communication,* vol. 58, no. 2, 2006, pp. 248-57.

—. *Responding to Student Writers.* Bedford, 2013.

Straub, Richard and Ronald Lunsford. *Twelve Readers Reading.* Hampton Press, 1995.

Straub, Richard. "Students' Reactions to Teacher Comments: An Exploratory Study." *Research in the Teaching of English,* vol. 31, no. 1, 1997, pp. 91–119.

—. *The Practice of Response: Strategies for Commenting on Student Writing.* Hampton Press, 2000.

Stewart, Kathleen. *Ordinary Affects.* Duke UP, 2007.

Tobin, Lad. *Writing Relationships: What Really Happens in a Writing Classroom.* Heinemann, 1993.

—. "Opinion: Self-Disclosure as a Strategic Teaching Tool: What I Do—and Don't—Tell My Students." *College English,* vol. 73, no. 2, 2010, pp. 196-206.

Webb, Nathan G. and Laura O. Barrett. "Student Views of Instructor-Student Rapport in the College Classroom." *Journal of the Scholarship of Teaching and Learning,* vol.14, no. 2, 2014, pp. 15-28.

Worsham, Lynn. "Afterword: Moving Beyond a Sentimental Education." *A Way to Move: Rhetorics of Emotion & Composition Studies,* edited by Dale Jacobs and Laura R. Micciche, Heinemann, 2003, pp. 161-163.

# "So, that's sort of wonderful": The Ideology of Commitment and the Labor of Contingency

Sarah V. Seeley

Abstract: *This article explores the emotional outcomes related to language commodification within an organizational context: the first-year writing program at Binghamton University, which is a public research university in upstate New York. In this setting, the meanings of effective writing instruction are discursively constructed in terms of a multi-faceted commitment to 'the process.' This entails an ideological commitment to both recursive process writing and the process of collaboratively evaluating the product that derives from it. I first offer an overview of the Binghamton context, including the details of collaborative portfolio assessment. I then analyze a specific sociolinguistic strategy: pep talking. I argue that pep talking is integral to cultivating localized technologies of the self through simultaneously bolstering the ideology of commitment and effacing instructors' emotional outcomes.*

Introduction

Much recent work across the social sciences has examined the employment and organizational contexts in which "care" is performed (Pugh; Lane; Murphy). In particular, Arlie Russell Hochschild's work has been foundational for contemporary discussions of emotional labor and the work of caring. Feelings are, of course, rule governed: people are socialized to express, repress, or act on their feelings based on context. What's more, workplaces are key sites for examining these socialization processes and their attendant outcomes.

Workplace contexts have also served as the location for linguistic anthropological analyses of language labor and language commodification. In particular, Bonnie Urciuoli and Chaise LaDousa as well as Monica Heller offer reviews of each respective body of literature. We are thinking here about language as a kind of cultural capital: as a framework for socioeconomic success. Following Judith Irvine, studying language in this way means that we conceptualize it as "a complex social fact that can be looked at from many angles, including the economic" (250). Given the complexities surrounding contemporary job (in)securities, it is unsurprising to see that material approaches to language are increasing (e.g. Shankar and Cavanaugh).

Publications on the subject of emotional labor in writing program contexts have been similarly increasing (Caswell; Adams Wooten, Babb, Costello, and Navickas). The work of assessing and commenting on student writing is an obvious location for examining "the toil of feeling." In particular, Jacob Babb and Steven Corbett have analyzed writing instructors' emotional responses to different kinds of student failure. They found that guilt was a common emotional response to student failure, with one survey respondent stating that, "I feel I have failed to support the student adequately." In effect, feelings of guilt reorient the concept of "failure" by shifting the evaluative gaze from a material stack of papers back onto oneself.

While guilt is not the specific focus of this essay, these circumstances may prompt us to ask: how are we socialized into feeling and expressing work-related emotion? How does language function as a social framework wherein socioeconomic success is linked to whether we possess, express, or repress particular emotions? Here, I take a synthetic approach to analyzing language-focused work. Drawing on the results of two years of ethnographic fieldwork, I will be considering the emotional outcomes related to language use within one specific organizational context: the first-year writing program at Binghamton University, which is a public research university in upstate New York.[1]

In the Binghamton case, language becomes a commodity as instructors participate in the program's system of collaborative portfolio assessment. This system tasks instructors with the continuous discursive negotiation of what effective writing instruction "looks like." Furthermore, these negotiations often unfold as enactments of one's commitment: to effective teaching practices, to objective writing assessment, and to the program's administrative goals. This is, in short, what I will refer to as an ideology of commitment, which functions like all language ideologies in that it enacts ties of language to the negotiation of the self.

In this case, we are observing how emotions— ranging from anger and annoyance to fear and uncertainty— shape individual negotiations of the self. This ideological stance functions as an uptake of Michel Foucault's technology of the self, which he describes as a tool for pragmatic self-transformation (18). Urciuoli and LaDousa have characterized technologies of the self as "means for fashioning a subjectivity compatible with dominant practices, institutions, and beliefs" (177). In short, we are thinking about subjective means for self-fashioning that are wholly context dependent. Social contexts are, of course, multiple, overlapping, and hierarchical. This is why Foucault's concept can be productively dovetailed with Terry Eagleton's assertion that ideologies often work by construing particular beliefs "as arising not from the interests of a dominant class but from the material structure of a society as a whole" (30). At its core, ideological commitment is a multi-faceted means of reconciling the social activities demanded by one's

---

1. I conducted fieldwork during 2013 and 2014 while also teaching for this first-year writing program as a graduate student. As such, I was a participant in the Pedagogy Group system that I will go on to describe in detail. The names of all study participants, with the exception of myself, have been anonymized. My contributions to the conversation represented in the Extract 2 transcript are labeled as "Sarah." Further, I have applied pseudonyms in a way that disguises gender. I made this choice in order to protect the integrity of the study.

Institutional anonymity is, on the other hand, not possible. In order to maintain methodological integrity, I must contextualize my own positionality as a participant observer which makes any attempt at institutional anonymization a very thin veil. In addition, there are a number of published texts associated with this writing program and having to avoid citing them would negatively impact this argument. Finally, institutional anonymity is not stipulated in the IRB-approved research design.

work. Because of this, the writing program presents itself as an ideal organizational context for observing real time manifestations of this ideological stance.

For example, the ideology may manifest through the tacit commitment to maintaining what Brad Hammer has critically referred to as a "'worker vs. intellectual' construction for compositionist inquiry and teaching" (A5). It also underpins what Kelly Ritter has critically described as "train[ing] new [writing] teachers to unquestioningly accept these often-crushing pedagogical practices as ethically, or even morally, superior to other methods" (412). Regardless of why teachers of writing become/remain committed to their work, it is important to recognize that the degree to which an ideology overlaps with, supports, or reflects social actors' views of the world is an indicator of how successful or powerful it is. This idea, then, may complicate our efforts to reject "worker" subjectivities, and it may actually thwart our ability to do the work of revising our pedagogical choices.

The particulars of language use have always formed an integral part of how success is measured across a variety of employment contexts, but applying this idea within the Binghamton context is to say that we are witnessing an intensification of the general principles of process writing and portfolio assessment. Instructors are continuously discussing how each other's students should be coached through the writing process, and eventually how each other's students' portfolios should be evaluated. As I will illustrate, these activities discursively expand the limits of instructors' responsibilities to include a variety of undue time investments. Instructors deploy the ideology of commitment as a means of reconciling the emotional responses that emerge from this expansion of responsibility.

Insofar as the social activities demanded by one's work are potentially inconsistent with one's own best interest, the emergence of negative emotional outcomes is not particularly surprising. In order to frame these emotional responses, it may be useful to think in terms of Niko Besnier's assertion that, "the activities that take place 'around' literate communication (i.e., simultaneously, in the same social space, with the same people) provide a specific flavor to the literacy activity, a flavor that becomes part of its inherent meaning" (142). We can, then, expect to see how the activities that take place "around" writing assessment contribute to the "flavor" of the writing program.

When we consider the origins of and socialization into labor-intensive process writing pedagogies, it is important to note that such methods are dominant for a reason: because they tend to yield positive results. This success is, however, quite problematically contextualized by the fact that contingent laborers most often enact this work. It has, for example, been estimated that contingent faculty were teaching over 80% of first-year writing classes at public institutions in 2007 (Ritter 388). The American Association of University Professors further confirms that, as of 2015, "non-tenure-track positions of all types now account for over 70 percent of all instructional staff appointments in American higher education." The AAUP also notes that, "contingent appointments are often clustered in programs with very high levels of predictability— such as freshman writing courses that are required for all students." It's no wonder that the "worker" subjectivity is hard to disavow. It is similarly unsurprising that the "hyper-caring" or "super-committed" writing professor persona may be easily reconciled by contingent laborers within the context of what Alison Pugh has referred to as "insecurity culture" (218). These character traits map directly onto likely-to-be renewed contracts for the new faculty majority.

As an example of the self-fashioning that comes along with the ideology of commitment, we can consider this comment made by Natasha, who was a graduate instructor of first-year writing at Binghamton University:

> I warn them in the beginning. I tell them I'm going to be making them feel uncomfortable about a lot of the things that they're going to write. I tell them that I'm not invalidating their experience, but that I'm challenging how they're going to communicate their experience to us. It's really uncomfortable at times, but it often seems to work out if they're receptive. But you always have some students who just maybe aren't going to be there yet, right? I mean in terms of their life and how they can perceive themselves. And then there are the people who write a draft, and I read it. They write another draft, and I read it. Then they write another draft, and all of a sudden they come running into the class and they're like, "aaah! I get it!" So, that's sort of wonderful.

In reading Natasha's words, the tensions between time, generosity, and remuneration emerge quite clearly. Yet the process she describes does not exclusively hinge on student receptivity, as her words may suggest. Rather, process writing is defined and enacted based on her receptivity, her willingness to undertake hours of work for a single student. Yes, the results certainly can be "sort of wonderful," but these labor-intensive expectations can simultaneously become "sort of taxing," which is to say the very least. Natasha's words illustrate how faculty contingency can lead to situations where "positive" or "care-based" types of emotional labor may be accepted as simply being a part of the job. Here we can see hierarchical circumstances and pedagogical values working in tandem to push forward a powerful ideology. Natasha's willingness to give of her time may map directly onto those likely-to-be renewed adjunct contracts and hopefully-to-be secured tenure-track contracts, but she may be betting on a labor system that scarcely exists anymore. In this case, "positive" emotional labor is being problematically elided with the effort process paradigms exact from instructors.

In what follows, I draw on a data set comprised of dyadic, semi-structured interviews and 50 plus hours of naturally occurring group conversation that took place among writing instructors in order to argue that the meanings of effective writing instruction are discursively constructed in terms of a multi-faceted commitment to "the process." In the Binghamton case, this entails an ideological commitment not only to recursive process writing but also to the process of collaboratively evaluating the product that derives from it. Moving forward, I will first offer an overview of the Binghamton context, including the specific details of collaborative portfolio assessment. This background will be essential to a discussion of one specific sociolinguistic strategy that simultaneously bolsters the ideology of commitment and effaces instructors' emotional outcomes. I will refer to this communicative strategy as pep talking, and I will illustrate how it is integral to cultivating the technologies of the self that yield the very specific "flavor" of first-year writing at Binghamton University.

The Writing Initiative and Collaborative Portfolio Grading

At Binghamton University, first-year writing courses are taught primarily by graduate teaching assistants, in addition to a small number of senior faculty members who are almost all off the tenure track. Although this type of staffing is standard at many public research universities, it merits further examination here because of the assessment system in place in Binghamton's program. When the Binghamton University Writing Initiative was established as an independent writing program in 2008, a collaborative portfolio grading system[2] was implemented. This system is relatively unique and based on the one in use at Grand Valley State University (Kinney and Fenty 2; Royer and Schendel).

In order to promote consistency within and among approximately 50 sections of first-year writing each semester, the program uses collaborative grading, which requires instructors to meet weekly in Pedagogy Groups, each consisting of five or six instructors. The main purpose of these meetings is to discuss individual evaluations of student writing and come to consensus about evaluation criteria. The former writing program administrators described the meetings in the following way:

> All of our teachers gather in small groups for weekly meetings led by experienced full-time faculty or graduate student administrators. Our Pedagogy Groups instill a sense of community and support for instructors through candid discussions among beginning and experienced teachers. In sum, Pedagogy Groups allow us to discuss classroom dynamics, share teaching activities, examine scholarly trends and—most centrally—practice effective strategies for responding to and grading student writing. (Kinney and Costello)

In a move intended to support programmatic standardization, the Pedagogy Group-based collaborative grading structure is supposed to provide an opportunity at the end of the semester for "teachers to reflect on how successfully they have internalized the grading criteria embraced by the program as a whole" (Kinney and Costello). Dan Royer and Ellen Schendel further describe this collaborative work:

> Despite our profession's familiarity with the concept of "portfolio group grading," our approach at Grand Valley is unique. We are unaware of any other program that weekly norms teams of teachers as graders for reliability over the course of the semester and then requires two- and three-reader agreement on student letter grades (not merely pass/fail) at the end of the term. At the end of the term, a group of five or so teachers of this class that have been grade-norming all semester using drafts from the students and finished portfolios from previous semesters determine the grade as a team for each student. The grading standard is in this way a very public standard, not based on a once-a-term workshop norming session or, worse, private, teacher-specific standard that allegedly adheres to a program rubric. Instead we have a two- sometimes three-reader grading group that is hyper-local to the five teachers' sections that

---

2. This assessment system was implemented in response to a series of institutional deficiencies. See Kinney and Costello 2010 for a full discussion.

has been communicating this achieved public grading standard back to these students in these sections throughout the semester. (28-29)

This system is still in place at Grand Valley and, as they do "not have graduate teaching assistants to rely on for staffing," it is currently enacted by a combination of full-time writing instructors and Affiliate Professors (Royer and Schendel 27). Their description of the process merits quotation at length because it expresses the very same rationale that guides the Binghamton application. The Binghamton University Pedagogy Groups, then, offer specific contexts for examining precisely how the charge of "communicating this achieved public grading standard" is experienced in real time by contingent faculty. On a very basic level, this charge is shaped by a series of negative assumptions about individual instructors. The existence of the Pedagogy Group assumes an unproductive binary between the individual and the group, with the former being characterized by potentially flawed perspectives, incomplete knowledge, or problematic motives. This binary clearly presupposes that individual actors are unreliable, and therefore casts individual choice as being incompatible with the best practices in the teaching of writing. While objectives like mentoring new teachers and cultivating a community of writers are a part of the Binghamton Pedagogy Group rationale, the common experience of participating in these groups does not appear to be that of receiving mentorship. Because the group system relies on the assumption that homogeneity is both desirable and attainable, group meetings were more often experienced as a form of surveillance and/or an undue draw on instructors' time. In turn, those realities yield their own emotional entailments and sociolinguistic responses.

To put a finer point on what collaborative portfolio assessment at Binghamton involves, all instructors read and evaluate their own students' portfolios at the end of each semester, but they also read an equal number of their colleagues' students' portfolios as well. Most graduate students teach two sections of the course. These sections are capped at 16 students each, and since the portfolios are about 20 pages apiece, this means we read and evaluated a pile of portfolios amounting to approximately 600 pages of writing. Then, we read and evaluated another 600 pages of writing produced by students from other instructors' classes before finally convening to hash out all the grades. All of this work continues to take place in the span of a week or less and it raises an important question: how do individuals move within a system like this, continuously participating in something they tend to recognize as not necessarily being in their own best interest? We have an idea why this happens. Perhaps we do this because we love to educate, or perhaps we do this because educating is a part of our identity. In another sense, we do this because teaching is our livelihood. Graduate students do this because their education and career prospects depend on it. Yet the question of why is only one piece of the puzzle.

Defining teaching effectiveness in terms of commitment importantly echoes the idea that writing is best taught through hands-on engagement with individual students. As Chris Anson has suggested, being open to such engagement allows educators to move beyond a "passion for sharing high-mindedness with high minds," and start "getting down close to the ground with young people who needed someone to help them discover literacy for themselves" (167). As an educator who loves teaching writing, I can easily recall my experiences of working with countless students and say: yes, this kind of discovery is a powerful thing. It is "sort of wonderful." Yet, insofar as the work done in writing classrooms is understood in terms of this commitment, which is mobilized in the service of large-scale learning outcomes, we are participating in a powerful ideology. As Tony Scott says, "writing is always ideological because discourses and instances of language use do not exist independently from cultures and their ideologies" ("Writing Enacts" 48). So, too, the curricular and the assessment choices that shape the teaching and learning of writing are always ideological. To this end, we can also frame our understanding of this case study in terms of Clifford Geertz's assertion that ideologies attempt to,

> render otherwise incomprehensible social situations meaningful, to so construe them as to make it possible to act purposefully within them—this accounts both for the ideologies' highly figurative nature and for the intensity with which, once accepted, they are held. Whatever else ideologies may be—projections of unacknowledged fears, disguises for ulterior motives, the phatic expressions of group solidarity—they are, most distinctively, maps of problematic social reality and matrices for the creation of collective conscience. (220)

The Writing Initiative's collaborative assessment policy not only shapes pedagogical practices and pursues uniformity in evaluation. It also shapes how individuals understand and perform their roles as writing teachers. In turn, the ideology of commitment becomes a tool for reconciling these social realities.

This program's "separate, but together" ethos of support, mentorship, and standardization offers an important opportunity to listen to stories about how programmatic assumptions trickle down to be experienced by instructors themselves. As one graduate student instructor, Louie, stated in our interview:

> I don't know that the program encourages us as instructors to voice opinions. I know that when putting forth different ideas or concerns, that's when the toe the line comes about. This applies to us [the instructors] more than for the students. If a student does it, okay. But if we do it, then it starts to get a little funky. What I don't like is the straightjacketing, especially when we're told that we're not being straightjacketed.

Louie's words illustrate the importance of seeking out and paying attention to individual experiences. As Scott has argued, it is important to recognize that, "discussions of academic labor and writing program management rarely touch on the specific effects of faculty hierarchies and pervasive managerialism on day-to-day pedagogy" ("Dangerous Writing" 38). By illustrating one such case, I suggest that language use is not merely a reflection of the systematic work of teaching and assessing writing within a particular hierarchy. Rather, language is actually constitutive of that work. Since "talk" is at the center of this collaborative enterprise, it is important to understand how a "collective conscience" is discursively constructed within these Pedagogy Groups. Such an understanding is meant to highlight the need for reexamining our labor assumptions in the same way we rightly reexamine our pedagogical approaches and assessment mechanisms.

Another graduate student instructor, Vivian, echoed Louie's words: "there's more than lip service to the [idea of] autonomy. It's problematic though, right?" She went on to note that, "a lot of people have never done this [before]. The best way to do anything is to fail, but this is not just a job. Your funding for your education also depends on it, so it's a weird place." Winston, who was a member of the senior faculty, expressed similarly mixed sentiments:

> I am a teacher in the program, but, you know, the curriculum was decided before I got here. If you think of expressing yourself as a teacher through the way you organize curriculum and classroom activities, then this isn't possible quite as much as [at] other places. As far as curriculum goes, it seems to me that teachers have a lot of room to do what they feel works within the strengths of the program and that the people who made the curriculum were thinking about that when they did it.

We can see a range of opinions over whether there actually is room for making the class "one's own." Yet, insofar as instructors do feel able to make individualized pedagogical choices, their choices are directed and constrained by the nature of the Pedagogy Group. Since individual approaches must be explained and accepted by one's Pedagogy Group, these choices must be adapted to conform to the program as a whole. As a result, instructors experience a dissonance between the creativity that characterizes teaching and the standardization that characterizes the program. While such constraints exist to some extent in any department or program, the Binghamton University model compels a particularly high degree of normalization. Frankie, a graduate student instructor, expressed her experience of this dissonance:

> I think that the Writing Initiative thinks that it's creating a really good space to hear the concerns of students, myself as a student. But I don't think that I feel very heard [as an instructor]. I think that Pedagogy Group is something that is probably designed to try to hear the voices of the students that are teaching its classes, but I don't feel particularly heard. It feels sometimes more like a big brother than something that is concerned with solving the problems that we confront in the classroom.

Despite the opposite intended outcome, the collaborative grading policy, as brought to life by the complexity and dynamism of Pedagogy Group talk, makes a standardized experience of first-year writing—whether for students or for instructors—an impossibility. As I will illustrate in the coming section, the pursuit of standardization creates negative emotional outcomes not only because of the social cost of what it takes to conform, but because conformity is often unsuccessful.

The "Community Standard" as Unstable Signifier

In what follows, I analyze two extracts from naturally occurring Pedagogy Group conversations. These extracts are meant to illustrate how the programmatic intensification of labor creates new affective demands. In other words, Pedagogy Group contexts dictate that it is not sufficient to only engage one's own students in recursive process writing. In addition, instructors are also called upon to commit their time and energy to enacting this objective at the programmatic level. My analysis of the following extracts aims to contextualize a specific sociolinguistic strategy, or speech genre: the pep talk. Pep talking is, of course, a common managerial speech genre that responds to problematic situations of one variety or another. In the present context, pep talking constitutes an attempt to filter, unify, and reconcile programmatically specific expectations. Pep talking also denies workers' emotional responses while simultaneously doubling down on programmatically specific emotional demands. This deny/amplify framework, as we will see, seems to define the experiences of teachers at all levels: both Pedagogy Group leaders and members.

To construe the "community standard" as a stable signifier—as an ontologically secure position—denies the fact that individual classrooms are distinctive social microcosms: sites of fluidity and multiplicity. Because of this, I have approached Pedagogy Group conversations as a discursive system of knowledge that is being continuously rearticulated and reshaped through individual practice. In doing so, I illustrate how deployments of ideological commitment attempt to preserve social stasis, which results in the denial of instructors' varied emotional reactions. Invoking the ideology also serves the larger goal of keeping the collaborative grading system intact, which results in the creation of additional emotional demands.

Extract 1: "Binghamton Writes is frustrating me"

In the conversation that follows, Pedagogy Group participants are discussing the student-written sample essays that are published in Binghamton Writes: A Journal of First-Year Writing. This is a required course text that contains genre samples written previously by former students. Everyone participating in this conversation is concerned, in one way or another, with the question of a community standard. This question is constantly at stake within a system where people do not seem to agree, and yet they need to agree. We are looking at how the group's leader, Josh, invokes the idea of commitment as he engages in pep talking in response to one particular group member's criticisms.

> Stanley: Binghamton Writes is frustrating me. So far, they [the researched arguments] are both not very good at all. And I'm just kind of wondering: why we are selling this to our students? Like, this [one] essay has totally unprovable claims. There's no evidence. The claims are ridiculous. I mean I have no idea how this – this is a C, if it's lucky. The second researched argument is a glorified op-ed with no real argument. It's very conversational in tone. It's kind of an informative essay. It never really makes an argument. These [essays in Binghamton Writes] are supposed to be what I'm like: hey, look… And I did, stupidly, because I hadn't read them yet. I was like: you guys need to read the Binghamton Writes essays and we're going to talk about them. It's going to help clarify things and see where the bar is set. And now I have to come back and say, well: this is garbage.
>
> Nick: I say that all the time.
>
> Josh: It's perplexing. A lot of that is contingent upon the editorial team for that semester, for that particular genre. A lot of it is dependent [….] A lot of it is subjective but, I mean, we can fix that by encouraging our own students to submit. And by being on the editorial staff, which counts for all kinds of brownie

points toward the teaching certificate. But that is surprising. I guess not too surprising. I have seen some of that myself, in previous editions, so... To your point about it having no argument, that is one of the basic requirements of it [the assignment]. And, you know, we can use Binghamton Writes in other ways. I've actually had them read things and say, you know, these are picked for a variety of reasons, not just because they're the best of the best. In many cases, it's about variety. It's about trying to find and encapsulate their voices. But, you can look at it critically and I'm sure you have.

Stanley has drawn attention to the problem of having to teach essays that he feels are poorly written, and Josh attempts to reorient this criticism through invoking the ideology of commitment. Josh argues that the members of his group can "work within the system to make it better" through further investing their own time in "the process," writ large. Specifically, he notes that the members of the group can fix this "problem" through encouraging students to submit and by volunteering as editors in the future. He reminds the group members that working on Binghamton Writes constitutes professional experience that is institutionally validated in the form of a Certificate in Teaching College Composition. In proposing these fixes instead of engaging in a critical dialogue, Josh's management of the meeting works to efface the root of the problem: the journal of first-year writing is a highly visible artifact that implies what effective uptakes of the course assignments should look like, and it is under fire. Instead of engaging in a critical dialogue, he suggests that the members of his group should assuage their frustrations by further committing themselves to the program in order to effect change from the bottom up as team players.

Stanley's problem is structural in nature: it derives from the unstable community standard. This fact accounts for not only how Stanley experiences his work, but for how the Binghamton Writes editors experience and enact theirs. All parties are equally constrained by the "rules" of the program. In other words, the unstable community standard is not a symptom of the Binghamton Writes selection process. Rather, the selection process and its material expression— the journal itself— are interrelated symptoms of the instability. Instructors' critiques and disagreements are similarly interrelated symptoms of the instability. The same rubric is used for selecting essays for publication and for assessing live student writing, and so the tension surrounding the question of a community standard permeates all programmatic activities.

As he voices his frustrations, Stanley calls the rubric into question by implication, yet the rubric is rarely criticized explicitly. The slipperiness of the rubric manifests in two contexts. First, it emerges throughout the process of assessing "live" student writing, which will become particularly evident in the next extract. Second, it emerges throughout the processes of selecting and teaching genre samples, which is evident in this extract. Since these essays continue to be produced and edited by a local community of writers, it is unproductive to degrade them as "garbage," as Stanley and Nick have done. That said, Stanley's frustrations are quite understandable. Even leaving aside the issue of quality, he is required to teach a prescribed set of texts, which erodes his authority to teach.

Further, Stanley likely derived very little satisfaction, let alone any sense of renewed authority, from voicing his complaints because Josh's replies skirt his feelings in favor of bolstering the program rationale. Yet, Josh's communicative strategies are also constrained by the system. He is, perhaps, unable to entertain Stanley's critiques even if he actually agrees with them because such an acknowledgement would contribute to their collective work truly going off the rails. Josh is, after all, doing the job of trying to create consensus. As a member of the senior faculty he may not—ironically—have felt that he had access to the same freedoms as Stanley and the others (myself included) because we were part of a continuous stream of graduate students who continue to cycle in and out of the program. In contrast, a position like Josh's has different stakes. His motivations were surely complex and reflective of his own compromised status. In real time, however, his pep talk was experienced as an ill-fitting Band-Aid. As he deployed the ideology of commitment in order to smooth out differences of opinion, the primary entailment was a denial of Stanley's frustrations, which he nonetheless continued to voice:

> Stanley: More often than not, I've been using these [Binghamton Writes essays] to teach them what not to do. Which, the way this [book] was sold to me in orientation is that this is something I can rely on to teach them what to do. And so that's really disappointing, because I do want examples. I want A papers that I can show them, and that's what I was promised that this was going to be and it's absolutely not.
>
> Nick: Over the years and over the semesters, I've had essays come through where I'm like: this is really good. But the problem is, they push you to use this one [the current edition] because of, well, they pay a lot of money for it. But it's kind of hard. I definitely see the frustration. I see it becoming more about the topic and less about –
>
> Josh: [stuttering] I mean …
>
> Nick: the craftsmanship. I would much rather see an essay every semester about violence and video games that's written very well.
>
> Josh: A lot of it is clearly different interpretations of requirements of the assignment.
>
> Stanley: Which I guess is a little concerning. For all of the management in this program and for all of the ways that we're trying to get standardized, just how wildly divergent these opinions still are.
>
> [silence]
>
> Josh: These are all interesting conversations, but I would tell you that – I would encourage you to work within the system to make it better if you're frustrated by this. So these tensions are really interesting and what I think is most important is – in the small – like these are all big picture things that maybe we can address long-term, but what really matters to us now, and that's what we're doing today, all that really matters right now is that we're all on the same page [regarding assignment criteria]. We can set the bar where we want it and we can articulate that to each other and we can talk about that. And another thing that I think is fair, as long as we're aware of it, and we discuss it and hash it out early – we don't even have to come to a consensus about that, y'know? Part of the norming thing is to understand what is important to each of us. If I can get a sense of what [you] really care about and I was evaluating one of [your]

portfolios, I would try as much as possible to consider that in my evaluation of those portfolios, and likewise for [all members of the group].

Here, Stanley has called direct attention to the fact that there is no "community standard." Meanwhile, this idea is the centerpiece of the collaborative grading system. Recall, the very existence of the Pedagogy Group format is underpinned by what I have identified as an unproductive binary between the individual and the group. Insofar as collaborative grading is conceptualized as an intervention against the flawed perspectives, incomplete knowledge, or general unreliability of individual actors, Stanley's critique is particularly noteworthy. Yet Josh skirts it again: he neither acknowledges nor discusses the fact that members of the program can be seen working from "wildly divergent" interpretations of the assignment criteria. In this case, his pep talk unfolds a little bit differently: he attempts to redirect everyone's attention back to the "task at hand." Whereas Josh's first pep talk denied Stanley's emotional reaction, this pep talk actually creates an emotional demand. In denying larger programmatic incongruities, Josh thrusts Stanley's problem back upon him by implying that the absence of a standard somehow doesn't matter: let's just ignore our frustrations and have faith in the process. This position serves a very particular semiotic function. It attempts to re-cast the tensions of the conversation, so that the group members may be repositioned in places of power. Instead of feeling constrained or strained, they should, rather, try to control collaborative outcomes through committed expressions of logic, reason, and collegiality.

The problem is this: Stanley and the others did not actually have the power to merely "set the bar where they wanted it," either as individuals or as a stand-alone Pedagogy Group, because the material artifacts and discourses that bring the entire program to life were all indexing the shifting nature of the "standard" as a meaningful signifier. This collective work is characterized by wild divergence, and so it is necessary to continuously smooth creative, individualistic wrinkles into the face of standardization. In this way, the content of group discourse becomes evidence of the very need for collaboration. As they disagree, critique, and emote, instructors are either enacting or being propelled toward a commitment to the collaborative process.

Extract 2: *"I'm concerned about my ability to keep from creating problems"*

In what follows, we will observe how discussions of live student writing similarly reify instructors' commitments to their collaborative work. During a discussion of a researched argument in progress, Pedagogy Group leader George engages in extended pep talking. His encouragement is primarily directed at one member of the group, Patti, who is teaching the course for the first time. At the beginning of the meeting, the five members of the group were split among three flat letter grades: one A, two B's, and two C's. By the end of the meeting, the balance had shifted to two B's and three C's. Patti is the instructor who brought what she believed to be the A essay. After everyone else had stated their grades, she immediately remarked, "Oh wow, I'm concerned about my ability to keep from creating problems." The conversation unfolds from there:

> George: No, don't be concerned about that. What I can tell you is that I've never seen any group just come to consensus. But, I've also observed that it gets a lot easier after the first semester. It's a skill. And you practice it and you norm

with different groups. What did we like about the paper? What did we want the student to do more of?

Patti: I liked how he included all the different types and compared the pros and cons. It was thorough. I thought it was thorough.

Cecelia: I think it had some good discussion. It's clearly written, with focused paragraphs, and some good use of sources.

Sarah: The focus was clear. And in most cases, there's good integration of sources.

George: But you mentioned you had thought C originally. Why was that?

Sarah: Because it's borderline report-like.

George: Do you want me to change your grade to a C?

Sarah: Yeah, I do. I wrote in my notes that I think it's borderline on meeting the assignment criteria, but that I could see it being part of a solid C portfolio.

James: I liked that the argument is not a myopic one. It's not making an either/or argument. I appreciated the complexity and I think that's a sophisticated move. There are transitions that advance the focus of the essay – I thought that was done well at the end of each paragraph. I saw a "yes, but" construction happening in a lot of paragraphs, and I thought that was very successful. [But] what kept it from being an A for me was [the fact] that the writer didn't integrate and put sources in conversation with one another. And in terms of the reportish thing... looking at the citations, you can see that most of the paper is [based on] one particular source. Once we get to the bottom of page three, that source dominates the rest of the essay. Also, I thought that there were a lot of unsubstantiated claims. I don't really think that argument is fully supported.

Sarah: There's a lot of good information, it's just that you're left to read between the lines.

James: I agree. But, these are things that, I don't think it would take too much for the student – in terms of coaching for the student – to really work on those characteristics. The paper has a lot of potential.

This stretch of the conversation goes quite a long way toward illustrating Stanley's problem with pervasive differences of opinion. The instructors' initial assessments range from thorough, clear, focused, and in control of sources on one hand, to report-like and not fully in control of sources on the other. This range of characteristics becomes more noteworthy once it is mapped onto grades ranging from A to C. Preliminary discussion of the essay indicates that the draft exhibits some potential, and the writer needs more coaching. Yet when George immediately indicates that Patti need not be concerned about causing problems, he foregrounds a tension between theory and practice. In theory, collaborative work is necessary because outlier opinions are 1.) presupposed to exist, and 2.) understood to be inconsistent with the best practices of teaching writing. In practice, however, it is not always possible to veto an outlier opinion because the ideas and assessments presented in Pedagogy Group do not exist in a vacuum: they are constituted by the underlying work performed in individual classrooms. The conversation continues to unfold:

Sarah: I'm kind of curious – just because we're so close to the end [of the semester] – about how everybody teaches this? Since we have a pretty solidified split between all of us here, this would almost certainly go to a third read, which is fine, but ... For me, I teach students that this essay tasks them with describing and analyzing a social phenomenon – more analysis than description. And like what's been said – this should involve putting sources into conversation with one another. And, all the bits and pieces for that are here, but it's not done. But at the same time, if it wasn't taught that way, then I can't just come in and give it a C.

Patti: And that's one of my biggest struggles – I'm not even familiar with these genres as I'm teaching them. So, this is probably why I don't recognize these things and teach to them.

George: Your students will not be sanctioned for that.

Patti: Well, yeah, because that has concerned me...

George: I think I'm answering your question [Sarah] and also addressing it in the context of this essay: how I teach it is, you have to see where the current scholarly debate is and there is no indication to me that this paper was written within the last three years. There are three scholarly sources here – one was from the 1980s and two were from the 1990s, so it misses the genre in terms of that, and I think a C is generous.

Cecelia: That's probably true. In thinking about it, I have a lot more here that is wrong than what is right. And so, I don't actually know if this would go to a third read, because after somebody told me the reasons, I'd be like: yeah – I guess I can see that. This is more like a C.

In this stretch of the conversation it becomes clear that George's pep talk is not only for Patti's benefit. He is strategically addressing concerns that I had voiced, which were of an order that usually emerges toward the end of each semester. In this particular case, Patti may be amplifying these concerns through continuously indexing her own uncertainty, but regardless, this is the point when instructors begin to wonder whether the final portfolio meeting will go smoothly. Such thoughts include: will the students actually receive the grades that I believe they've earned? Will there be conflicts? Will my time be wasted? Several types of emotional labor are being performed here. Pedagogy Group surveillance compelled Patti's self-disclosure, which eroded her authority in the eyes of the group. Group surveillance similarly compelled me to acknowledge how the collaborative grading system erodes everyone's authority. Despite the fact that consensus will be impossible because we must account for how a student was taught in the context of their own classroom, we must still participate in the process.

As George reassures Patti that this process will become easier in time, he is also tacitly reassuring everyone else that they will be able to have principled conversations and that all students have an opportunity to do well if they meet the criteria set out in their own classrooms. He is trying to reintegrate Patti's pragmatic classroom choices back into the more normative framework that seems to exist for the other members of the group. Like Josh, George is sincere, but his responses similarly skirt the program's reliance on a shifting standard. Examining any set of pedagogical principles or learning outcomes across educational space and time will always yield diversity. This is the kind of diversity that is to be expected when comparing the experience of taking a particular class with Professor X, versus taking that same class with Professor Y. This is the case in any discipline. Professors X and Y will teach different things. They will use different approaches and styles. They will privilege different lines of thought and modes of inquiry in their students' work. Yet, in most contexts, Professors X and Y do not sit down together and evaluate their differentially educated students using a shared grading rubric. And even if they did, it is unlikely that they would feel compelled, let alone be required, to come to consensus regarding each other's students' final grades. So where do the students land in all of this?

> George: The last thing I want to do is punish a student for not being my student, right. I want all students to do well, and if they fulfill the criteria in your classroom, then you would need to tell me that. And I think that's the kind of thing we could have a good negotiation about – a principled one – in the final meeting. I think if it were an A/C split then it would probably just go to a third read, but if there's still this outcome where you're [Patti] seeing something as an A and you can't see it as a C, and, more importantly, if you've conveyed to the student: "this is A quality work," then, you know, we would have to take that into account.
>
> Patti: I've been really careful not to convey grades to them, other than telling them what characteristics the essay exhibits. And, you know, when I hand them [rubric] sheets, the bulk of almost everything I've indicated is in the C column, but this... I considered him my best student... But, I'm also influenced by classroom behavior, too, so to know that this essay does not actually fit the criteria, I need to hear that. Because, that means I'm not clear myself.

On one hand, George's comment about not wanting to punish a student for not being in one's own class was a widely repeated, valued, and acted upon sentiment. Instructors in this program were, in general, very keen to avoid negative student impacts. On the other hand, frustration comes easily when an immutable part of one's work becomes a mechanism for devaluing one's time and effort. Insofar as instructors ought to respect their colleagues' assessments of their own students' work, a situation like this one really foregrounds how futile "the process" can feel. What's the point of reading Patti's student's portfolio and assessing it as C quality work, only to learn about the context surrounding her class and be compelled to swallow that opinion? George's pep talking, then, functions very similarly to Josh's. It simultaneously skirts the problem at hand, ignoring any associated feelings the instructors may have, in order to underline the programmatic rationale. In both cases, the pep talk ironically creates a new and different emotional demand. In denying larger programmatic incongruities, George skirts the "Patti problem" just as Josh thrust Stanley's problem back upon him. In both cases, instructors are compelled to ignore their frustrations and have faith in the process.

Patti might be seen by some as a "soft grader" for her different valuation of her student's work. Of course, the problem isn't really Patti. There are many other examples of soft and hard graders. In another context, Patti's judgment might be chalked up to inexperience: she would assess her students based on the instruction they received, learn from the process, revise her teaching strategies, and move on. Yet, in the Binghamton case, the work of collaboration consistently compels instructors to report on, contest, and align their practices and performances against a shifting, yet omnipresent standard. This has the potential to heighten the disenfranchisement that is often associated with contingency. Patti's students are producing work that others identify as "missing the mark," and in response to this recurring condition, she notes, "I'm not clear myself." In making this candid admission, she comes to embody the source of the problem because her struggles to clearly express and teach to the genre criteria are being broadcast publicly. Just as when Stanley expresses his frustrations in Extract 1, when Patti indexes her status as a newcomer, we see unfortunate examples of how collaboration yields unexpected layers of frustration and stress. Patti's struggles registered with a degree of embarrassment. Stanley's peers consistently interpreted his frustrations and criticisms as evidence of a bad attitude. The Pedagogy Groups are a kind of recurring performance among one's peers, and it is easy to see how exhausting that level of performativity might become for these instructors.

While it is unfortunate that Patti seemed to struggle so much with teaching the genres of the course, the question of whether "everything would be okay" tended to emerge at the close of each semester, regardless of whether there was an explicit catalyst. As George's pep talking unfolds, we can see an attempt to amalgamate everyone's values and concerns and to reassure the group that everything will, in fact, work out. In a similar manner to Josh's replies to Stanley, George's comments also ignore larger programmatic incongruities in favor of recuperating social stasis. When George asserts that Patti's students "will not be sanctioned," he makes a very important point: the pursuit of consensus in the name of a community standard cannot supersede the goal of assessing students fairly based on the instruction they've received in individual classrooms. Regardless, the problem is this: the pursuit of this elusive community standard persists. It is the instructors who are sanctioned in the process. The "wildly divergent" opinions create working conditions that are marked by frustration and inefficiency.

It is, unsurprisingly, clear that Pedagogy Group leaders like Josh and George occupy tense positions within this program. They, too, are simultaneously constrained and strained by the ideology of commitment. Their work also requires counterintuitive subjective self-fashioning. Each week, the Pedagogy Group leaders deal with the unenviable task of making the system work in real time. As Josh has put it: "we do our best, and hope it all works out. But, you know it's the system that we're – it's the system that we have." It is a stressful system. This is the case not only because of labor expectations, but also because it has a unique ability to discursively construct difference, and in some cases, judgment. For example, one graduate student, Chet, made the following comments in an interview:

> [The Pedagogy Group leaders] are most inclined to start conversations with questions like "where are the sticky wheels that are keeping this machine from going?" And everyone else, either at the very top or at our level, seems to want to help design the machine. And those middle managers just seem to want to push it forward as is.

Chet's comments illustrate how easy it could be for graduate students to implicate their Pedagogy Group leaders as the source of their discontent. While it is not unique for workers to blame their bosses for problems, this instance has some additional complexities. The mood of each group is discursively constructed throughout a given semester. However, group membership changes each semester, and so each instructor carries the accretions of other values, management styles, and general experiences with them as they move through groups over time. This experiential fact works in direct opposition to Josh's assertion that, "we can set the bar where we want it." Yes, the bar can be continuously re-set, but that is merely a temporary fix that re-enlists all instructors— graduate student instructors and Pedagogy Group leaders alike— by compelling them to navigate new stressors each semester. As Frankie has suggested, "this all kind of comes back to Pedagogy Group:"

> I felt like I had more problem students, not necessarily because I had problem students, but because discussing the student writing in Pedagogy Group – that's what made me feel like had more problem students – because I was disagreeing about how I would work with my students on their writing. I had different opinions than the other people in the group and the team leader. I've had a really good last semester with the Writing Initiative – and I know that they're not sitting there like – how can we exploit our graduate students? [How can we] get the most out of them that we possibly can? But with the shared syllabus and the group grading and the daily schedule, sometimes it does actually feel that way.

Conclusion

While the Binghamton case is a relatively unique one, it demands our attention nonetheless. It reveals the ways in which managerialism, as experienced in and reflected through real time discourses, unwittingly creates unexpected layers of additional work and stress that remain inadequately unaccounted for in the labor paradigm of higher education. These narratives may form a question mark in our minds: what are the experiences of contingency in my writing program? The Binghamton case illustrates how an already labor-intensive pedagogical orientation—as enacted largely on the backs of underpaid graduate students—has been problematically intensified. This intensification is not merely a "rough patch" to be endured. Rather, insofar as "we make sense of the world around us through the ideologies to which we have been exposed and conditioned" (Scott, "Writing Enacts" 48), this intensification socializes nascent professionals to accept an ideology of commitment as a governing principle of their work. It socializes us to level those expectations on our colleagues and students. It socializes us into a bootstraps mentality, wherein vertical movement is the only goal, and questioning or terminating our own participation in this managerial culture is emotionally painful, if not financially untenable.

In order to understand how ideologies take hold, circulate within, and, in some cases, dominate the discourses of higher education, it is necessary to examine the hierarchical circumstances, capitalistic purposes, and pedagogical values that cement them in real time conversation. Here, we have looked at the experiences of a group of educators who persist within the context of a strange double bind. Their work is deeply presupposed by very specific uses of language, yet their possibilities for authoritative verbal expression are programmatically delimited. The Binghamton case constitutes an ethnographic uptake of Allison Laubach Wright's critique of how rhetorics of excellence intertwine with apprenticeship narratives to efface graduate student labor. She writes:

> the narrative we hold to—that of the graduate student as an apprentice who is learning a trade—helps create the conditions which erase the work of graduate students and make it that much harder to change the system. Nowhere is this tension more obvious than in English departments, where four year universities have graduate students teaching the labor-intensive first year writing course while minimizing both the presence of the course and the work of the graduate students. (276)

In the Binghamton case, the labor demanded of graduate students is simultaneously minimized and amplified by the ideology of commitment. Continuous talk about writing configures, but also denies, instructors' claims to power, authority, and even the control of their own time. Here we have seen how the ideological underpinnings of one writing program—as brought to life in the social context of the Pedagogy groups—simultaneously efface emotional reactions, while creating new, counterintuitive emotional demands.

Instead of presupposing such demands, we must listen to ourselves. While there are a number of potential benefits associated with collaborative models, it is important to solicit and value narratives of the real time experiences of enacting such models. I have argued here that attempted standardization is not necessarily guided by stable signifiers, yet the call for standardization is a perennial response to all manner of academic problems. Given this, it is important to listen to and engage with the actual experiences of contingency. I follow Seth Kahn here: "by 'listen,' I mean more than just nod, smile, and wring your hands in empathetic frustration when contingent faculty bring problems to your attention" (266). Solutions to acknowledging uncompensated labor— emotional or otherwise— will not be realized through individual expressions of empathy. Rather, they will arise out of structural and material institutional change.

Dorothy Smith and Alison Griffith have argued that institutional ethnography is a method "designed to discover how our everyday lives and worlds are embedded in and organized by relations that transcend them" (10). Institutional ethnographies, such as the larger project of which this argument is a part, offer much potential for understanding how the real time experiences of academic work are shaped by a complex tangle of pragmatic choices, agentive strategies, affective stances, and institutional demands. Disentangling such circumstances in localized contexts offers an important inroad toward better material and emotional working conditions.

In the Binghamton case, the collaborative grading structure presupposes individual deficiency. Maintaining such a low opinion of the individual is, I hope to have illustrated, neither defensible nor tenable. Whereas collaborative grading is problematic from a labor perspective, the core of the Pedagogy Group ethos does offer many options for preserving the best parts of an imperfect system. For example, truly "listening" in the Binghamton case could mean retaining the weekly Pedagogy Group meeting structure but reinvigorating the agenda in order to focus entirely on teaching strategies in lieu of collaborative norming and grading. "Listening" may, in the Binghamton case, be an exercise in loosening the white-knuckle grip: it may be as "simple" as trusting each other. Regardless of the institutional setting, "listening" is an exercise that involves questioning how programmatic structures may differentially impact contingent faculty.

Again, as Seth Kahn indicates, truly listening, "is to recognize that almost anything we say is likely an overgeneralization, or a misrepresentation of at least some of the contingent faculty population" (268). A major step in moving beyond overgeneralization and misrepresentation is, of course, working with locally specific "pictures" of contingency. Are we thinking about adjunct faculty who earn $1k per credit hour with no health insurance? Are we thinking about graduate students who are teaching classes, taking classes, and earning $15k plus benefits annually? While the definitions and experiences of contingency are diverse, insecurity culture is not going anywhere. Because of this, questions related to graduate student socialization and professional development should be at the forefront of disciplinary debates. Disciplines across the social sciences and humanities are turning out exponentially more job candidates than their bespoke job markets can handle. Therefore, building a body of particularistic accounts of how contingency is experienced constitutes an important step beyond overgeneralization and misrepresentation. It may, rather, represent a step toward action.

Work Cited

American Association of University Professors. "Background Facts on Contingent Faculty Positions. https://www.aaup.org/issues/contingency/background-facts

Anson, Chris M. "Who Wants Composition? Reflections on the Rise and Fall of an Independent Program." *Field of Dreams: Independent Writing Programs and the Future of Composition Studies*, edited by Peggy O'Neill, Angela Crow, and Larry Burton, Utah State University Press, 2002, pp. 153-169.

Babb, Jacob and Steven J. Corbett. "From Zero to Sixty: A Survey of College Writing Teachers' Grading Practices and the Affect of Failed Performance." *Composition Forum*, vol. 34, Summer, 2016.

Besnier, Niko. "Literacy." Journal of Linguistic Anthropology, vol. 9, no.1/2, 1999, pp. 141-143.

Caswell, Nicole I. "Emotionally Exhausting: Investigating the Role of Emotion in Teacher Response Practices." *Literacy in Practice*, edited by Patrick Thomas and Pam Takayoshi, Routledge, 2016, pp. 148-160.

Caswell, Nicole. "'I still grade objectively': Emotional labor of response." *Ohio Journal of English Language Arts*, vol. 54, no. 2, Winter 2014-2015, pp. 33-39.

Eagleton, Terry. *Ideology: An Introduction*. Verso Books, 1991.

Foucault, Michel "Technologies of the Self." *Technologies of the Self: A Seminar with Michel Foucault*, edited by Luther H. Martin, Huck Gutman, and Patrick H. Hutton, University of Massachusetts Press, 1988, pp. 16-49.

Geertz, Clifford. *The Interpretation of Cultures*. Basic Books, 1973.

Hammer, Brad. "The "Service" of Contingency: Outsiderness and the Commodification of Teaching." *College Composition and Communication*, vol. 64, no. 1, 2012, pp. A1-A5.

Heller, Monica. "The Commodification of Language." *Annual Review of Anthropology*, vol. 39, 2010, pp. 101-114.

Hochschild, Arlie Russell. "Emotion Work, Feeling Rules, and Social Structure." *American Journal of Sociology*, vol. 85, no. 3, 1979, pp. 551-575.

Irvine, Judith T. "When Talk Isn't Cheap: Language and Political Economy." *American Ethnologist*, vol. 16, no. 2, 1989, pp. 248-267.

Kahn, Seth. "The Problem of Speaking for Adjuncts." *Contingency, Exploitation, and Solidarity: Labor and Action in English Composition*, edited by Seth Kahn, William B. Lalicker, and Amy Lynch-Biniek, University Press of Colorado, 2017, pp. 259-270.

Kinney, Kelly and Kristi Murray Costello. "Back to the Future: First-Year Writing in the Binghamton University Writing Initiative, State University of New York." *Composition Forum*, vol. 21, 2010.

Kinney, Kelly and Sean Fenty. *Coming to VOICE: Writing Personal, Civic, and Academic Arguments*, 2nd ed., Hayden McNeil, 2015.

Lane, Carrie M. "The Work of Care, Caring at Work: An Introduction." *Anthropology of Work Review*, vol. 38, no. 1, 2017, pp. 3-7.

Laubach Wright, Allison. "The Rhetoric of Excellence and the Erasure of Graduate Labor." *Contingency, Exploitation, and Solidarity: Labor and Action in English Composition*, edited by Seth Kahn, William Lalicker, and Amy Lynch-Biniek, University Press of Colorado, 2017, pp. 271-278.

Murphy, Ryan Patrick. "The Political Economy of Care: Flight Attendant Unions and the Struggle over Airline Deregulation in the 1980s." *Anthropology of Work Review*, vol. 38, no. 1, 2017, pp. 18-27.

Pugh, Allison. *The Tumbleweed Society: Working and Caring in an Age of Insecurity*. Oxford University Press, 2016.

Ritter, Kelly. "'Ladies Who Don't Know Us Correct Our Papers': Postwar Lay Reader Programs and Twenty-First Century Contingent Labor in First-Year Writing." *College Composition and Communication*, vol. 63, no. 3, 2012, pp. 387-419.

Royer, Dan and Ellen Schendel. "Coming into Being: The Writing Department at Grand Valley State University in its 13th Year." *A Minefield of Dreams: Triumphs and Travails of Independent Writing Programs*, edited by Justin Everett and Cristina Hanganu-Bresch, WAC Clearinghouse, 2017, pp. 23-41.

Scott, Tony. *Dangerous Writing: Understanding the Political Economy of Composition*. Utah State Univerity Press, 2009.

—. "Writing Enacts and Creates Identities and Ideologies." *Naming What We Know: Threshold Concepts of Writing Studies*, edited by Linda Adler-Kassner and Elizabeth-Wardle, Utah State University Press, 2015, pp. 48-50.

Shankar, Shalini and Jillian R. Cavanaugh. "Language and Materiality in Global Capitalism." *Annual Review of Anthropology*, vol. 41, 2012, pp. 355-69.

Smith, Dorothy E. and Alison I. Griffith. *Under New Public Management: Institutional Ethnographies of Changing Front-Line Work*. University of Toronto Press, 2014.

Urciuoli, Bonnie and Chaise LaDousa. "Language Management/Labor." *Annual Review of Anthropology*, vol. 42, 2013, pp. 175-190.

Wooten, Courtney Adams, Jacob Babb, Kristi Murray Costello, and Kate Navickas, editors. *The Things We Carry: Strategies for Recognizing and Negotiating Emotional Labor in Writing Program Administration*. University of Colorado/Utah State UP, forthcoming.

Complaint as 'Sticky Data' for the Woman WPA: The Intellectual Work of a WPA's Emotional and Embodied Labor

Anna Sicari

Abstract: *There is rich scholarship on emotions in writing program administration, and the labor this work requires from WPAs (Holt; Micciche; McKinney et. al; Ratcliffe and Rickley; Vidali) and on the feminized nature of writing programs and the way gender informs this type of emotional work (Enos; Flynn; Miller; Schell). Many WPA scholars advocate that our administrative work is intellectual work, yet little attention has been given to the emotional and embodied labor of WPA work as intellectual and as defining components of WPA work. Drawing from Sara Ahmed's recent work on complaint and data I collected from thirty interviews with women WPAs in a two-year IRB approved qualitative study, I bring attention to the emotional and embodied knowledge of WPAs and the need to take more seriously this issue of complaint as a scholarly topic and source of knowledge. Through insight from this archive of complaint stemming from the institutional stories told by the participants, I will explore how critical attention to the embodied experiences of the people doing the work (WPAs) is necessary scholarly work, particularly for feminist scholars and activists who wish to work toward institutional change.*

Introduction

A body of rich scholarship exists on emotions in writing program administration, the labor this work requires from WPAs (Holt; Micciche; McKinney, Caswell, and Jackson; Ratcliffe and Rickley; Vidali), and on the feminized nature of writing programs and the way gender informs this type of emotional work (Enos; Flynn; Miller; Schell). In *The Cultural Politics of Emotion*, Sara Ahmed writes, "Thought and reason are identified with the masculine and the Western subject, emotions and bodies are associated with femininity and racial others" (141). She goes on to argue that this type of projection works to "conceal the emotional and embodied aspects of thought and reason." Knowledge cannot be separated from our bodily and emotional experiences, and in fact, these bodily and emotional experiences make up our knowledge in ways that have not yet been properly documented in the field of writing studies. Many WPA scholars advocate that our administrative work is intellectual work ("Evaluating the Intellectual Work of Writing Program Administration"), yet little attention has been given to this intellectual work as emotional and embodied labor that defines components of WPA work.

One reason for this failure to acknowledge that embodied and emotional knowledge is intellectual labor is that this type of knowledge stems from the personal; and discussing the personal experiences of working within the institution often reads as "whiny" or, rather, as "complaint." Marginalized identities, including and perhaps specifically women, often hear that they are "making it personal" when discussing issues of sexism, racism, abliism (as well as other isms). Drawing from Sara Ahmed's recent work on complaint and data I collected from thirty interviews with women WPAs in a two-year IRB approved qualitative study, I bring attention to the emotional and embodied knowledge of WPAs and the need to take more seriously this issue of complaint as a scholarly topic in which knowledge and reason can be generated. I argue that if we are to not acknowledge complaint as a scholarly endeavor, and the emotions and bodies that draw from this work, we will fail at making any type of institutional change, as emotional and embodied work is exhausting and can be all-consuming (and I will discuss exhaustion as a certain type of emotion that is used to curtail any activist work in academia). Because embodied and emotional knowledge stems from lived experience, and complaint allows us to understand power dynamics, this type of knowledge is especially important for feminist scholars and researchers. Through insight generated from the archive of complaint I created from the data, I will explore how critical attention to the embodied experiences of the people doing the work (WPAs) is necessary scholarly work, particularly for feminist scholars and activists who wish to work toward insitutional change.

Emotional and Embodied WPA Work

In *Doing Emotion: Rhetoric, Writing, and Teaching*, Laura Micciche explores embodied emotion and advocates that emotion is a skill to be taught in the writing classroom. Micciche writes, "To understand emotion as embodied is to know that it is not static or fixed or predictably available for analysis...Making explicit that emotion and bodies merge enables students to work with 'the appeal to pathos' differently" (57). Micciche argues that embodied emotional work can serve as a basis for critical thought, that our strong feelings (often stemming from bodily reactions and understandings) on topics can serve as a resource for analysis—and that writing instructors can and should teach embodied emotions in our writing classrooms to create better writers and rhetors. While Micciche argues for teaching emotional literacy, many feminist scholars and pedagogues argue that good teachers themselves are affective, and that the identity and performance of the instructor must be embodied and emotional. bell hooks writes, "Teaching is a performative act...To embrace the performative aspect of teaching we are compelled to engage 'audiences,' to consider issues of reciprocity" (11). This type of performance requires an awareness and acknowledgement of the body, of both the instructor's body and the students' bodies, in order to fully engage and produce emotions and feelings, to create the type of engaged pedagogy that critical pedagogues such as bell hooks, Paolo Freire, and Ira Shor advocate. Other scholars such as Beverly Moss, Eileen Schell, and Andrea Lunsford have discussed their own emotional experiences of the shame they experienced in graduate school and as educators in academia, and how their intersectional identities stemming from gender, race and class informed those experiences and the ways in which emotion both worked with and for them as they navigated the institution. These embodied experiences, and the emotions that generate both from the experiences and the physical emotions connected to such experiences, inform how the WPA and writing instructor operate and perform—and how they are responded to. In *Living A Feminist Life*, Sara Ahmed writes, "Think with bodies. Bodies think" (48). WPA bodies think, and we must learn to recognize and learn from this embodied thinking for the field to be sustainable; I argue that to learn from the bodies of WPAs, we must be attuned to complaint and the emotional knowledge it brings.

Emotional and embodied labor is difficult to teach and prepare graduate students for, which is a topic that has been explored in WPA scholarship. In their book, *The Working Lives of New Writing Center Directors*, Jackie Grutsch McKinney, Nikki Caswell, and Rebecca Jackson reveal that emotional labor was not only a significant component of a writing center director's job but was also the aspect of the job for which these directors were least prepared. In "Writing Center Administration and/as Emotional Labor," these same authors discuss how surprisingly little has been written on emotional and affective labor in writing center scholarship; in their empirical study, in which they followed nine writing center directors, these authors found that it is important for directors to be "prepared to expect it [emotional labor] and negotiate it." They state towards the end of this brief essay, "We pay attention to how the emotional labor of each of the nine directors intersects with their everyday and disciplinary labor.... [L]ong days of putting on a friendly face, mentoring, and negotiating leave little time and energy for our participants to do disciplinary labor." As they address, writing center work is driven by the relational, and the one-to-one context of teaching is centered on establishing connections with the writers we meet through the use of embodied emotions. Micciche's foundational chapter on emotions and WPA work, "Disappointment and WPA Work," also suggests that we are not teaching or training graduate students and junior faculty for the emotional component of WPA work and of academia more broadly. The central emotion she focuses on is disappointment: "To deny the negative emotional realities of the academy does a disservice to faculty and graduate students we train, for it leaves all of us unprepared to navigate our way through the material, including the affective realities of academic life" (85).

The emotional and relational aspect of writing program work is perhaps, as I suggest, the most important aspect of WPA work, and as I argue, this type of emotional and embodied work is intellectual work: analyzing how WPAs situate themselves, learning to read and understand multiple audiences, recognizing the importance of purpose and context in different situations as you work with and for people in all aspects of the job. Amy Vidali writes of the importance of incorporating emotional labor into job descriptions, promotion and tenure files, and any documentation in which WPAs describe, and perhaps justify, the work that they do. In "Disabling Writing Program Administration," Vidali discusses the extensive literature on mental illness, anxiety, and depression in WPA narratives, specifically as effects of the job itself, and as obstacles to overcome, and how this excludes WPAs with disabilities, as many of the narratives suggest a WPA needs to be of heroic strength (both physically and mentally). She writes, "If disability is only ever something bad that happens to WPAs…there is scarce space for the disabled WPA to articulate her value…but more than this, there is no space to articulate an interdependent model of WPA work where we care for ourselves, and each other, in the ways disability studies teaches" (40-41). Vidali is specifically bridging embodied and emotional work and the ways in which WPA models continue to exclude through a patriarchal lens of ability and strength. Vidali explores the way her disability shaped her as a scholar, thinker, teacher, and administrator. Although not enjoyable, the experience was fruitful and productive for her scholarship and the writing program. My work here extends Vidali's argument that embodied and emotional labor is intellectual, and that specifically complaint, while unpleasant and often a catalyst for eye rolls and audible sighs from others, is a generative site for WPAs.

The Importance of Complaint in WPA and Feminist Work

Complaint is gendered, and this is an important topic that Ahmed is currently researching as she explores how complaint is feminist work. Complaint, according to Ahmed, is necessary in revealing power dyanmics embedded in our institutional positions and policies, particularly for marginalized bodies. In many ways, complaint is gendered because it is women who are put into positions that require complaint; or, when women are pointing out issues with problems and policies that other people do not want to address, their concerns are easily dismissed as "complaint." In a recent blog post, "Why Complain?" Ahmed writes, "Discrediting is often performed by giving the complainer motives.... She is assumed to complain because she has a will to power or because she wishes to deprive others of a power they enjoy." This essay examines the embedded power dynamics grounded in complaint and the bodies of those who complain, and ways in which complaint is both easily dismissed and yet has the potential to be subversive precisely because of the emotions connected to this type of work.

In our analysis of WPA work as emotional and embodied labor, it is necessary to think about gender and the gendered history of the field, and the bodies of those who primarily do the work. WPA work and the teaching of writing is gendered, as advanced by scholars such as Susan Miller, Sue Ellen Holbrook, Therese Enos, Eileen Schell, and Deidre McMahon and Ann Green, and these women have connected the feminized aspect of the profession (i.e., heavily female dominated) to the feminized construction of the work that we do, often utilizing Donna Haraway's concept of feminization. As Haraway writes in her foundational text "A Cyborg Manifesto," to be feminized is to "be made extremely vulnerable...leading an existence that always borders on being obscene, out of place, and reducible to sex" (449). This feminization is often linked to the contingent issues the field faces and the labor issues that come with contingent and administrative positions. In "Gender, Contingent Labor, and Writing Studies," McMahon and Green write, "If we seek more equitable and thus sustainable solutions to academic supply and demand, we must recognize that gender and labor concerns are one and the same" (19). Many WPAs, particularly those who identify as rhetorical feminists (Glenn; Micchiche; Ratcliffe and Rickley) and those who see writing programs as activist sites (Adler-Kassner; Charlton, Charlton, Graban, Ryan, and Ferdinandt; Müeller and Ruiz), believe that the field can and should respond to systemic issues of contingent labor, racism and academic exclusion, and the growing corporatization of higher education, in order to foster democratic education and accessibility for all writers.

Very often, however, feminist and activist principles seem to be in direct contradiction to successful administrative work, as explored by WPA scholars such as Jeanne Gunner, Hildy Miller, and Krista Ratcliffe and Rebecca Rickly, particularly with regard to large writing programs that include required first-year writing. Because of this mandatory component, the very creation of writing programs is built on the corporatized principles such programs try to address in their curriculum. Ahmed (*Living*) speaks similarly of her work in building women's studies programs: "The point of women's studies is to transform the very ground on which women's studies is built. We have to shake the foundations. But when we shake the foundations, it is harder to stay up.... If we cannot sustain the labor required for some things to be, they cannot be" (112-113). In many ways, Ahmed's analysis and exploration of women's studies programs applies to FY and other writing programs and the issues that WPAs, particularly feminist WPAs, face. How do WPAs transform the ground on which they were built? And how can we sustain the labor in ways that do not compromise the ethos many of us wish to create in our programs, when we know the multiple and serious issues those doing the work face? A more in-depth exploration of complaint, as a scholarly endeavor, and an interrogation of the emotional and embodied work of those complaining, is necessary for us to understand and learn from in order to seriously think about institutional change.

Institutional Ethnography: A Methodology for Complaint

"A complaint is sticky data," Ahmed writes ("Warnings").

To conduct my research into complaint, I utilized institutional ethnography as my methodology to organize and analyze data I collected from thirty interviews with women[1] WPAs. Institutional ethnography is a methodology developed by Dorothy Smith in 1987 which started as a "sociology for women" in the workplace, although this methodology has a much wider application. As Marjorie DeVault and Liza McCoy write of institutional ethnographers, "the aim is to explore particular corners or strands within a specific institutional complex, in ways that make visible their points of connection with other sites and courses of action" (17) and to explore the everyday activities of people. "The researcher's purpose in an IE investigation is not to generalize about the group of people interviewed, but to find and describe social processes that have generalizing effects" (193). Institutional ethnography takes the standpoint of those who are being ruled, and as Michelle LaFrance and Melissa Nicolas discuss in "Institutional Ethnography as Materialist Framework for Writing Program Administration," IE explores "how our institutional locations situate, compel, and organize our bodies" (131). Nicolas and LaFrance advocate for the field of writing studies to utilize institutional ethnography as a research methodology "because it takes into account situated variability of experience within institutions, casting individuals as active and interested, mindfully negotiating the competing priorities and material conditions of their work day" (133). Along with these authors, I argue that the field of writing studies is often concerned with issues of institutional politics and the role of the everyday in the workplace, and therefore IE is a good research methodology for those invested in understanding the dynamics by which such programs constitute themselves. Institutional ethnography asks researchers

---

1. I must acknowledge that I use the categories woman or women in this article; however, I am mindful of the way these categories fail to acknowledge the broad spectrum of gender identity and expression. The women I interviewed all identified as cis-gender women, as do I, and I believe more work is needed to be done to explore the complexities of gender expression and WPA work.

to identify an experience, identify some of the processes and practices that shape that experience, and investigate those processes to describe analytically how they operate. As this work starts with individuals and what they are doing in and with their actual bodily being, this methodology is particularly useful for reseachers invested in studying embodied experiences and the emotional labor of institutional work. Smith writes, "People are the expert practioners of their own lives, and the ethnographer's work is to learn from them, to assemble what is learned from different perspectives, and to investigate how their activities are coordinated" (41). In this article, I use IE as the methodology to look to the discourse of complaint made by women WPAs in order to analyze and theorize the institutional politics that inform such complaint and theorize the knowledge to be gained from such relations.

By analyzing the "sticky data" collected in a two-year qualitative study, I highlight the importance of learning from the embodied and emotional work of complaint. Institutional ethnography is very much an embodied methodology, particularly in the way this methodology asks researchers to approach and analyze interviews. IE asks us to consider the embodied actuality of the research question, as we are always in our bodies. People's descriptions of their work activities and lived experiences are often produced "gesturally as well as verbally" (Devault and McCoy 24). Our understanding of that work and their expertise arises for us, in part, through our bodily responses to their gestures. In this way, the bodies of the research participants are part of the actual data, as the data takes into account both their experiences as bodies, as well as their bodies in the actual conversations (Devault and McCoy 24-25). I argue that this is especially important in thinking about complaint—the ways our bodies respond when complaining, the physical gestures we make and the responses we have when we are complaining, the emotional responses that come with it (anger, sadness, laughter, embarrassment). It's not just the words but how the words live in an embodied experience. The participants in this project, a group of thirty women WPAs ranging widely in their institutional rank from senior to junior WPA and the type of institutions they came from (R-1s, SLACs, public regionals, HBCUs, and community colleges), all experienced this type of embodied and emotional response when discussing their positions and the ways in which gender informs the everyday work that they do, in particular, how their leadership is institutionally recognized (or not). Institutional ethnography in these cases helps make visible the social relations in institutions and brings to the forefront the actions and emotional responses of those working within professional standards.

The interviews lasted forty-five minutes to an hour and were conducted either in person or through Skype and the phone. Data was collected over a duration of two years. The women interviewed were also in charge of different writing units: many were WPAs and at some point WC Directors, some were WAC directors, and some were the only "writing expert" on campus. Utilizing the standpoint of woman WPAs, I sorted through and coded the data to identify repeated experiences of complaint, repeated institutional processes that are shaping those experiences of complaint, and investigated those processes in order to describe analytically how they operate as the grounds of experience. Through these embodied and emotional responses on complaint, I argue that these experiences speak to the gendered responses these women receive on a regular basis at work as WPAs and that when voicing these experiences, they are often met with gendered responses, such as, "Well, you are just complaining," or small head nods, or justifications as to why they were treated the way that they were. Not only does this speak to the way women are continually treated by the institution (and we can argue other marginalized bodies although my data cannot verify that) but also to the way the field is viewed, as these women are in leadership positions; the data shows how complaint about real issues, such as contingent labor being a problematic practice, can get tossed aside as mere venting, as a woman who is upset, as trivial and non-important.

The data that I will highlight in the next section will be a data of complaint, more specifically, of women complaining, and is therefore highlighting the emotional, relational, and embodied work of a WPA. I will then analyze, through IE, the institutional politics that shape these complaints, and how these institutional politics operate in order to control, and further exhaust, these bodies, as a way to maintain practices and policies that keep bodies in check. However, I will show how complaint, when viewed in light of exposing a problem, or posing a problem, can be generative when we do not view complaint itself as a problem but rather as experiences pointing to a generalized issue to be explored. As I coded the data, in the aim of proposing a theory grounded in people's experiences, three different and equally important themes of complaint arose: women WPA's expertise dismissed as complaint, colleagues' responses to complaint, and what I am defining as affective complaint, complaint that stems from bodily experiences in the academy. In this particular article, I will argue that through the complaint gathered, a case can be made that better and stronger support and mentorship for junior faculty is needed, particularly junior faculty who are otherwise marginalized in the academy through race, class, or gender. This complaint archive speaks to the need for a greater network of leadership in WPA work and supports an argument that the most effective leadership stems from emotional and embodied knowledge of experience. I argue that we need to think about who is in leadership and that marginalized bodies need to be in leadership positions, not merely because we need greater representation but because the lived experiences of these bodies offer unique perspectives on the issues at the root of complaint; these embodied experiences can help in stopping cycles of harassment and abuse, so long as those in leadership recognize these are experiences to stop and not merely to suffer through.

Many of the women that I interviewed discussed their concerns about how they sounded throughout the interview. One woman, following the interview, said, "I feel like all I did was complain." Another woman was concerned that she got too emotional at a certain point when she was discussing harassment she experienced from colleagues, and yet another said that the interview was a good venting session to get her anger out. Many women discussed with me that this interview was cathartic, a chance to discuss these experiences and possibly theorize them, and yet at work they subscribe to a more professional approach to these experiences. This is not surprising, nor can I say that I am any different, for as Jane Detweiler, Margaret Laware, and Patti Wojahn argue in "Academic Leadership and Advocacy: On Not Leaning In," the current leadership models we operate under are Western, male, and individualized (463). However, I do believe there is power in complaint: complaint directly speaks into power, the way complaint is handled addresses power, and the potential of what complaint—collective complaint—can do is particularly powerful, which may be one reason why complaint often becomes individualized and invisible and difficult to capture. This essay suggests that a complaint archive made by and for women can have significant impact for institutional change, as "complaint can point to those who come after, who can receive something from you because of what you tried to do, even though all you seemed to have done was scratch the surface" (Ahmed, "Why Complain"). This complaint archive, and the power of collective complaint, requires a new rhetorical advocacy that WPAs, particularly marginalized ones, must take up: an advocacy grounded in the personal, in authentic dialogue, and deep listening as we learn from the emotional, and intellectual, insight gained from complaint.

The Complexities with Complaint and the Daily Lives of a Woman WPA

Expertise Dismissed as Complaint

Many women discussed the issues of complaint and how voicing their opinions based on their writing expertise was often viewed by others as "complaining." One woman, both the WC and WAC director at a SLAC, had just come back from a rather frustrating meeting when I interviewed her. This meeting was a discussion of the need for writing intensive courses at the college level, and she went in thinking she would be the point person in this conversation. However, it soon became clear to her that she was merely supposed to be present and that her input was not welcome. She explains, "*It is so frustrating—I am the writing expert, they know nothing about writing, and yet every suggestion I made was shot down—I got shot down three times in that one meeting, 'Yeah, well, we don't have the funding to do this.'*" When we discussed her responses and reactions to being shot down, she told me she remained silent throughout the rest of the meeting. "*It feels like a losing battle. Why should I speak up? Oh, [participant name withheld], she always complains.*" Many women in this study complained about this very issue: that their expertise and opinions were not valued but rather, as this participant succinctly puts it, seen as complaint. These experiences, and this particular individualized experience, says quite a lot about the discourses that shape our field: how expertise gets viewed as complaint. It is important to note how much gender influences views of expertise and how women attempting to take leadership positions, or voice their expertise, get easily dismissed in meetings. The women often felt their gender to be a factor in the reception of their opinions and that their requests for additional funding and labor to create sustainable programs with long-term success were relegated to mere complaint. "Shooting down" ideas at a meeting is one way to ensure that an opinion is seen as complaint, not to be taken seriously by others, and it is a way to ensure that the woman "complaining" is silenced. As this participant went on to say, after being shot down by the upper administrators in the room, she remained silent—and this was not a new experience for her, nor was she an outlier in the data set. She herself recognized that her expertise was being interpreted and read as complaint and no longer saw the importance in voicing her opinions, as people just see her as a "whiny woman" (this in quotations as I am borrowing language from another participant speaking on this topic). In this way, she is silenced and so is the complaint silenced. Ahmed writes, "When a complaint has been made, silence can sometimes be achieved by *silencing*, you have to silence someone because they are talking, or because they are talking in the wrong way, perhaps in a way that has too many implications for the organization" ("Damage Limitation"). Complaint often addresses very real issues and inequities, or in this case, issues involving the lack of writing instruction across the disciplines and lack of support for helping those teach writing.

However, because complaint often challenges the status quo of academic institutions, it is often deemed trivial, whiny, and emotional—and therefore unprofessional and out of place in academic settings that value *logic* and *reasoning*. This distinction and divide is particularly important when we analyze *who* is doing the complaining and the type of work that is being valued (or not valued). Another interview participant told me, "I remember saying things at [English] departmental meetings and having that outer body experience where nobody listens, or they think you're just whining or complaining, and you know, a man says the same thing—then everybody listens. It really was happening to me." I find it important to highlight here how this one participant described this experience as an "outer body" one, and how this one woman remembers these experiences through the body, even if she was explicitly describing them as disassociated from her body. From this transcript, we see how a woman experiences the invalidation of her opinion as a gendered experience, in which masculine voices are invested with more authority than her own. This participant however is now an upper administrator at an R-1 institution, as well as directing a large academic success and writing center, and has, in her own admission, "a considerable amount of power." Throughout the interview, however, it was clear this woman consistently reflected on complaint: complaints made by her or complaints made about her, and recognized the embedded institutional politics within complaint and gender. This particular participant felt that she was not valued in her English department, where she was housed as an assistant professor in Rhetoric, while directing a writing program, and felt she was deemed as a "complainer." Instead of becoming isolated, or feeling devalued, she made it a priority to utilize complaint in order to break from the English department; after tenure, this participant worked with her now supervisor, an associate provost at the institution, to create a proposal for the writing program to be separate from the English department. Much of the proposal was based on the years of ideas she had from her experience and expertise, which were ignored or deemed as "complaint" when she brought them up at the faculty meetings she earlier discussed. Ahmed writes, "A complaint is a way of not being crushed. Complaints…can lead you to form new partnerships" ("Why Complain"). This woman's own experience with complaint ultimately led her to a position of institutional authority, as she engaged in the emotional labor of processing complaint.

Responses to Complaint

What I found surprising, and disappointing, in the data was the way that other colleagues, specifically other women, responded to the complaints shared by the women in this study. As mentioned earlier, many of the participants were quick to make visible their complaints, in the form of pushing back at faculty members or more formal complaints of going to HR. Many women expressed to me their disappointment with the HR process, and while a thorough treatment of this important topic lies outside the scope of my current project, I wish to note briefly that many of the HR responses to the women's concerns were similar to the dismissals enacted by their colleagues. In this section I will be focusing on the responses of female colleagues. The reactions from these women were, in effect, non-responses, or responses that merely shrugged the complaints off, justified the behavior of the person being complained about, or expressed that they experienced similar issues when they first entered the institution and the woman WPA needs to "learn how to deal with it." One woman complained to me about another male colleague in her department:

> *There is an older male faculty member in my department who literally asks me to make photocopies for him. Sometimes I think he doesn't know who I am, and he confuses me for an administrative assistant, I think because I appear young and am a woman. What is more troubling is the way my colleagues, particularly the female colleagues in my department, respond when I tell them about this, "Oh that is just Jim". 'Oh he's just like that. The women covered his ass!*

Again, we know that "social relations don't just happen" (Nicolas and LaFrance 138). They are constructed and shaped and informed by historical discourses; we can certainly view the reactions and responses from the female colleagues in this situation as responses grounded in second-wave feminism about how to deal with emotions and complaints in the workplace, that is to conform to the "norm" of sexist workplace behavior and to focus on how the individual responds to the behavior, as opposed to creating a collective that pushes for institutional change (hooks). In this sense, we see the women justifying the bad behavior of Jim, and placating the complainer with an understanding that the women working with Jim need to adjust their expectations based on how he operates. In many ways, we see these women referring back to being the "pleasing" women (and we know how it is easier for certain women, particularly white women, to perform this task of the pleasing woman) and encouraging their colleague to do the same, albeit in a sympathetic manner. Of placating, Ahmed writes, "To placate is to calm or soothe. Placate derives from the word please, to be agreeable. Being placated is another way complaint is stopped" ("Nodding as a Non-Performative"). Ahmed writes of the danger, particularly for women, and specifically marginalized women, of happiness in many of her works, and in *Living a Feminist Life*, she says, "Happiness as a form of emotional labor can be condensed in the formula: making others happy by appearing happy.... Institutional passing as appearing to fulfil the happiness duty, softening one's own appearance, smiling because or when we are perceived as too harsh" (131). The women in this study certainly felt as if they had to perform the emotional labor of happiness (and smiling) in order to successfully pass in the institution; they especially felt they had to perform their happiness duty when they were complaining about serious issues, as they were not fulfilling their obligatory role of the happy woman WPA. Another participant shared a similar experience of her complaint being dismissed, as she wanted to go to HR regarding colleagues harassing her in the department. "An older senior woman told me, 'Oh, honey, don't let one bad person ruin your time here.'" As many WPA scholars have addressed, there is a narrative of WPAs taking up heroic type performances (Charlton, Charlton, Graban, Ryan, and Ferdinandt; Micciche; Vidali; Schell) despite the realities of the institution and their personal lives in order to institutionally pass; complaining, voicing concerns about structural issues and problems, does not fit into this type of performance, and especially does not work for a woman WPA. Women responding to their fellow women colleagues in this way further perpetuates the issues we have with complaint as valid, as data, and attempts to placate conceal institutional deficiencies in problematically gendered ways.

Other women discussed the exhaustion that came with voicing complaint and the repercussions they experienced when pushing back. One woman discussed with me an experience that happened to her when she was a junior faculty member and a relatively young woman. This woman was the WAC director and interim WPA at a small, liberal arts college. This is a very similar situation to the previous experience, except in this case the repercussion which came from her voicing her expertise was more damaging and directly connected to her gender; while silence was a tactic used in the previous experience, actual discrediting of this woman was used in this situation, and she expresses her powerlessness:

> *A much older male faculty member stood up and said [to me], 'Well that's just your opinion, why should we listen to you' and I said, 'Well I spent six years of graduate coursework studying composition theory and practice…so while it is my opinion, it is grounded in theory and research…you should put a little more weight into my opinions.' I heard back from people—he went around telling people that my office should be in his building because his office needed [pause]* **beautification***. He would say things like that repeatedly—he would call me things like, "little girl."*

Once again, the emotional labor and work of complaint is directly connected to intellectual work of a WPA (and we can see how heavily gendered this situation is). In this situation, we see the ruling relations at play. As Nicolas and LaFrance write, "Akin to powerful social or workplace norms, ruling relations draw on complexes of power and authority-expertise, marginality, influence, decision making that coordinates us with particular daily practices. Social relations are not accidental; they do not simply happen to people" (138). The ruling relations of this experience—an older, tenured, male faculty member resisting the authority of a junior, female faculty member—is one steeped in social and historical norms of power; this particular faculty member was also not familiar with the field of rhetoric and composition, and we can see here the historical conditions of the feminized nature of the field, particularly in English departments, at play. And again, we see this woman pushing back, or complaining, to the man that she is an expert in her field, that her opinions are credible, and that she should be listened to. Instead of taking this complaint seriously as one grounded in theory and research, he chose to respond by objectifying her, discrediting her authority, and harassing her. Ahmed writes about discrediting complainers and harassment and claims, "Discrediting a complainer is about damage limitation…. Harassment can be the attempt to stop someone from identifying the harassment that implicates the institution in wrong doing" ("Damage Limitation"). While this junior faculty member professionally called out this man for not listening to her because of both her gender and her expertise, and therefore discrediting his opinion, he used a stronger tactic of harassment, calling her "beautiful" to colleagues and a "little girl," in order to limit the damage her open complaint did, and bully her into silence. Later on in the interview, the woman spoke about the effects this dismissal had on her as a junior faculty member and how it informed her professional identity as the WPA at that institution, "So it was hard to establish [pause] any authority there. And I wasn't tenured…so…I don't know how much I could have said or done." Again, the emotional labor of complaint is directly tied to intellectual labor, both to the disciplinary expertise of the field and the way social relations work, and we see the complicated ways complaint is at play in the life of a woman WPA.

Affective Complaint

Other women discussed with me professional experiences that I categorized as complaint, in that they were sharing memories that were both emotional and affective, and were recognizing the issues that stemmed from these experiences throughout the interview. Ahmed writes in *Living A Feminist Life*, "To share a memory is to put a body into words" (23), and many of the women shared memories in which they were discussing their emotion and embodied experiences in the academy and voicing their complaints to and with me. One of my participants, a senior faculty WC director, recollected of her career,

> *I got everything from male colleagues telling female colleagues to tell me about how I should be, 'Make sure she approaches it this way,' or 'To always wear hose.' Truly. The chair of my department was very prone to greeting me, honestly, with a pat on the head…that got very uncomfortable.*

As I relistened to the recording, I heard myself asking her how she dealt with the "pats," especially since they continued despite her vocalized discomfort, or complaint, and again she smiled. Even in the moment I knew it was not a smile of happiness or contentment. It was a knowing smile, a weary smile. A smile that so many of the women participants of my study had on their faces when they answered my questions about their experiences as a woman WPA: the smile that helps them exist in their institutions, the type of emotional and embodied labor that remains invisible, perhaps because it is in an attempt to appease, and yet I argue that attention to this type of work is critical in our intellectual endeavors, particularly for those invested in institutional change. The participant went on to tell me that she started responding to his pats on her head with her pats on his belly. We laughed together again, and while humorous, this personal experience speaks to physical bodies in the space of the academy and what a woman WPA will most likely experience during her career. The pats on the head are condescending to this participant as an individual and as an academic professional. The discussion of her legs and the need for her to cover them, or perhaps even make them look more appealing (as hose can do), objectifies and reduces this WPA to her body. As a woman and as a writing center director, she is not being respected in the academy. Yet, later, I learned how she dealt with this particular situation, how she pushed back at this gesture in her own, somewhat comical way, embodied way, putting a complaint into action through a small gesture. Again, this is one transcription from one participant that is representative of how one's body, particularly a woman's body, is read and policed by the institution and the type of emotional and embodied labor that stems from such experiences.

Other participants spoke with me about their own bodily experiences as women WPAs, and it was interesting to note how these experiences were framed by them to me. One woman told me of a personal experience of being pregnant on campus, and how aware she was of her body at that time, how aware she was of other people's hyperawareness of her body, and the ways this impacted her professional work:

> *I was walking around with big, giant boobs on campus and a growing belly. I had a male colleauge, who I always got along with, start to treat me with a fatherly gentleness. He even would place his hand on my stomach during conversations.*

Similar to the particpant who spoke about pats on her head, this woman laughed with me as she was telling this story, even patting her stomach as she was talking. We both were aware that this invasive gesture made by her male colleague was not funny and was harassment, and yet we also knew this experience was all too common for women. Several other participants discussed their hypervisible bodies during pregnancy, and complained to me about the way they were treated on campus, fearful that people no longer saw them as administrators but rather as vulnerable women needing protection, their bodies inviting pats and rubs. The participants did not, however, express to me that they voiced their complaint to the colleagues participating in these actions. In "On Not Leaning In," Detweiler, Laware, and Wojahn report that "women with children were 38 percent less likely to procure tenure than were their male counterparts with children" (457). While my essay is not addressing issues of tenure and gender, I believe the findings from this archive of complaint point to the affective and emotional component to having children, and the ways in which women WPAs navigate pregnancy in the institution. This participant who shared with me the story of her male colleague treating her as a child later told me, "I don't think he's ever looked at me the same since I had my children. I do not talk about my children at work now. It is so unfair that I need to remove my gender." These are powerful words, and a complaint expressed most explicitly by this particular participant, but also representative of the way women felt as pregnant women, as mothers, in the academy. I believe this shared complaint is one that needs to be vocalized and more present in conversations about emotional labor, gender, and WPA work, as these embodied and affective experiences have impact on how women view their leadership on campus through how they are treated. Ahmed writes, "Not complaining because it would be too costly to complain does not mean it is not costly not to complain. Those costs can be personal- you might find it hard to live with yourself if you had grounds for a complaint…. Costs can also be institutional: the grounds remain" ("Why Complain"). These bodily experiences, if voiced and archived as complaint, can provide insight into how the emotional becomes intellectual; the ways in which the body informs our identity and informs our work, particularly our changing bodies. Institutional forces of sexism, racism, and classism exist and are ever-present, and the academy plays a major role in enforcing exclusionary power systems. I believe that open exchanges, voicing complaints and hearing them, about bodily experiences in the academy enable us to have complex and nuanced conversations about intersectionality and how racism, sexism, classism, and ableism (among other "isms") stem from patriarchal systems of power—in ways we have not quite yet been able to do in the field, as we do not view these conversations as intellectual and integral to the daily work we do as WPAs.

Complaint as Insight for Institutional Change and Rhetorical Advocacy

While these women often were concerned that their stories were "mere" complaint, this is the very issue that needs to be further explored in documenting and studying complaint. We see in these experiences women attempting to push back and voice their concerns only to be told that they are "complaining" or discredited in some other way. We also see women who have worked around verbal complaint to push back through embodied gestures—as seen with the woman who patted her chair's belly when he would pat her head. Complaint moves beyond disappointment in our working lives, although I certainly believe that disappointment is a necessary emotion to explore. Micciche asks, "Enroute to hope, can we speak candidly about professional inequities and disappointments without being regarded as doomsayers, as spoilers of the democratic identity that composition studies has constructed of itself?" (98). I argue that the emotional and embodied work of a WPA is directly connected to complaint, or as Micciche writes, disappointment, and that through complaint, we can learn how to get to the hopefulness many writing studies scholars crave as we work to better the lives of the people we work with. Hope, as feminist rhetoric and composition scholars, such as Paula Matthieu and, more recently, Cheryl Glenn, argue can be viewed as a feminist goal, and hope cannot be accomplished without complaint, without listening to a growing archive and collective that we can learn from as we aim to make for more hopeful futures. Through complaint, which is connected to calling out the daily institutional harms and harassments as seen through the data, we can understand how to be better equipped in situations in which we see our colleagues experience microaggressions, assault, and other embodied and emotional experiences that impact and inform our work. Through complaint, we can recognize who is experiencing these situations and what different forces of institutional power are at work, and how we can possibly change the paradigm by rethinking our leadership: who we put in leadership positions, what they have learned from their own personal embodied and emotional experiences, and how we can stop these experiences from happening. Complaint is intellectual work, that stems directly from the embodied and emotional experiences, and it is a topic that needs to be more fully explored by researchers, as complaint will inevitably vary depending on the types of bodies being interviewed. While this article focused on gender, and delineated gender as one aspect of identity that is necessary to explore, more research is needed to be done on WPAs of color, queer and LGBTQIA WPAs, WPAs with disabilities, and complaints connected to their experiences.

Of complaint and feminist work, Sara Ahmed writes, "One of our most important tasks as feminists is to ensure that making a complaint does not mean closing the door. We need to do this work together: a complaint requires a feminist collective" ("Complaint"). In other work on complaint, Ahmed states that, "listening to those who have made or tried to make formal complaints about abuses of power is teaching me about institutional mechanics; how institutions work; how different parts fit together. By institutional mechanics I am referring to the mechanics of power" ("Damage Limitation"). The act of listening can be understood as a feminist act in and of itself, particularly listening to those with different standpoints and perspectives, and it is an embodied act, and we can draw on the work done by Ratcliffe on rhetorical listening to understand the importance of listening. However, very often complaint—as Ahmed and I both argue—is not listened to (although often there is a performance of listening to complaint through the gestures of nodding and verbal cues of saying, "yes, yes"), and is certainly not seen as a generative site for learning. For Ahmed complaint becomes a way to better understand the operations of institutional power, the important perspectives that those who are complaining offer, and the need for their complaints to be listened to, and learned from. In our field, we can see complaints via the WPA listserv and the need to take such complaints seriously and to understand what they are telling us about the field and the work that we do. For example, when the CCCC 2019 CFP on performativity was announced which included the acronym AAVE, a listserv thread developed that no doubt seemed like complaining to some members. Eric Smith responded, "As a black man, I find the use of code-meshing in the conference a bit gimmicky, cosmetic, and a little offensive...The term 'blaxploitation' comes to mind." This, then, was the start to multiple emails, many from those responders who also took the time to complain about the CFP, many who then decided to complain against those complainers. The issue with complaining is not that it isn't a productive activity (it can be), or a scholarly endeavor (again, it can be), but that people very often do not listen, deeply and rhetorically, to those who are doing the complaining, when such listeners are not, as Ratcliffe describes it,

> consciously standing under discourses that surround us and others, while consciously acknowledging all our particular and fluid standpoints. Standing under discourses means letting discourses wash over, through, and around us and then letting them lie there to inform our politics and ethics. Standing under our own discourses means identifying the various discourses embodied in each of us and then listening to hear and imagine how they might affect not only ourselves but others. (205-206)

The complaints on the WPA listerv, and here I am thinking specifically of Smith's initial complaint of the 2019 CFP (it is important to note here that I often disagree with Smith's viewpoints and perspectives), can certainly be starting points to scholarly conversations (as I am using them in an article). However, we are not rhetorically listening to "stand under," particularly when people point out perspectives we disagree with or are not fully attempting to imagine. Smith's's critique, as he deliberately points out his own perspective and standpoint as a black man in academia, was certainly not given the attention it warranted. Not enough time was allowed for his own embodied discourse to "wash over" those reading, and to think about ways in which his perspective informs or contradicts the politics and ethics of the field. In fact, perhaps because the WPA is text-based in a way that makes it difficult to imagine a full human being writing and responding, Smith's complaint became both simultaneously disembodied and extremely individualized. The problem with complaints is that we often do not go very deep with them in the way that Ahmed suggests, and this is because we are not understanding in the way Ratcliffe calls for; while we honor an individual's complaint and what that complaint signifies, we also know that the individual is often voicing an embodied and historical discourse of power that we too often dismiss as just being "one person complaining, one person's viewpoint." I use the example of Smith not because he is an outlier in the field, a black man critiquing AAVE and discussing "blaxploitation," but because of his discussion of needing to perform in a certain way and because of the way many white people view him as a black man. This experience is real and embodied. We must learn to recognize, understand, and learn from these embodied and emotional experiences, as they can teach us and inform our ethics and politics to help us better understand institutional power and oppression in ways that text may not. Complaining, as I briefly mentioned earlier, is often gendered, but it is also raced and classed. Ahmed writes, "Complaints are immanent: they are *about* what we are *in*" ("Nodding as a Non-Performative"). We must learn to recognize and study complaints so that we do not "hear complaints so they can disappear" (and we see this often with the WPA listerv complaints), but rather create an archive of complaints in the field to understand the situations, local, global, historical, contextual, and embodied, that we are in right now.

The complexities of the complaints shared by the woman WPAs, and the gendered experiences directly connected to such complaints, are necessary to listen to and draw from if we are to revise the way we approach working with our colleagues and how we navigate our everyday experiences. The emotional and embodied labor of complaint can teach us how we think about the institutional positioning of our field, the way women leaders are viewed in the academy (and how they are being heard or not heard), and the everyday negotiations women and other marginalized bodies perform and take on in order to survive in the institution. We can also learn from this archive of complaint how this work is being listened to, and how people respond to complaint; that is, very often when the women perform this difficult and emotional work of voicing their concerns and issues, of pushing back, the genre of complaint acts to marginalize the experience of dissatisfaction so that it can be safely ignored by others (in these cases, especially by older men). A feminist collective of complaint, however, can show repeated patterns of bad behavior that occur everyday in the institution and ways in which we can start calling out people on such behavior together, as opposed to an individual, isolated act. I argue that complaint, as it is grounded in lived experience, allows for marginalized bodies to have more authentic dialogue by connecting stories and learning from differences; complaint, too, allows us to see ways in which we are all complicit in participating in bad behavior. Detweiler, Laware, and Wojahn in their discussion of the real need for changes in feminist advocacy, call us to rethink the way we view leadership, as our current models are deeply embedded in patriarchal structures: "Feminist leadership capitalizes on awareness and sensitivity to material, embodied experiences…as marked by social categories, embedded in hierarchical structures, and providing points of connection, of common political cause…. [T]his means reflectively locating our administration at the intersections of our personal…lives" (460). In her article "Is it Worth it to 'Lean In' and Lead? On Being A Woman Department Chair in Rhetoric and Writing Studies," Schell advocates for the need for further research to be done on embodied leadership and administration. Complaint as an archive allows feminists and advocates to understand not just how the personal is political but how emotion is also intellect and provides insight for the type of rhetorical advocacy needed in the current structures of the institution.

Complaint, as it is stemmed in emotion, is the explosive data that is needed for institutional change; moving from the individual to the collective by collecting and categorizing complaint made by marginalized bodies can be the type of intellectual work for newer generations of WPAs, those who come after the complaint. Complaint is forward-thinking, and points to experiences that can change. Complaint, as Ahmed and I argue, is hopeful, even if it is a "weary hope" ("Why Complain"). As Cheryl Glenn writes in *Rhetorical Feminism and This Thing Called Hope,*

> When rhetoric and feminism become allies in contention with the forces troubling us all, our shared goal is to articulate a vision of hope and expectation. Toward such a future, we can support our friends, colleagues, and students as they come to voice; feel empowered in critical discussions; and write, speak, and teach the words that reshape (and repair) the world and pave our future. (212)

The critical discussions that are needed and that we are starting to see in the field derive from our personal, embodied, and emotional experiences in our professional, academic lives (and in the way in which we live in this world). Complaint, as we live in a contentious society with troubling forces, is necessary emotional and explosive data to study and learn from as we think about hope, or what it would it mean to get on together a little bit better than we have been. Complaint goes beyond dialogue, which Carmen Kynard critiques as "whitewashing," in that it immediately addresses embodied experiences, as we see from the data, and calls to action. It is "calling out" and voicing problems that need to be addressed. We can see that complaint asks us to "stay with the trouble," as Haraway has suggested ("Staying"), to create sustainability in the currently embattled climate of higher education: "Staying with the trouble, yearning toward resurgence, requires inheriting hard histories for everybody, but not equally and not in the same ways" (114). Complaint reflects the hard histories that we need to reconcile and allows us to understand that histories are different for different bodies. Ahmed writes, "Those who are willing to hear will end up hearing more and more; you are providing those whose sphere of influence has been restricted with a place to go. A feminist ear can be what we are for" ("Complaint"). The emotional and embodied work of a WPA can often lead to complaining, but this complaining is the path towards the hope and resurgence that higher education needs; WPAs, with their highly relational work and the focus on bettering the lives of those we teach, are in prime positions to complain, not only because of their experiences that cause complaint, but because their complaint speaks to the everyday patterns and behaviors of people in academic institutions. We know that gender informs WPA work and complaint, and this is why feminist work is so important to WPA work; through complaint, and a new rhetorical advocay of authentic dialogue and listening deeply to lived experience, we can form a feminist collective that is necessary, one that requires "inheriting the hard histories" and recognizing our own implications in such histories as we try to carve out a better space through our writing programs/centers.

Works Cited

Adler-Kassner, Linda. *The Activist WPA: Changing Stories about Writing and Writers.* Logan, Utah State University Press, 2008.
Ahmed, Sara. "Complaint." *SaraAhmed,* www.saranahmed.com/complaint.
—. *The Cultural Politics of Emotion.* Routledge, 2004.
—. "Damage Limitation." *Feministkilljoys,* 15 Feb. 2019, www.feministkilljoys.com/2019/02/15/damge-limitation.
—. *Living a Feminist Life.* Duke University Press, 2017.
—. "Nodding as a Non-Performative." *Feministkilljoys,* 29 April 2019, www.feministkilljoys.com/2019/04/29/nodding-as-a-non-performative.
—. "Warnings." *Feministkilljoys,* 3 Dec. 2018, www.feministkilljoys.com/2019/12/03/warnings.
—. "Why Complain?" *Feministkilljoys,* 22 July 2019, www.feministkilljoys.com/2019/07/22/why-complain/.
Charlton, Collin, Jonikka Charlton, Tarez Samra Graban, Kathleen J. Ryan, and Amy Ferdinandt Stoley. *GenAdmin: Theorizing WPA Identities in the Twenty-First Century.* Parlor Press, 2011.
Detweiler, Jane, Margaret Laware, and Patti Wojahn. "Academic Leadership and Advocacy: On Not Leaning In." *College English,* vol. 79, no. 5, 2017, pp. 451-465.
DeVault, Marjorie L. and Liza McCoy. "Institutional Ethnography: Using Interviews to Investigate Ruling Relations." *Institutional Ethnography as Practice,* edited by Dorothy Smith, Lanham, Rowman & Battlefield Publishers, 2006, pp. 15-45.
Enos, Theresa. *Gender Roles and Faculty Lives in Rhetoric and Composition.* Southern Illinois Univeristy Press, 1996.
"Evaluating the Intellectual Work of Writing Administration." *Council of Writing Program Administrators,* www.wpacouncil.org/positions/intellectualwork.
Flynn, Elizabeth A. "Composing as a Woman." *College Composition and Communication,* vol. 39, no. 4, 1988, pp. 423-35.
Freire, Paolo. *Pedagogy of the Oppressed.* Bloomsbury Publishing, 1970.
Glenn, Cheryl. *Rhetorical Feminism and This Thing Called Hope.* Southern Illinois University Press, 2018.
Gunner, Jeanne. "Decentering the WPA." *WPA: Writing Program Administration,* vol. 18, no. 1/2, 1994, pp. 8-15.
Haraway, Donna. "A Cyborg Manifesto." *Sex/machine: Readings in Culture, Gender and Technology,* edited by Patrick D. Hopkins, Indiana University Press, 1998, pp. 434-468.
—. *Staying With the Trouble.* Duke University Press, 2016.
Holbrook, Sue Ellen. "Women's Work: The Feminization of Composition." *Rhetoric Review,* vol. 9, no. 2, 1991, pp. 201-29.
Holt, Mara. "On Coming to Voice." *Kitchen Cooks, Plate Twirlers, and Troubadors,* edited by Diana George, Boynton/Cook, 1999, pp. 26-43.
hooks, bell. *Teaching to Transgress: Education as the Practice of Freedom.* Routledge, 1994.
Kynard, Carmen. "Racial Intruders and Closed, White Shops: Reading Collin Craig's and Staci Perryman-Clark's Troubling the Boundaries." *Council of Writing Program Administrators,* 5 Nov. 2012, www.wpacouncil.org.

Lunsford, Andrea. "Refiguring Classroom Authority." *The Ethics of Writing Instruction: Issues in Theory and Practice*, edited by Michael Pemberton, Ablex Publishing, 2000, pp. 65-78.

Mathieu, Paula. *Tactics of Hope: The Public Turn in English Composition*. Heinemann, 2005.

McKinney, Jackie G., Nikki Caswell, and Rebecca Jackson. *Working Lives of New Writing Center Directors*. Utah State University Press, 2016.

—. "Writing Center and/as Emotional Labor." *Composition Forum*, vol. 34, 2016.

McMahon, Deidre and Ann Green. "Gender, Contingent Labor, and Writing Studies." *Academe*, vol. 94, no. 6, 2008, pp. 16-19.

Micciche, Laura. *Doing Emotion: Rhetoric, Writing, Teaching*. Boynton/Cook Publishers, 2007.

Miller, Hildy. "Postmasculinist Directions in Writing Program Administration." *WPA: Writing Program Admnistration*, vol. 20, no. 1/2, 1996, pp. 49-61.

Miller, Susan P. *Textual Carnivals: The Politics of Composition*. Southern Illinois University Press, 1991.

Moss, Beverly. "Intersections of Race and Class in the Academy." *Coming to Class: Pedagogy and the Social Class of Teachers*, edited by Alan Shepard, John McMillan, and Gary Tate, Heinemann, 1988, pp. 157-69.

Müeller, Genevieve and Iris Ruiz. "Race, Silence, and Writing Program Administration: A Qualitative Study of US College Writing Programs." *WPA: Writing Program Administration*, vol. 40, no. 2, 2017, pp. 19-39.

Nicolas, Melissa and Michelle LaFrance. "Institutional Ethnography as Materialist Framework for Writing Program Research and the Faculty-Staff Work Standpoints Project." *College Composition and Communication*, vol. 64, no.1, 2012, pp. 130-150.

Ratcliffe, Krista. "Rhetorical Listening: A Trope for Interpretive Invention and a 'Code of Cross Cultural Conduct.'" *College Composition and Communication*, vol. 51, no. 2, 1999, pp.195-224.

Ratcliffe, Krista, and Rebecca Rickly, editors. *Performing Feminism and Administration in Rhetoric and Composition Studies*. Hampton Press, 2010.

Schell, Eileen. *Gypsy Academics and Mother-Teachers: Gender, Contingent Labor, and Writing Instruction*. Boynton/Cook Publishers, 1998.

—. "Is it Worth it to 'Lean In' and Lead? On Being a Woman Department Chair in Rhetoric and Writing Studies." *Peitho Journal*, vol. 21, no. 2, 2019, pp. 308-332.

Shor, Ira. "What is Critical Literacy?" *Jounal of Pedagogy, Pluralism, and Practice*, vol. 1, no. 4, 1999, pp. 2-42.

Smith, Dorothy. *Institutional Ethnography: A Sociology For People*. Altimira Press, 2005.

Smith, Eric. "Re: 2019 CCCC CFP: Is this the first CFP for a major/"flagship" conference to use AAVE extensively?" *Writing Program Administratiors Listserv*. WPA-L@asu.edu (22 March 2018).

Vidali, Amy. "Disabling Writing Program Administration." *WPA: Writing Program Administration*, vol. 38, no. 2, 2015, pp. 32-55.

Invictus: Race and Emotional Labor of Faculty of Color at the Urban Community College

Kerri-Ann M. Smith, Kathleen Alves, Irvin Weathersby, Jr., and John D. Yi

Abstract: *This article shares the counter-stories of four junior faculty members of color, whose lived experiences provide concrete examples of what emotional labor sometimes entails in higher education. Grounded in Critical RaceTtheory and antiracist methodologies, these academics identify four specific ways in which they experience emotional labor: guilt, silence, anger, navigating double-consciousness and liminality, and self-regulating physical and mental health. They seek to buttress their experiences with counternarratives and, consequently, recommendations for how community college leaders may help to alleviate the emotional labor associated with junior faculty members of color through promotion, leadership, mentoring, and recognition of diverse perspectives and contributions by faculty members of color to the landscape of academe.*

Introduction

In the rhetoric of diversity in academia, the verb "reflect" stands as a ubiquitous means of performing the work of diversity.[1] To reflect something is to embody or represent it faithfully. In the urban community college, this would mean that the racial makeup of faculty reflects the racial makeup of the student body. But within the current conditions of academia, where its full-time faculty is primarily comprised of white males, (US Department of Education), the ideals of diversity seem impossible. The authors of this article—an immigrant Filipino woman, an immigrant Black woman, a Korean American man, a Black man—reflect the promise and success of diversity work. As junior scholars at our institution, we are marking a different racial landscape that diverges from the homogenous past. Our hiring reflects well on the institution. Our hiring brings credit to the powers that be that made that happen. Our hiring is diversity work at work. Writing on diversity work in higher education, Sara Ahmed posits that "you *already* embody diversity by providing an institution of whiteness with color" (*On Being Included* 4). Our bodies of color become the embodiments of diversity work. And yet, our mere presence on campus is not enough.

Our counter-stories situate our experiences, as faculty members from marginalized minority groups, on the landscape of an urban community college, and in a department where the majority of our colleagues are white. These counter-stories draw on the concept in Critical Race Theory (CRT) that centralizes, legitimizes, and validates the lived experiences of people of color as "critical to understanding, analyzing, and teaching racial subordination" (Yasso 74). We share a commitment to highlight Otherness in

---

1. The authors respectfully request that all citations of this article include all of the names (not with et.al) of the authors to honor the collaborative nature of this project.

various ways at our institution and through our voices, to make visible the institutional barriers that may isolate or marginalize us as faculty members of color and that create complex layers of emotional labor. We also draw upon Arlie Hochschild's distinctions between the "'real" and "acted" self and the tests that come about as a result of our presence at an institution where we are few in number. We seek to explore, through these counter-narratives, the idea of being disconnected from the sources of power for which we "act" as members of marginalized groups.

We teach at a community college in one of the most diverse counties in the United States, which, according to institutional data, serves a student body comprised of people from over 127 countries, who speak 78 different languages. We serve a dynamic demographic of students, and in the past few years, we have seen our full-time student enrollment shift from having almost equal numbers of students from each race to a 7% decrease in the number of white students we serve. Like those at other urban community colleges (Carter; Levin, Levin, Walker, Haberler, and Jackson-Boothby), the demographics of the faculty, on the other hand, represent a stark contrast to the dynamic heterogeneity of our students. Our faculty is mostly white (64%), and for those in the minority, our presence at work is often met with scenarios that radically disturb and uproot our sense of belonging.

Community colleges serve students with diverse interests and backgrounds, most of whom enter the workforce immediately through technical and business-related fields. Thus, the impetus is upon the faculty to create a community where our students are exposed to and familiar with a wide range of experiences that reflect the dynamic racial, cultural, and political world in which we reside. There are long-term institutional, educational, and personal benefits for students when faculty members of color are permanent and present at their institutions (Levin, Walker, Haberler, and Jackson-Boothby; Mertes; Newkirk). Having faculty members who reflect diverse perspectives is one important way to help students discuss and confront issues that are unique to their circumstances. The paucity of faculty of color to serve the needs of a diverse college community may result in extensive emotional labor for that faculty. An institution that lacks diversity in its faculty maintains the status quo of academe, which by nature of its origins, marginalizes and excludes qualified faculty members of color, while relying on those who are present to extensively render emotional labor.

Derrick Bell identifies four strands of resistance that make the academy inflexible: white superiority, faculty conservatism, scholarly conformity, and tokenism. Other research (Ladson-Billings) validates and qualifies Bell's categories, while placing emphasis on patterns of exclusionary hiring, retention, and training that reflect practices historically in line with white supremacy. All four of us have experienced these features of our institution's culture, and thus attest that the culture of this institution fosters an environment where junior faculty members are often relegated to silence and compliance. For junior faculty of color, this distinction is more palpable and emotionally cataclysmic.

In a recent interview, Hochschild clarifies that emotional labor is "work for which you're paid, which centrally involves trying to feel the right feeling for the job. This involves evoking and suppressing feelings" (Beck). In extending Hochschild's definition through a theorization of racialized emotional labor in academe, we propose solutions to help ameliorate the effects thereof. We posit the necessity of unmaking institutional life centered on marginalization and power in order to create an environment that moves beyond the empty rhetoric of diversity. Rinaldo Walcott proposes that "something more radical and sustaining than diversity is now required if whiteness is to be understood as the foundation and barrier that preempts nonwhite others from the structural arrangements that currently govern human life" (394). Whiteness depends on phenotype, but whiteness is also a structure—*the* structure—that works to replicate white people's superiority through a set of ideas and practices that endow and affirm that superiority. We can no longer tolerate the myth of unconscious bias, for it moves the attention from the recipient of racism to empathy with the person who benefits from phenotype and social structure. Unequivocally, white faculty wear the face of and benefit from white supremacy. Walcott argues, "The structures that require radical transformation to change the ongoing global administration of life and death cannot be transformed without the transformation of whiteness, and such a transformation can occur only if people marked as white are implicated and fully understand their implication and are prepared to act on it" (398). This understanding and willingness to act by white faculty is requisite for change and transformation in institutional structure and human relations.

In this article, we offer the lived experience of four marginalized scholars and our counter-narratives depicting guilt, silence, anger, navigating double-consciousness and liminality, and managing our physical and mental health. We present these counter-narratives as testaments to the labor required to thrive in inequitable conditions. Occasionally, we have experienced moments of clarity through a willingness to allow room for growth, believing in our own labor as transformative, as a force that fosters transcendence and mobility. But, frequently, carrying this labor is a huge weight, one that threatens to crush our careers. If we manage to survive and embrace the struggle, however, we believe that we can effect radical change.

Alves: The Emotional Labor of the Tenured Professor of Color

On the tenure track for six years, I was granted tenure and promotion last year. I am one of two female associate professors of color in a department of 63. Since I was hired, more faculty of color have joined the department, but at the time of my hiring, there were no full-time men of color and only two women of color in the entire department. There were no full-time professors who identified as queer or disabled. Indubitably the department was homogenous, with the majority of full-time professors white. While the racial landscape in the department has definitely become more heterogeneous since my hiring, this change has positioned me in an unexpected political location, one resting on my racial identity.

When I was on the tenure track, I tried to be careful. I avoided conflict. There were many moments when I wanted to air my frustration, my disagreement, my opinions. I knew that to survive on the tenure track I had to play the game of civility. I did not want to be known as a shit-stirrer, someone who causes trouble, makes people uncomfortable, forces people to confront their own problematic prejudices and viewpoints. This "effort not to stand out or stand apart" is what Ahmed calls "institutional passing" (Cultural Politics127). I thought I played the game of institutional passing well. I silently considered every word, every gesture, every microaggression with care. I shrunk my body's occupation of linguistic and political space, a symptom of fear. Ahmed writes that "fear works to restrict some bodies through the movement or expansion of others," and "to contain bodies within social space through the way it shrinks the body, or constitutes the bodily surface through an expectant withdrawal from a world that might yet present itself as dangerous" (*Cultural Politics* 69, 79). Though I was on the tenure-track, the professional world I inhabited was precarious.

Silence and Silencing

"How does it feel to be a problem?" W.E.B. Dubois' words in *The Souls of Black Folk* continue to haunt us a century later. In higher education, faculty of color who expose racism within the institution become the problem. Ahmed writes, "To talk about racism is thus to be heard as making rather than exposing the problem: to talk about racism is to become the problem you pose" (*On Being Included* 153). If our bodies of color "fix" the diversity problem in academia, that we are the political solution, speaking out can mean becoming the problem that you bring. When we speak out, we become the problem. And in becoming the problem, we can see how diversity as a commitment to antiracism in the institution is a performance.

In the space of exclusion, we have two choices, both rooted in anger. We can bring up the problem, become the problem, and be seen as the angry women of color that they see us as anyway; or leave it alone and be angry at the performative dimension of antiracist work in the institution.

Ahmed observes that people of color are careful to avoid the language of racism because of the saturation of racism in institutional spaces: "If you already pose a problem, or appear 'out of place' in the institutions of whiteness, there can be good reasons not to exercise what is heard as a threatening or aggressive vocabulary" (*On Being Included* 162). Bringing up racism is aggressive. Embodying the figure of the angry person of color presents an impossible situation. When we criticize racism, it is perceived as an expression of anger, anger heard without cause: "It is as if we talk about racism because we are angry, rather than being angry because of racism" (Ahmed, *On Being Included* 159). And in transferring the burden of talking about racism onto us, whiteness is recentered.

Tenure and the Meritocracy Myth

Before tenure, I never would have asked pointed questions about race with my white colleagues. I never would have asked them to confront their own ways of enacting white supremacist practices in their teaching. I never would have asked them to think more deeply about their own whiteness, to call that whiteness into account. I never would have asked them to think about how inequity occurs through homogeneity, how as white people they are not aware of the barriers nonwhite people face, the barriers in thinking through and writing in the imperialist language of standard written English. I never would have asked them to think about how this homogeneity provides an advantage they feel entitled to as white people who wield the power of recognition.

We think of tenure in the future abstract, but tenure is rooted in material and concrete advantages: a promotion with higher pay. But tenure is *granted* by the college Personnel and Budget Committee (P&B), then the president. Whenever I speak up in meetings now, I feel that tenure has endowed me some power, a small space to speak from my position in the minority for the minority. I can say I earned that power. I can believe in the myths of individualism and meritocracy, but I can also say that the college P&B and the president (who is white) *allowed* me to stay and *allowed* me to move a step forward in my career trajectory. This distinction is crucial, for no matter how competent a professor is, that professor cannot stay if the institution does not allow it. Access is denied. Tanya Titchkosky notes that access is not merely a bureaucratic practice, but demonstrates how access opens toward specific bodies. Whiteness obfuscates racism by paradoxically presenting whites, white privilege, and racist institutions as unseen. As Robin Diangelo observes, whiteness creates and buttresses the dominant narratives in American society, such as individualism and meritocracy: "These narratives allow [whites] to congratulate [themselves] on [their] success within the institutions of society and blame others for their lack of success" (27). If I believe I *earned* tenure, then I do not have to think about the uncomfortable truth that I am a character of these narratives, narratives written by white people.

The Professional Consequences of Rage

A few days after a racially insensitive meeting held by the department's Composition Committee, where roughly half the full-time faculty were present, I decided to Tweet my thoughts, my anger and frustration palpable. A day or two after, my chair asked me in an email if I could stop by her office for a chat. I knew immediately that this chat would be over my Tweets.

My chair is a white woman. She is kind and gracious. We talk about our kids and the pressures of parenting. She has never given me any reason to fear her. But her position as chair and the power she wields as a member of the white community with the collective social and institutional power and privilege over people of color, people like me, frightened me. I was filled with dread. I was like a child called into the principal's office: The principal could deliver positive news, but that office symbolized power—a power usually imagined as punitive authority. Was I going to detention? Would I be expelled? Is it worth putting my partner and children under economic pressure if I lose this job to make a point? I fell into a chasm of guilt, resentment, and shame.

The meeting was awkward; both my chair and I acknowledged the discomfort. But she listened to the source of my anger. She recognized and validated my experience by asking how we could begin antiracist work in the department. We brainstormed some ideas, and one of the major changes instituted that semester was a department Diversity and Inclusion Committee. Junior colleagues of color on the committee insisted that two members should be senior faculty with their concomitant influence in the college, and she made this happen. In my entire professional career, this has been the strongest example of a supportive white person who demonstrated a commitment to breaking with white solidarity.

I am heartened by the positive direction in antiracist work in the department, but I still feel the weight of acting as an ambassador for the faculty of color who are on the tenure track or in contingent positions. I cannot say with certainty that my colleagues of color feel similar pressure to play the same game of civility and silence that I felt when I was on the tenure track. I can say that in the course of the two hours of that meeting, the majority of them did not say anything. Was this the work of "institutional passing," the kind of work I did and continue to do? Carrying this crushing weight of responsibility takes an enormous toll on my body, my spirit. It is an impossible balancing of what I feel is my obligations to them, to myself, and to my relationship with my white colleagues.

Smith: On Being Black and Young-ish

According to institutional data, I am one of 43 Black faculty members in a body of 415. That's 10.4% at a college where 26% of the students are Black. In my department, at the time of writing this, I am the only Black woman who is tenured and who has earned that distinction in recent history. The Department made a historic move by finally granting tenure to a Black man in 2019. These milestones are significant because only tenured members can hold leadership positions in our departments, and with the exception of one, everyone on departmental and college-wide personnel and budget committees must be tenured. The absence, over the course of many years, of a tenured Black person means that none of the key stakeholders in my department has ever been Black and, more significant, none has held a full professorship. The personnel and budget committee makes key decisions related to hiring, promoting, and funding faculty members. A committee that reflects only the culture of power reinforces the exclusionary tactics historically practiced in higher education.

Professors with tenure, especially those who have reached the highest rank of full professor, can advocate with impunity. They can lead, advise, advocate, and choose to say "no" when overwhelmed. College-wide, there are only six full professors who self-identify as Black.

Professors of color, in general, rarely occupy advocacy roles. Instead, we are often found in advisory or supporting roles where votes are not essential to the hiring, firing, or reappointment process at the college. Four years ago, however, only 8.9% of the overall faculty were Black, so we have grown in number, and our attrition rate has been fairly low in the last two years. The absence of faculty of color in key advocacy roles reinforces the foundation of white supremacy upon which higher education was built.

People on campus are not used to seeing us in leadership roles outside of student affairs. Pamela Newkirk notes that a 2016 study by the Teachers Insurance and Annuity Institute confirms that "administrators of color were disproportionately in diversity or student affairs positions" (93). It is, then, no wonder that when I enter offices, I'm sometimes met with strong animadversion and reproach. Incidents I have encountered reinforce the historical and stereotypical mindset of white supremacy and its agents on my campus. I often find myself suppressing rage and sarcasm for the sake of maintaining decorum in a professional world—something my offenders rarely seem to have to consider for themselves. This mindset is consistent with Austin Channing Brown's assertion that, "it's work to always be hypervisible because of your skin...it's work to do the emotional labor of pointing out problematic racist thinking," all while struggling to maintain a sense of worthiness and avoiding "bitterness and cynicism" (21). The double-consciousness of suppressing rage on the inside, and maintaining professionalism on the outside, is what John Levin, Laurencia Walker, Zachary Haberler, and Adam Jackson-Boothby describe as "the divided self," and what Hochschild identifies as "deep acting"—a method that is used to "'personalize' or 'depersonalize' an encounter at will" (133).

After about the third time, I began recording the instances when I would walk into offices and receive either the cold shoulder or be completely ignored while standing and waiting for assistance. The offenders were mostly college assistants—invariably older white women. Outside of campus office spaces, white men were the other prominent offenders.

Once I was assigned to share rooms with a white male colleague from my department for our final exams. I had arrived a few minutes before he did, and my students and I were enjoying a spirited conversation when he walked in with authority, declaring it was time to begin, while instructing me to take my seat before he distributed the exam. I registered my disapproval by ignoring his directives and continued to talk to my students, who were vocally and visibly annoyed. We were in a large lecture hall, with all of his students and all of mine, and his response to being ignored was to speak louder. I was standing in front of the lecture hall, facing students, wearing professional attire, and holding a stack of blue exam booklets. At the very least, his perception should have been that I was there to assist the professor. Yet, he continued to direct me to "sit down now," all while referring to me as "you."

Once he finally realized that we were colleagues, he came over to quietly apologize. He attributed his ignorance to my youthful appearance, stating (ironically) that times have changed and his children, who are around my age (whatever his perception of my age was) are also professors. I found it hard to separate this man's perception from that of other racists, who fail to see us or situate us, Black women, in the frame of the professoriate. I reluctantly accepted his "quiet" apology and noted to myself that he had not apologized as publicly and emphatically as he had imposed his misguided older-white-male authority when he insulted me in front of a large group of students. I walked away from the situation regretting that I had not insisted on a public apology with the same gusto with which he spewed his insults. The consequence of these unfortunate encounters is always ours to bear. We leave angry, agitated, and anxious about things we should have said and the offenders walk away bearing little to no emotional consequence.

I imagine that I did not represent, to him, the image of what a professor should look like, confirming Ahmed's observation that "being asked whether you are the professor is a way of being made into a stranger, of not being at home in a category that gives residence to others" (*On Being Included* 177). I am Black, and youngish, and while I dress "professionally" (again reinforcing the white supremacist mindset of what a professional embodies), I somehow did not represent what his mind conceived as a person worthy of the title, Professor.

The Diversity Hire

I define emotional labor through the lens of microaggressions that I experience before I enter my classroom. These microaggressions render me both hypervisible and invisible simultaneously, since part of my commitment to changing my surroundings now includes heavy involvement in all things connected to diversity on my campus. My hypervisibility in diversity work is what Amado Padilla calls "cultural taxation" and what Tiffany D. Joseph and Laura Hirshfield would describe as "pioneer" work, which in many cases comes with "important consequences for faculty of colour's academic performance, subsequent promotion and tenure" (129). Patricia Matthew issues a clear warning to faculty of color that we must maintain focus on scholarship, rather than attempting to solve problems of inequity that were created and maintained at our institutions long before we arrived. In 1992 Derrick Bell tackled the notion of hiring Black professors for the sake of "diversifying the academy." In *Faces at the Bottom of the Well*, he proposes that power brokers should consider an academy where the statistics were reversed and the number of Black faculty members outweighed whites. He asks, "what action, then, would whites take?" (138). In such a scenario, he says, those in power would certainly find solutions—and rapidly.

A white woman in a leadership role once casually referred to me as "a diversity hire," and by this she meant no harm, but I decided to embrace the title and proverbially "come whiffing through the tulgey wood" (Carroll 170) of white complacency and status "quoism" on my campus. Still, like Alice's fall down the rabbit hole in *Alice in Wonderland*, my desire for inclusion, coupled with my "pioneer" efforts may very well be "nonsensical" because issues of race are often disguised in policies, cultural practices, and "norms" that are part of a "deeply embedded ideology of White superiority and Black inferiority" (Newkirk 77) often perpetuated in the hiring, promoting, and retention of Black faculty members in the academy.

Nonetheless, as an appointed member of the president's faculty advisory committee for diversity, I use my voice as an advocate for change. Membership in this group is an emotionally taxing task that every member must undertake if change will ever transpire at our college. Since joining this committee, I have seen small shifts, but there is still much to be done. The composition of the select group of faculty members is worth noting. Of the ten selected faculty members, only one is white and male. There are three Black men, one Asian-American man, one Asian-American woman, one Latinx woman, and three Black women. Being a member of this select group allows me to be what Brown calls a bridge builder, though she reminds us that "the role of a bridge builder sounds appealing until it becomes clear how often that bridge is your broken back" (69). The task is laborious, and I may never see the full impact of the work in my lifetime, yet the work must be done.

As Newkirk points out, diversity is a buzzword in the academy, and despite the efforts and copious amounts of funding to help shift the tide, our institutions continue to be hostile spaces where our cultural capital is exploited in many cases (for example, we are called upon to use our networks for diversity talks, or are asked to join panels and discussions to fulfill a diversity quota, or are given the courses for which most students of color register) and devalued in others. Walcott reminds us that, "diversity interrupts and delays more radical calls for human transformation" (405), and oftentimes the term is used, but nothing radical occurs to impact change. Internalized racism and institutional racism (Bell, Funk, Joshi, and Valdivia) are interwoven in the seams of academia, and as a Black woman interested in making a difference, I must protect and preserve my position as a scholar. Even as much as my institution has made efforts to effect change in the area of diversity, I am reminded that "American college campuses have historically been inhospitable environments for people of color" (Newkirk 96), and even with the efforts put forward, there is much to be done to ensure true inclusivity. Much like the unnamed narrator in Ralph Ellison's *Invisible Man*, I am aware that although I have been so involved in the work of diversity on my campus, I have been doing it at the risk of being "sacrificed for my own good" while everyone else benefits. Ellison calls this the "sacrificial merry-go-round" (505).

Brain-Picking Without Benefits

Research on faculty experiences at American colleges and universities show that while they engage robust diversity initiatives, faculty of color persistently grapple with exclusion and marginalization (Joseph and Hirshfield). As a Black woman, I often rely on my navigational capital (Yosso) in order to cope with conditions that were never created to include or accommodate me in the first place. I must also be conscious of my status as a junior faculty member, and I must continue to grapple with the double-bind of the oppositional culture (Ogbu) that resides within me and the double-consciousness of holding my head down, while treading murky waters (Levin, Walker, Haberler, and Jackson-Boothby). This state of being is emotionally onerous, and morally degrading, yet like Paul Ruffins suggests, I must maintain decorum and "navigate minefields" (qtd. in Joseph and Hirschfield 123) to ensure financial and scholarly security, while defending my right to exist in the academy.

Equally emotionally exhausting is the fact that while navigating these spaces, I am still called upon to share ideas, gratis, for which others would be compensated or credited. For example, senior colleagues have asked me to share entire bibliographies on topics related to my specialty without an invitation to co-author a piece. The power differential, coupled with the unspoken demands of collegiality, can become complicated. I have had countless incidents where senior faculty members have scheduled meetings to "pick my brain" about a research project, with no consideration for my time or the fact that it would be beneficial for me, then an untenured faculty member, to earn co-authorship of the article or research project.

Furthermore, in exchange for the brain-picking, no mentoring is offered to help support my advancement as a junior faculty member despite the widely understood benefits of mentorship (Padilla; Laden and Hagedorn). Only once did a colleague—a senior faculty member who is a Black woman—deliberately invite me to co-author a now-published article, for which my expertise was requested. Her example speaks to the necessity and benefits of having senior faculty of color available to support, mentor, and collaborate with junior faculty members. As noted by Levin, Walker, Haberler, and Jackson-Boothby, Black faculty members often work collaboratively, and so when they are institutionally underrepresented, such support systems cannot exist and thrive.

Yi: Not Your Asian Ambassador

I am a co-coordinator of the Accelerated Learning Program (ALP) and have the opportunity to lead a cohort of faculty who teach a co-requisite ALP section designated for students who need to exit from reading and/or writing remediation. I am responsible for leading workshops, creating and updating the collective body of curricular and pedagogical work of ALP faculty that helps with student achievement and success. It is a role that I am both serious and passionate about; and one that I am really fortunate to have been given by the chair of the department.

Although I am a coordinator within the English department, I sometimes feel pigeonholed by my white colleagues whenever the topic of Asian, particularly Chinese English language learners, becomes the topic of discussion. These conversations embarrass and upset me because, for one, I am not Chinese and have no professional teaching background in working with Chinese English language learners, and secondly, I did not come to work for the English department to be an ambassador for Asian students.

Jane Hyun, in her seminal work, *Breaking the Bamboo Ceiling*, articulates my anxieties of balancing interpersonal relationships within the overly-ambitious American work environment. As a Korean, I demonstrate respect for my elders as is expected in my culture, but this approach often works to prevent Asians from reaching leadership positions. A former HR executive, Hyun has looked at the ways in which Asian cultural values may be limiting/hurting Asian professionals in career advancement and fulfillment. She presents numerous case studies and anecdotes on Asian professionals of diverse age groups and professions working in the US to highlight the ways in which one's cultural background plays into how they are perceived and treated in the American workplace.

Hyun looks largely at Confucian cultural elements that limit Asian Americans from excelling in the American workforce—such elements that center on deference to authority and elders, collectivism, and self-control/restraint. Hyun's work identifies and affirms the cultural nuances that I bring to the department as a Korean American who straddles both Korean and American cultures. My role as a co-coordinator allows me to "break," if not crack, the bamboo ceiling and both challenges and inspires me to no longer restrain myself before it is too late to say something, especially when I want to be heard. As one of only two Asian American male faculty members, I can see how my colleague and I both confide in each other, especially when navigating through our respective work. The bond that we have formed (re)affirms much of the internal tensions I feel as someone who may sometimes seem invisible in collegial conversations. When I do speak out, however, it seems as if I am moving out of that "other" space.

Seeing how my colleague is treated as less than, interrupted during meetings, and is reluctant to talk first, I get where he comes from. I understand what it is like to feel invisible in the presence of white colleagues. And yet I can see there is a difference in how each of us is treated. In a recent cohort meeting that was aimed at creating additional resources for ELL students, this Asian American colleague was rudely interrupted by a senior white colleague when he finally shared out his points, after patiently waiting for everyone to offer their feedback. I was very angry and regret not standing up for him in that moment like I wished I had stood up for myself in those moments when I have also felt silenced or interrupted. But DiAngelo writes that "White people often define as respectful an environment with no conflict, no expression of strong emotion, no challenging of racist patterns, and a focus on intentions over impact. But such an atmosphere is exactly what creates an inauthentic, white-norm-centered, and thus hostile environment for people of color" (127).

Balancing Two Halves

Being Korean American affords me a unique lens through which I understand the work that I provide to the department. ALP allows me to use my strengths of navigating this liminal space. I find particular enjoyment in my classroom conversations because my ALP students also navigate this world of two halves. At least 90% of students are either bilingual and/or bicultural, sometimes even tri-lingual, and belong to more than two cultures, not including American. Further, these students participate in an English composition course and a corequisite remedial reading and/or writing course simultaneously. Often our discussions extend beyond the scope of composition and literacy, and my students and I *really* talk about the things that matter most for us in the context of who we are, where we come from, what matters most to us, and how all those things inform the ways in which we approach our writing and reading identities.

I love to teach Freshman composition unlike many of my colleagues. Often, I find that they dislike it because of the work it requires of you as an instructor. You are not tasked with teaching composition alone. You are challenged to teach soft skills like notetaking, college etiquette, academic professionalism and other life skills. I suppose it is in this role that my liminal, Korean American identity becomes a strength and aids my effectiveness. There is always movement and flux between different modes and mediums related to identity, learning, philosophizing, interpreting, defining and sense-making. This fluidity complements my passion and contemplative practices which help me meet the demands and challenges of teaching an ALP course.

In a recent freshman composition course I taught, an Asian male student, who identified himself as both (and neither) Korean and Chinese, shared some insightful commentary on his identity. Although he was quiet during class, he came up to me once class was over and all the other students had left the room to express his feelings of not belonging within the Korean community, as well as the Chinese community at our college. He taught me that I am very privileged to not have to deal with the stigmas, fears, or labels of being accepted by neither the Chinese nor Korean community. We then got into language, and his own social fears of speaking in class. That day also happened to be the first day he actually spoke out during class discussion, and he was eager to seek my feedback since he was afraid that he was being inappropriate or too personal. It was a very illuminating conversation that lasted for about an hour, and I was able to share with him the very same feelings of what it is like to live in a very liminal space, and how sometimes being of two or more worlds and not fitting in perfectly in either one can be unique and uplifting. Our conversations made me think about the notions and meanings behind "Korean," "Chinese" and "American," as well as the other insights about the neighboring borders all around us.

When I establish connections with students on a personal, cultural level, we each straddle a liminal space wherein we are faced with identities that are often conflicting.

The spaces we occupy seem dissonant, not the norm, or what is expected. A part of the work is undoing notions of irrelevance or feelings of insignificance that many students feel. This work provides an opportunity for us to share and teach each other about our feelings of uncertainty and/or psycho-socio pensive moods that intersect race, ethnicity, religion and class. The opportunity to create dialogue around these meaningful discussions helps me to understand that emotional labor for a faculty member of color is not so different than the emotional labor (and trauma) that students of color face.

The reading and writing class I teach gives me such an opportunity. And while this happens I cannot help but wonder if I am good enough, if I am put into this role because of other reasons—because I look like the majority of ALP students enrolled in my class, that I am some sort of physical prop to reflect the demographics of ALP students. As an ALP faculty member, I am seen both as an "expert" and someone who may understand students. This duality often plays into and challenges me to reconsider my role. Still, I love giving students the opportunity and space to learn comfortably, in the way they best make sense of their own learning process—not to press them or see them as blank slates, or empty vessels. But to what extent do my peers really see me as just an expert of ALP or remediation courses?

The experiences of feeling out of place, or not deserving to be in a space with other "qualified" students is something that I have struggled with throughout my doctoral journey, which possibly stems from my own internal struggles I've had with being both Korean, as well as Korean American. I was raised in a household where I was encouraged to speak either Korean or English, unlike my two older sisters who were born in Korea. My father made it a point that they study Korean at an early age, but he deemed it unnecessary for me. As I grew older, I yearned to learn it, particularly when I became a teen and K-Pop, or Korean popular music, was becoming more popular, especially among second and third-generation Asian Americans. I vividly recall teaching myself how to read in Korean after spending an entire month just watching a Korean music show after school called *Music Bank* (a music show devoted to the hottest Korean music videos for the week, much like MTV's *TRL* or BET's *106 & Park*) where popular artists would perform live. In short, I learned to read in Korean without having to literally understand what I was reading. Essentially, my limited understanding of the Korean language in a way shapes how I perceive my limited access and entry into Korean culture and traditions. I do not entirely see myself as Korean, nor entirely American. I am neither, but I am also both in a sense. This in-between space is where I speak often from when discussions of identity surface around culture, race, and ethnicity. It is also a space where many of my students reside.

Being an ALP faculty member and now a co-coordinator within the program encourages me to see past all the internalizations that I have put up with. This role enables me to move beyond the space of seeing myself as less than to being a vital member of the department.

Weathersby: Denying Discomfort

When asked about being awarded a MacArthur Fellowship, Claudia Rankine has described the recognition as not necessarily about her work but its subject which centers on racism and the deconstruction of white supremacy (Begley). In *Citizen*, a collection of prose poems, Rankine mines expressions of racism and how they correspond with the imagination in vignettes that grapple with the quotidian experiences of Black Americans. Some of these experiences illustrate the racist encounters that she has been subjected to as a professor and speak directly to the racism that I have also experienced in academia. When she veers into these spaces, the psychic burdens I bear are revisited.

One of the most difficult incidents that I endured actually involved the teaching of *Citizen* during my formal observation. I hadn't planned for the text to fall on my observation date, but the professor assigned to assess my performance needed to reschedule, and in a way I was grateful for the change if for no other reason than for him to actually engage with racism and see me, not as a competent instructor, but more as a competent Black man, product of a rich legacy of pride and excellence. I had wanted to detail this much to him and more in our earlier exchanges but had demurred for the sake of my employment. I am untenured, and like many professors of color, I am fully aware of the tenuous circumstances that define my existence. "Unemployment rates for black workers have been consistently higher than for white workers over the past 60 years" (Perry), so causing a disturbance in the name of discomfort seemed impractical.

DiAngelo articulates many of the challenges that I face when people of color must confront their oppressors. Additionally, Rachel Alicia Griffin, Lacharles Ward, and Amanda Phillips have identified experiences of Black male faculty members, in which they, too, have managed racist structures, while navigating academic spaces. While DiAngelo offers "rules of engagement" when broaching racism, she also concedes that "the only way to give feedback without triggering white fragility is to not give it at all" (123). This revelation wasn't a new concept, for white supremacy has long taught me to keep my mouth shut when I feel compelled to describe the regular offenses perpetrated against me. It goes without saying then that I couldn't detail my grievances to someone entrusted with rating my performance. How could I tell him that my name is not Irwin after not correcting him in so many exchanges? How could I tell him that his glowing description of the joy that his son receives from participating in Civil War reenactments is offensive, that my ancestors' suffering is not the subject of pageantry? Even if I had questioned him, I'm sure he would have relayed that his son fought on the right side, that he's progressive and voted for Obama. But as DiAngelo suggests, "white progressives cause the most daily damage to people of color," which explains why I felt so powerless to describe my feelings at every step of the observation process (5).

At every meeting and in every email, I wanted to speak up for myself. Even more, I felt doubly burdened by shouldering the task of detailing his racism, especially after learning that he had requested to observe me again after having done so years before when I was an adjunct. bell hooks underscores that bad feelings about racism or white privilege work as a kind of self-centeredness, returning the white subject back to itself, back to the one whose feelings matter. On this point, Ahmed asserts that "happy whiteness" allows racism to continue to press on the backs of racialized others. In my observer's eyes, we maintained an amicable relationship, so how could I heed DiAngelo's advice and tell this well-intended white man to be "less white" (150)?

The Imagery of Racism

Fortunately, I let Rankine's *Citizen* do the talking. In the excerpted poem I selected for discussion, Rankine depicts the causal assertion of Black inferiority as she drives with a colleague who bemoans the hiring of a Black writer "when there are so many great writers out there"; Rankine's subsequent reflection of the exchange as she sits in her driveway alone, hoping the solitude would mitigate her pain; a scene at Starbucks wherein a white man standing ahead of her in line casually refers to a boisterous group of Black teenagers as "niggers"; the quiet strength in numbers that emerged in the aftermath of a Black boy being knocked over on a subway platform without regard for his well-being; a trip to see a therapist who mistakes Rankine for an intruder and screams "Get away from my house?" until Rankine reminds her that she made an appointment to see her.

My goal for the excerpt was to focus on imagery, and from Rankine's vignettes, I asked my students to identify the sensory language employed and describe the corresponding feelings that Rankine hoped to convey. Their answers were mostly accurate but guarded as many of them had never been asked to discuss racism openly. They felt themselves "slam on the brakes" in a fit of rage so that their faces could crash through the windshield of Rankine's car and "be exposed to the wind." They saw the black boy being unseen by a man who "has never seen him, has perhaps never seen anyone who is not a reflection of himself." They smelled the rosemary plants lining the pathway to the door of Rankine's therapist before hearing her scream like "a wounded Doberman pinscher or German shepherd" (from *Citizen*). Viscerally, they experienced the poem but denied my requests to expound.

In the end, my post-observation report was complimentary and effusive which was unsurprising as this is the case for all of my observations. I never doubt my ability although I often doubt my place. It was obvious that my students learned to interpret imagery in poetry, but what I don't know is whether my colleague was able to see himself in the poem and in turn, see me.

John Henryism and the Adjunct's Plight

In one of the excerpted selections, Rankine details a medical term called John Henryism, "for people exposed to stresses stemming from racism. They achieve themselves to death," she continues, "trying to dodge the build up of erasure." I first read this as hyperbole until I came across "The Death of an Adjunct" (Harris) and began to see myself reflected in the story of a promising professor who resigned from a tenure-track post due to the overwhelming stress of the racism she encountered on campus.

Thea Hunter earned her doctorate in history from Columbia University, and by many accounts, was a pioneer in her field of study. But at Western Connecticut State, she was subjected to many of the same microaggressions detailed by my co-authors. Her credentials were questioned by her students, she was mistaken for a janitor, and eventually the emotional toil became too much to bear. In search of a more welcoming environment, she left her post optimistic that she would find another full-time appointment. What she found was the unrelenting life of an adjunct. After a year of filling in for a professor on leave at Princeton, she worked at the New School, NYU, Montclair State University, Manhattan College, City College, and even at a private high school. She often taught five to seven sections to support herself which effectively left her no time to do what she was trained to do—research and write.

Before her untimely death, she shared the costs of the years devoted to doggedly pursuing another tenure-track position. In an email to a friend she wrote, "I have been saying I am done, emotionally drained and without reserves. There has just been too much going on in my life that has been drawing upon whatever emotional reserves I have. That plus the constant financial crisis that has been my life for years takes its toll" (Harris). The tragedy of her death could and should have been avoided. She died of respiratory failure after battling asthma, a condition that became more severe and undetected because she lacked the security of health insurance. Had she been employed full-time, she wouldn't have succumbed to the racist practices infecting the academy.

When I think of Hunter's story, I ask myself if the unjust treatment I accept is worth it. Was she not strong enough to weather the storms, or am I just an unprincipled fool? Even more, why must I be burdened by such a zero-sum proposition? I have earned my professorship after working as an adjunct for seven years at my institution. I've schlepped from campus to campus on the subways and busses of New York City—sometimes for two hours one-way—teaching composition courses at hosts of schools as an adjunct. My resume is just as scattershot as Hunter's, and I recognize that I'm no more deserving than she. The tragedy of her life then emerges as a cautionary tale that instructs me to embrace the occasional comforts of my full-time status, for if I don't, if I don't learn to manage the stress of being Black in an unwelcoming space, John Henry will surely chop me down.

Conclusion: But We Are Brave

In *Teaching to Transgress*, hooks reminds us that in order to create the kind of academy that we hope to see, we must embrace both the "struggle and sacrifice." In order to transform the spaces that so violently bludgeon us with words and oppressive policies and practices, we must be steadfast. hooks counsels, "we cannot be easily discouraged. We cannot despair when there is conflict." She reminds us that "our solidarity must be affirmed by shared belief in a spirit of intellectual openness that celebrates diversity, welcomes dissent, and rejoices in collective dedication to truth" (33). What hooks leaves us to solve is the problem of true solidarity through inclusion. Faculty of color are susceptible to burnout (Bellas), isolation, silencing, and tokenism as a consequence of the lack of representation, resulting in extensive emotional labor.

We offer these ways in which the emotional labor of faculty of color can be allayed. First, institutions must hire and promote more full-time faculty of color. Newkirk highlights the many benefits of hiring a diverse faculty. The norms of whiteness are reproduced and maintained when there is a lack of access, and for those who manage to break through, their presence in a sea of whiteness is a demoralizing reminder of the lack of access. Power lies in the ability to serve on personnel and budget committees, speak without fear, object with impunity, and lead without feeling marginalized (Levin, Walker, Haberler, and Jackson-Boothby.). Without the security of tenure and promotion, faculty members of color lack the agency to conduct any of the above, thus finding themselves in a cycle of emotional labor, with very little support or security. Weathersby relates his own and Thea Hunter's struggles to land a tenure-track job, and Alves' tenure and promotion gave her the space to honestly articulate the racist conditions in her department to her Chair, which became the catalyst to the formation of the department's Diversity and Inclusion Committee.

Second, as a testament to the collaborative effort placed into creating this piece, faculty of color must be present in order to provide affinity groups and engaging scholarly communities for other faculty of color. Environments that support active and collaborative techniques, in both teaching and scholarship, are beneficial to students and the college alike. Smith's report of senior white faculty requesting her time and expertise without recognition or compensation, while the senior faculty member of color provided opportunities to collaborate, is a strong testament to the importance of this support. Faculty members of color are often called upon for their cultural capital in the name of collegiality, which has very little bearing on whether they will secure tenure and, subsequently, promotion. Such practices reinforce oppressive structures that facilitate the exertion of emotional labor on the part of faculty of color, often resulting in a loss of valuable research and preparation time needed to secure tenure and promotion.

Third, faculty of color should have substantial leadership roles in which key decisions are made beyond their respective departments and outside of committees centered on diversity and race to avoid tokenism. Their Black and brown bodies are not the beginning and the end of diversity work. As an antiracist act, structures must be set in place to protect faculty of color when their white colleagues exercise their privilege. Yi highlights the importance and positive impact on his emotional health of this action in his account as a co-coordinator in the ALP program. Institutions must recognize the work of faculty of color outside of white centeredness as legitimate and also recognize the contributions of faculty of color to the scholarship of their colleagues.

Finally, junior faculty members of color must have consistent access to a senior faculty mentor with whom the mentee can build racial trust. The proper guidance and support from a senior faculty mentor would help lead the mentee in making strategic professional and scholarly moves for promotion to associate and then full professor. In this way, institutions will have more faculty of color in higher positions, thus allowing access to advocacy roles. In such advocacy roles, faculty of color gain opportunities to unmake the status quo and reduce the amount of emotional labor tied to their presence as diverse members of the faculty.

These suggestions by no means serve as a wrecking ball to the fortress of white supremacy embedded within academic institutions. Perhaps they may open the door a few inches. If our colleagues are to truly engage diversity, then they must also consider inclusion as its byproduct. The push to hire and subsequently boast about diverse faculty members should work in tandem with an effort to ensure that the spaces in which these diverse faculty members operate are not hostile or harmful to their emotional health or scholarly pursuits. To do this, there must be a shared commitment by all stakeholders to enacting change and allowing faculty of color to present their authentic selves in the workplace, without fear of retribution. In order to transform the academy, the academy must perform brave acts by investing in a commitment to undo oppressive structures that result in emotional labor for faculty of color. A shared belief cannot transform the academy until the academy dedicates itself to decimating the racist practices at its core—those that deny faculty members of color their right to be included in the policies and procedures, the conversations, the spaces, the scholarship, and the new and more colorful fabric of the academic quilt. What we as faculty members of color can no longer continue to do, however, is to wear a mask while proverbially "setting ourselves on fire" just to keep the academy warm.

Works Cited

Ahmed, Sara. *The Cultural Politics of Emotion*. Edinburgh University Press, 2014.

--. *On Being Included*. Duke UP, 2012.

Beck, Julie. "The Concept Creep of 'Emotional Labor'." *The Atlantic*, Atlantic Media Company, 26 Nov. 2018, https://www.theatlantic.com/family/archive/2018/11/arlie-hochschild-housework-isnt-emotional-labor/576637/

Begley, Sarah. "Claudia Rankine: Society Is 'In a State of Emergency." *Time*, 7 Sep. 2016, http://time.com/4503473/claudia-rankine-macarthur-fellow/.

Bell, Derrick. *Faces at The Bottom of the Well*. Basic Books, 1992.

Bell, Lee Ann, Michael S. Funk, Khyatu Joshi, and Marjorie Valdivia. "Racism and White Privilege." *Teaching for Diversity and Social Justice*, edited by Marianne Adams and Lee Ann Bell, Routledge, 2016, pp. 133–181.

Bellas, Marcia L. "Emotional Labor in Academia: The Case of Professors." *The ANNALS of the American Academy of Political and Social Science*, vol. 561, no. 1, Jan. 1999, pp. 96–110, doi:10.1177/000271629956100107.

Brown, Austin Channing. *I'm Still Here: Black Dignity in a World Made for Whiteness*. Convergent, 2018.

Carroll, Lewis. "Jabberwocky." *The Random House Book of Poetry for Children*, edited by Jack Prelutsky, Random House, 1983, p.170.

Carter, Tara Yvonne. *A Change Is Gonna Come: Critical Race Theory and African American Community College Faculty Narratives*. 2011. Walden University, PhD Dissertation.

Diangelo, Robin. *White Fragility: Why It's So Hard for White People to Talk About Racism*. Beacon, 2018.

Dubois, W.E.B. *The Souls of Black Folk*. Penguin Classics, 1996.

Ellison, Ralph. *Invisible Man*. Vintage, 1995.

Griffin, Rachel Alicia, Lacharles Ward and Amanda Phillips. "Still Flies in Buttermilk: Black Male Faculty, Critical Race Theory, and Composite Counterstorytelling. *International Journal of Qualitative Studies in Education*, vol.27, no. 10, 2014, pp.1354-1375.

Harris, Adam. "The Death of An Adjunct." *The Atlantic*, Atlantic Media Company, 8 Apr. 2019, https://www.theatlantic.com/education/archive/2019/04/adjunct-professors-higher-education-thea-hunter/586168/

Hochschild, Arlie Russell. *The Managed Heart: Commercialization of Human Feelings (Twentieth Anniversary Edition)*. University of California Press, 2003.

hooks, bell. *Teaching to Transgress: Education as the Practice of Freedom*. Routledge,1994.

Hyun, Jane. *Breaking the Bamboo Ceiling*. Harper Business, 2006.

Joseph, Tiffany D. and Laura Hirschfield. "'Why Don't You Get Somebody New To Do It?' Race and Cultural Taxation in the Academy." *Ethnic and Racial Studies,* vol. 34, no. 1, 2011, pp. 121-141.

Laden, Berta Vigil and Linda Serra Hagedorn. "Job Satisfaction Among Faculty of Color in Academe: Individual Survivors or Institutional Transformers?" *New Directions for Institutional Research,* vol. 105, 2000, pp. 57-66.

Ladson-Billings, Gloria. "The Evolving Role of Critical Race Theory in Educational Scholarship." *Race, Ethnicity, and Education,* vol. 8, no. 1, 2005, pp. 115-119.

Levin, John. S., Laurencia Walker, Zachary Haberler, and Adam Jackson-Boothby. "The Divided Self: The Double Consciousness of Faculty of Color in Community Colleges." *Community College Review,* vol. 41, no. 4, 2013, pp. 311-329.

Matthew, Patricia. *Written/Unwritten: Diversity and the Hidden Truths of Tenure.* University of North Carolina Press, 2016.

Mertes, Scott. "Community College Retention: A Critical Race Theory Perspective. *Journal of Applied Research in the Community College,* vol. 21, no. 1, 2013, pp. 25-30.

Newkirk, Pamela. *Diversity, Inc.: The Failed Promise of a Billion-Dollar Business.* Bold Type Books, 2019.

Ogbu, John. "Understanding Cultural Diversity and Learning." *Educational Researcher,* vol. 21, no.8, 1992, pp. 5-18.

Padilla, Amado. "Ethnic Minority Scholars, Research, and Mentoring: Current and Future Issues." *Educational Researcher,* vol. 23, no.4, 1994, pp. 24-27.

Perry, Andre M. "Black Workers are Being Left Behind by Full Employment." *Brookings,* The Brookings Institution, 26 Jun. 2019. https://www.brookings.edu/blog/the-avenue/2019/06/26/black-workers-are-being-left-behind-by-full-employment/.

Rankine, Claudia. "from *Citizen*: 'You are in the dark, in the car…'" *Poetry,* March 2014. *Poetry Foundation,* https://www.poetryfoundation.org/poetrymagazine/poems/56848/citizen-you-are-in-the-dark-in-the-car.

Smith, William A., Jalil Bishop Mustaffa, Chantal M. Jones, Tommy J. Curry, and Walter R. Allen. "'You Make Me Wanna Holler and Throw Up Both My Hands!': Campus Culture, Black Misandric Microaggressions, and Racial Battle Fatigue." *International Journal of Qualitative Studies in Education,* vol. 29, no.9, 2016, pp. 1189-1209.

Titchokosky, Tanya. *The Question of Access: Disability, Space, Meaning.* University of Toronto, 2011.

U.S. Department of Education, National Center for Education Statistics. *The Condition of Education 2019* (NCES 2019-144), Characteristics of Postsecondary Faculty.

Walcott, Rinaldo. "The End of Diversity." *Public Culture,* vol. 31, no. 2, 2019, pp. 393-408.

Yosso, Tara J. "Whose Culture Has Capital? A Critical Race Theory Discussion of Community Cultural Wealth." *Race Ethnicity and Education,* vol. 8, no. 1, 2005, pp. 69-91.

Rhetoric and Emotion Save Science: Lessons from Student Eco-Activists

Jesse Priest

Abstract: *This essay is a qualitative study of the experience of undergraduate students learning how to teach issues of sustainability to their campus communities through an innovative outreach program at a large northeastern research university, while at the same time learning to navigate complex emotional labor required by their outreach and activist work. While most previous work on science writing and rhetoric focuses on disciplinary, publishing, or genre practices, I examine the holistic student experience by placing outreach, writing, and the classroom in conversation with each other, illuminating how discourses can cross institutional and contextual borders. Additionally, while most previous work involving student engagement has focused on its positive and rewarding aspects, I examine how tension and critical moments can also be productive learning experiences for students, suggesting ways in which teachers might recognize the often-invisible aspects of students' emotional labor that impact their learning experiences. I consider ways in which moments of tension represent productive opportunities for education, wholly separate from traditional notions of success in learning. I propose a re-orientation towards how we view engagement and success in educational contexts to allow for and even welcome moments of frustration as valid and productive representations of emotional labor.*

Introduction

This essay is concerned with how student activists in Sustainability Studies at a large northeastern research university participate in roles that may function to re-orient how we talk about emotional labor in educational settings. Specifically, I examine how student activism and outreach in science represents a re-orientation in the circulation of scientific knowledge to include the explicit recognition of emotional labor as a component of scientific knowledge production. I am curious how these movements may suggest a popularization that gives us a better understanding of how those removed from traditional knowledge-making roles in the academy can both access and influence the creation of scientific knowledge. Here, students are outside the role of expert in traditional discussions of both scientific expertise and public intellectualism; however, their relationship with publics outside of their classrooms in their outreach work allows them to function as experts.

Because of its explicit focus on communicating to and informing the public, the field of Sustainability Studies is situated in a way that makes it a hybrid of the academic and non-academic. Examining the way academic and public sites are related in this field might help us address ongoing questions of public intellectualism that revolve around its appearance, necessity, and practicality in the 21st century (see Warner; Farmer). That is, if we are to consider the relationship between the Academy and outside publics in a way that might best reflect (and foster) outreach and sharing of knowledge, we might discard the traditional notion that one specific kind of solitary intellectual must reach a specific kind of mass audience in order to be considered doing the work of public intellectualism, and also consider the ways in which localized, community efforts also fall within the realm of public intellectualism. In that sense, Sustainability Studies often positions relatively new initiates to the discipline as content knowledge experts when communicating to publics outside of the field, and these communicative contexts are often localized, personal, and community-oriented.

My understanding of the typical notion of public intellectualism borrows from Michael Warner, who writes that the public as a cultural form is "a matter of uptake, citation and recharacterization. It takes place not in closely argued essays but in an informal, intertextual, and multigeneric field" (145). As uptake is a crucial component of engaging with public audiences (i.e., engagement assessed in terms of what the audiences do with expert knowledge), then one of the key aspects of public intellectualism is learning; the public intellectual is a kind of teacher who seeks to educate people outside of the speaker's discipline. Unlike the necessity of mass audience appeal, this notion of the public intellectual is one that I do not believe needs to be discarded in order to redefine the idea, as it accounts for local, communal, and even individual levels of uptake.

Because persuading outside audiences to care about the disciplinary content knowledge of the field is such a clear stake of disciplinary success in Sustainability, teaching and research are not as formally separated as is traditionally the case for many academic disciplines. To clarify: public understanding of such issues as climate change and renewable habits, is, quite literally, a matter of survival of our planet. Those engaged in any aspect of Sustainability Studies are pursuing what may be one of the most vital educational projects of our time. Student-driven outreach in sustainability is horizontal, not vertical; instead of the already-established and successful disciplinary expert attempting to pass on knowledge to the uneducated in a top-down fashion, the kind of outreach often done in sustainability involves students just as likely as it might involve advanced experts. Outreach in this context creates a removal of the traditional hierarchical relationship necessitated by the idea of the public intellectual; novice initiates to the discipline, as part of their process of becoming disciplinary experts, teach the issues of sustainability to other audiences just as easily considered novices. At the same time, it is important to recognize the ways in which disciplinary expertise is not the only kind of expertise relevant to our contexts within Higher Education: students are, of course, the experts of their emotional labor, and we should recognize this expertise as equally valid to disciplinary expertise, as it is, of course, equally present.

This project is relevant to those within Higher Education teaching and administration who are concerned with inter-disciplinary pedagogy and student engagement. I posit suggestions for how writing pedagogy might help scientists and activists better formalize their outreach practices, and general suggestions for teachers and administrators who are curious about fostering increased disciplinary engagement with their students through increased recognition of the complex and rich emotional work that our students put into their learning experiences.

Literature: Science, Rhetoric, and Emotion

Science communication with the public relies on both scientific experts understanding their audience and their intended audiences understanding the experts' messages, which is what Philippa Spoel and Chantal Barriault define as the "rhetorical challenge" of public engagement (87). Diana Wegner expresses the frustration often present in "studies of public participation in environmental decision-making...[which] yield scenarios of unproductive processes of public participation, usually generating frustration among citizens (114). "Frustration" among citizens is, I will discuss later, one of the recurring themes even in the microcosm of my study, and represents one of the common problems in scientific communication at both the micro and macro levels. As any teacher of technical communication well knows, the sharing of expert knowledge to non-experts always represents a multifaceted (if often exciting) challenge. As Michael Zerbe claims, however, it is to scientific discourse that "our society assigns the responsibility of performing the day-to-day work of making sense of ourselves and our surroundings, both epistemologically and ontologically. This authority should be reason enough to make scientific discourse a central component of rhetorical study for all students." (43)

Zerbe notes that one issue with science rhetoric is its relative inaccessibility to those in the humanities due to vast differences in disciplinary knowledge. This resonates with a perennial problem in scientific communication, namely, non-experts feeling either patronized or ill-informed (or both), and the combination of public frustration with a culturally dominant discourse creates a complex and always-changing rhetorical situation. Zerbe's notion of science as a culturally *dominant* discourse is a productive inquiry in part because it allows for an ideological awareness of power in society. The ideological dominance of scientific discourse elucidates how discourses and publics function together and can be examined from an inter-disciplinary perspective to consider questions of the Humanities' so-called crisis of cultural relevancy. Conceptualizing science as the epistemological and ideological giant of our society, however, misses scientific practice done in the name of outreach and activism that typically do align more clearly with our own disciplinary notions of rhetoric, including agent-driven communicative acts, community-oriented kairotic moments, and emotionally-driven persuasion. Furthermore, the emphasis on local, communal, grassroots efforts in Sustainability Studies and related fields reveals a different possibility of scientific discourse as one that does not necessarily function in ways that are ideologically marginalizing or exclusionary. In scientific discourse, this often takes the form of "gendered vocabulary" (Keller 33) or publishing practices that gesture towards interdisciplinarity while still failing to include ethical and other considerations from the Humanities (see Truana 1964).

One crucial aspect of student engagement is emotional work, as outreach by nature is frustrating, uneven, and even troublesome at times for those who attempt to engage audiences in issues in which the audiences perceive they have no stake. As such, my discussion is directly following a growing recognition within composition and rhetoric to take emotion more seriously as a category of analysis, to borrow Laura R. Micciche's phrase. Micciche writes that "to figure emotion as a critical term that can illuminate perspectives on the content of intellectual work in new, refreshed ways...is to take seriously the work that emotions do in the context of disciplinary formation" (7). With regards to disciplinary formation, emotional work represents a combination of an individual's motivation to participate in the discursive practices of their field and the resulting knowledge production and sharing that comes from their participation. In adopting emotion as one of my methodological investigations (which, as I outlined, happened recursively as I explored my data), I am extending Micciche's claim that rhetoric benefits when expanded to the realm of the emotive. Disciplinary participation can itself be represented by the emotional responses of those engaged within the discipline, and a way of negotiating the means of communicating within the discourse community. As such, the goings-on of disciplinary participation necessitates engagement, and engagement necessitates emotion.

Compositionists who believe in the possible benefits of attempting to fold emotion into the realm of the rhetorical need to be careful not to, as Micciche suggests, "collapse" (3) it into a generalized abstraction. In order to do this, we may borrow from suggestions within affect theory regarding the relationships between emotion and work, while at the same time establishing modes of inquiry that rely on our already-established and perhaps *safer* methodologies. Here, as I will outline later, I have mostly done this by sticking to places where my case study participants have self-identified emotional responses. In doing so, I hope to help in a small way the larger project of developing research methodologies within composition that can be inclusive of emotional affect. In this area, compositionists can borrow from classical and modern rhetoric, which have long since recognized the primacy of emotion within the rhetorical situation. Regarding the relationship between emotion and persuasion, Aristotle writes that "the emotions [*pathe*] are those things through which, by undergoing *change*, people come to differ in their judgments and which are accompanied by pain and pleasure, for example, anger, pity, fear, and other such things *and their opposites*" (121, emphasis added). In *Rhetoric*, Aristotle realized that emotion was itself embedded into rhetorical situations through the interplay of ideas, thoughts and feelings between speaker and audience. In this project, my findings about the emotional responses and affective experiences I observed in my students draws on the way Aristotle conceives of the emotional realm of persuasion being developed through change and through the individual speaker's negotiation of disparate and conflicting feelings.

While rhetoricians have long since recognized the importance of emotion within the rhetorical situation, compositionists have been slower to recognize the possibility of emotion as a pedagogical and disciplinary bridge between the Humanities and the Sciences. Within composition, perhaps the closest we have come to formally crossing the disciplinary divide between us and the sciences is through the work of ecocomposition. While WAC draws together interdisciplinary concerns around writing (and often creates programs that are concerned with pedagogies within both the Sciences and the Humanities), ecocomposition seeks to establish an explicit connection between composition studies and ecology, as Sidney Dobrin and Christian Weisser write that "composition's roots do indeed tap into ecological sciences in their current incarnations…composition studies is very much an ecological inquiry" (*Natural Discourse* 259). Ecocomposition functions both as a theoretical frame and a possible methodological approach to the relationship between agents and systems. The ecological perspective argues for a conceptual framework where difference *is* the norm, as networks and ecologies are only made up of relational differences. Ecocomposition remains the closest endeavor in Composition to move towards explicitly discussing environmental and scientific issues, and shares some of the concerns of the WAC movement with regard to the need for interdisciplinary examinations of writing and its contexts. Dobrin and Weisser suggest that ecocomposition must "become a site for... public intellectualism," and they argue that "ecocomposition sees the university as the public, all part of the same system, all the same place" (*Breaking Ground* 95). Furthermore, Dobrin and Weisser also claim that "compositionists already talk about the consumption and production of discourse in much the same way ecologists discuss the consumption and production of energy" (*Natural Discourse* 18). As a subfield, ecocomposition draws explicitly from earlier movements within the field to recognize the importance of considering physical location as part of our definition of context, as ecology is by necessity dependent on location. Ecocomposition provides for both a theoretical lens (writing-as-ecology) and a methodological framework for positioning disciplines of composition and disciplines of science in direct conversation with each other.

The combination of disciplinarities that results from considering rhetoric and emotion as two emergent necessities of communication also draws attention to another cognitive domain: the ethical. Alan G. Gross and Arthur Walzer write that, in the *Challenger* disaster, the failings of scientific deliberation revolved around "an ethical dilemma, a problem that required that a cognitive dilemma be viewed from an ethical perspective. This ethical dilemma was not even perceived" (86). Earlier, I outlined the importance--more simply, the urgency--of sustainability. The insufficient public appreciation of the importance of climate change may be seen as a failure of scientific discourse to adequately create ethically-informed systemic change. The failure to include the ethical domain is something that feminist scholars such as Nancy Tuana have criticized (1963) with specific regard for how science can benefit from becoming increasingly interdisciplinary. As such, if disciplinary success in the sciences relies on some form of what we might call uptake in the form of public change, it is evident that scientific inquiry alone is not enough to create mass persuasion. What seems to be missing in scientific inquiry, *especially* as it relates to interactions with its publics, is the ethical and emotional as a domain of critical thought equal to the rational.

The Study

In order to address these concerns, I spent a semester conducting a case study of the writing, pedagogy, and outreach practices of the "Ecology Representatives" (henceforth "Eco-Reps") program at what I am pseudonymously referring to as Northeastern Research University. The Eco-Rep program is an innovative opportunity that combines coursework with outreach in an attempt to train undergraduate students to become skilled at raising community awareness of sustainability issues. According to institutional description, the Eco-Rep program is an opportunity for students to become engaged in

> environmental literacy and leadership both within the program, and on the campus at large… Eco-Reps build a foundational knowledge surrounding issues of sustainability and explore how best to raise awareness about these

issues amongst their peers. Focusing on the role and impact of the individual, Eco-Reps work to promote environmentally responsible behavior in the campus community.

The Northeastern Research University Eco-Rep Program represents a localized site for the now-national Eco-Rep movement that began at Tufts in 2001. In 2015, the Association for the Advancement of Sustainability in Higher Education (AASHE) created specific criteria for universities seeking to establish their own Eco-Rep program, which individual universities can adapt to their own communities' needs. The AASHE, however, dictates that each nationally-recognized Eco-Rep program must include components of "training peer educators, educating residential students, educating populace who practice environmentally-sustainable behaviors," with the goal of a "stabilized, decreased ecological footprint of campus operations; tangible cost savings; and greater understanding of facilities and infrastructure issues of the campus" (Erickson). At Northeastern Research University, the Eco-Rep program consists of a 2-credit College of Natural Sciences course which includes student participation in projects and outreach across campus. There are six sections of the course every semester, with each section being offered across campus in a different residential area. Each section typically has 6 to 8 students in it. The course is a dialogue-based seminar that is taught by undergraduate course facilitators who are themselves former Eco-Reps. Each section is overseen by a program manager, who is also an undergraduate and former Eco-Rep and course facilitator. Together with a faculty advisor, the program manager and course facilitators collaborate to develop pedagogy through training and regular meetings. The goal of the Eco-Rep program is for students to build a foundational awareness of issues of sustainability and use that knowledge to foster sustainability awareness within their communities on campus.

The Eco-Rep program classroom overlaps with students' involvement in their residence halls and campus community with the course facilitators spending class time collaboratively developing outreach activities. Students use their Eco-Rep work in the class to craft activities and material explicitly addressed to the larger campus community. The classroom emphasis is on the individual's involvement in sustainability and critical consideration of the best way students can impact their own communities. Working collaboratively, students are tasked with developing, over the course of the semester, a variety of materials to achieve this. Students create outreach materials like videos and posters, and host awareness-raising social or outreach events. The goals of these activities are twofold: educating their peers on sustainability issues and suggesting individual behavioral changes to address these issues. Students work closely with Residence Life staff and other on-campus departments and offices in developing, promoting, and publishing these events and materials. These outreach projects often directly reflect the thematic content of the class; examples include innovative recycling programs, student-led educational activities across campus, increased access to green resources in academic offices, and visible campus events designed to spread awareness of the dangers of pollution and waste mismanagement.

In this paper I examine what the student Eco-Reps are doing with the knowledge and identity of the Eco-Rep program; identities that are strongly identified by an orientation towards the importance of sustainability and sustainable outreach. As members of the Eco-Rep program, each of my five case study participants engage in numerous moments of explicit and implicit self-reflection that suggest how the role influences their own evolution and growth as students, scientists, and activists. Furthermore, participating as active members of the Eco-Rep program also creates moments of tension with other discursive identities; moments that are, understandably, handled differently by each of my case study participants.

The study involved eight course visits; four interviews with current student Eco-Reps; and three Eco-Rep outreach activities on campus which I attended. I collected writing and outreach material produced in the class and Eco-Rep work, totaling approximately 30 pages of written and visual material from the students. I also collected written pedagogical material from the course facilitators, including lesson plans and activities and their own reflective writing written for their lesson planning meetings, totaling approximately 20 pages of written material. When analyzing my research data, I coded for important themes and ideas that seem suggestive of how the Eco-Reps themselves view their work. Following Anne Haas Dyson and Celia Genishi (85), I allowed my coding process to lead me from larger ideas to more specific ones as I re-read the interview transcripts. As I will discuss later, this recursive coding process led me to realize that my initial consideration did not account for the importance of emotional labor within the students' activist work.

This study directly extends some ongoing conversations within the field of composition and rhetoric. Specifically, examining my students' outreach work in conversation with their academic writing answers calls made by scholars concerned with student engagement (see Tinberg); I also seek to provide an addition to the important conversation regarding the relationship between engagement, literacies, and transfer (see Bacon; Depalma). Both of these disciplinary threads are concerned with what students take from the classroom setting or, rather, what students *do* with the knowledge they gain from the classroom.

During my time observing the Eco-Rep Program, I began to realize just how seriously the students take their own emotional experiences, often attaching their emotions, at least in part, to the kind of audience response their activist work was receiving. It became impossible for me to ignore the vast degree to which my students, in their outreach work, were grappling with complex and immediate emotional experiences that greatly influenced both the work they produced and their experience learning the content knowledge of sustainability. Through recursive coding and analysis (explained below), the emotional work in all of my student participants' experiences became impossible to ignore. My first rounds of coding did not count for emotion, and I believe this is partly to blame for my initial constricted coding schema; the students' performance of discourse and knowledge of sustainability through their outreach is very emotion-laden. So the added investigation based on emotion led me to consider: what is the role of emotion in students' engagement with sustainability? This became the guiding research question for the study.

Case Study Participants

During my course visits, I offered my informed consent documents and explained the nature of my study to the students. I allowed for students to approach me if they were interested in participating. I ended up with five student Eco-Rep case study participants. Their spread of majors as well as their mix of class standing make them an adequate, if not exhaustive, representation of the program.

Zhi

Zhi was the first student to approach me with an interest in being a case study participant. At the time of my study, Zhi was a freshman with an undeclared major, although she plans on studying "Business Marketing with a minor in Environmental Science." She tells me that she finds this combination attractive because, in her view, many businesses that claim to pursue sustainable practices "are not very aware of what Environmental Science is about and focus more on the business aspect. I think that's sometimes disappointing." As a second-semester freshman, she also took the Eco-Rep seminar her first semester, meaning that her outreach work became a year-long project.

Jaime

Like Zhi, Jaime was in her second semester as a freshman as well as her second semester in the Eco-Rep program at the time of our interview. When finalizing her class schedule at the beginning of her first semester as a Business major, she as well as her roommate decided to take the Eco-Rep class due in part to their Resident Assistant (RA) being a Sustainability Fellow. Like Zhi (and like all of my student participants, in their own way) she discusses some aspects of *difference* between her experience in the class and her experience in other contexts. However, for Jaime these moments do not seem to be ones steeped in disappointment or tension. For her outreach work, Jaime was able to work alongside her RA, meaning she had more of a ready support system in place for her outreach experience than Zhi did.

Ann

A second semester transfer student studying Psychology, Ann discovered the Eco-Rep program because she was visiting a friend's dorm on campus and she began talking to someone already involved with the program. She's interested in eventually becoming a course facilitator, and cited this possibility as part of her reason for initially wanting to be involved with the program. She also mentioned her course facilitator as being an inspiration for the kind of teacher she would like to be because she found the dialogue-based nature of the seminar to be very effective. Ann is also currently enrolled in a Sustainable Living class, and much of her discussion with me is focused on discussing how these opportunities allow her to see connections to sustainability that other students don't have. Broadly, Ann is very concerned with appealing to the widest possible audience with her outreach and spent a lot of time enlisting the help of residents in her chosen residence hall to try to maximize the effectiveness of her recycling advocacy project.

Pat

Pat is a nontraditional student majoring in Social Justice, who decided to add a concentration in Environmental Science because they felt that there was not enough attention to issues of sustainability in the Social Justice program. Pat's outreach work, as well as their writing, focus largely on two topics; the specific interdisciplinary connections between sustainability and computer science, and the role of personal responsibility in trying to improve the world.

Laura

Laura, an Ecology Major, was a late-comer to participating in my study; I first talked with her at the Eco-Rep end of semester potluck gathering, where she presented her outreach project. Laura went against the rules of the Program in choosing her sorority house, technically not part of campus, as the site of her outreach work. She pushed back against both the program's Faculty Advisor's request and the governing body of the sorority to create a recycling program in her sorority house.

My revised coding schema led me to look for a set of common referents based on what I found in recursively reading and annotating my interview and writing samples. These codes were as follows: "positive emotion," "negative emotion," "work/labor," "sustainability/science," "success," and "failure." This set of codes allowed me to examine cross-referents in each student's writing and interviews, as well as finding where and to what degree they expressed positivity or negativity with regard to their experiences. The following table represents a breakdown of how these codes appeared in each student's data.

Analysis: Investigating Emotional Labor in Activism

In my investigation of emotional labor in student activist work, I draw on Patricia Ticineto Clough's definition of the affective turn in composition and rhetoric as being driven by "information/communication systems including the human body…including the circulation of value through human labor… and in biopolitical networks of disciplining, surveillance, and control" (3). The outreach work my students participated in represents affective work in that it is embodied by each individual student engaging in their own labor; further, this work happens in the specific context of the Eco-Rep program. Following Sara Ahmed, my examination of emotion necessitates considering how emotion and affect influence and are influenced by students' relationships with their communities. As such, I am less concerned with defining emotional responses and more with looking at the "work" of the emotions (Ahmed). In other words, as I recursively engaged with my data, I came to realize that it would have been impossible (or at least reductive) to talk about the richness of the outreach work my students were doing without talking about the emotional context for this work.

Table 1: Coding Breakdown and Frequency

Case Study Participant	Frequency of Emotional Expression (percentages indicate comparison of positive and negative referents)	Frequency of success/failure referents (percentages indicate comparison of success and failure referents)	Most commonly used referents	Most frequent cross-references
Zhi	Positive: 55% Negative: 45%	Success: 30% Failure: 70%	Work/labor ("living wages," "doing more work than in a lecture"), Failure ("What did I get for my work?")	Positive emotion + negative emotion ("overpower the negativity," "people may not care but it's still worth it")
Jaime	Positive: 63% Negative: 37%	Success: 57% Failure: 43%	Sustainability/Science, Work/labor: ("we're talking about inequality," "environmentalism is in everything")	Positive emotion + Work/labor ("I'm going to force people to notice the poster,"We drove around encouraging people to recycle and it was a big success")
Ann	Positive: 55% Negative: 45%	Success: 52% Failure: 48%	Negative emotion, ("I use things that are harmful,") Sustainability ("I've learned to care about the environment and it makes things a lot harder")	Negative emotion + Work/labor ("The happy posters didn't work so I'm gonna make the next ones sarcastic")

Pat	Positive: 33% Negative: 67%	Success: 54% Failure: 46%	Sustainability, ("I was better at sustainability before I came to college," Work/labor ("It takes real effort to bring sustainability to computer science")	Sustainability + Negative emotion ("I tried to teach them about e-waste but they didn't seem engaged," "People tend to be cynical about others but not themselves")
Laura	Positive: 64% Negative: 36%	Success: 59% Failure: 41%	Positive emotion ("I felt good after doing the trivia night,") Success ("People were surprised at told me they learned something")	Sustainability/Science + Positive emotion ("The event was a fantastic idea because we felt good getting people to donate")

In order to identify emotions in my students' writing and interviews, I coded for places where emotion was either specifically mentioned (e.g., Ann writing that the work of sustainability can be "saddening") or implicitly expressed (e.g., Laura writing that the low attendance to one of her projects was "tough for me to see"). As such, I try to identify emotional responses in each students' experience that seem to be clearly present and intentionally expressed. As I suggested earlier, these emotions seem to be connected to the ways in which my students both define sustainability and perform sustainability outreach. The relationship is not a causal one; to infer that these students are simply feeling positive or negative emotions based on how their work is going would be to reduce the complexity of the dialogic connection between emotion and knowledge, and how emotional labor influences the material realities of students' work. As Aristotle explains, inhabiting emotions during a persuasive action often requires a speaker to feel opposites (121), and the nature of rhetoric itself requires a speaker to combine "analytical knowledge and knowledge of characters...of mental faculties [and] sciences" (53). The emotions I refer to here from my data analysis are, again, ones that have been directly and specifically expressed by my case study participants and, as such, represent only one aspect of their discursive performance of outreach.

For Zhi, her feelings of frustration are directly connected to why she also feels hope. Feeling "frustration" when she entered her chosen Residence Hall to find the recycling bins mis-labeled and inaccessible allowed her to find positive motivation to work against a perceived injustice. "I thought I would get in trouble," she says in our interview, "because I was crawling up these recycling bins trying to move them and change the labels" (Interview 2/20). In her reflection on her outreach experience, appropriately titled "Recycling: A Myth in Sycamore Hall," Zhi again emphasizes both frustration and the importance of personal responsibility in her conception of what it means to work in sustainability. Zhi writes: "consciousness, leadership, awareness – these are all qualities and characteristics thought to be associated with Honors students. However, in the case of recycling, that does not ring true whatsoever, especially not in Sycamore Hall." This is reflected in the higher representation of "failure" referents in her data while at the same time still having a higher overall frequency of "positive" emotional referents. For Zhi, the tension between her expectation (perhaps magnified by her subject position as an especially eager and motivated first-year Honors College student) of what it means to be in the Honors College and the material reality she encountered during her first Eco-Rep reconnaissance venture is especially difficult for her. Consciously drawing on the University's own philosophy of the Honors College experience, Zhi here uses her awareness of that mission statement to emphasize her frustration with the messy and disorganized (and therefore ineffective) state of recycling in her chosen outreach area. Reflecting on how her role as an Eco-Rep has changed her idea of what it means to be a student, Zhi says: "I feel more responsible" and "I feel like my decisions are more important now" (Zhi Interview 2/20). Furthermore, the language of these statements possibly reflects the personal and intellectual development in progress of a first-year college student, which may account for some of her challenges and frustration throughout her outreach work.

In Jaime's case, her knowledge of sustainability as an interdisciplinary, performative action helps her to feel both pride and community inclusion as someone working towards positive change. Because Jaime sees more positive connections between her work as an Eco-Rep and her experience in other classes, she doesn't express tension between these two different sets of experiences. Instead, her experiences create for her a holistic and interconnected educational setting where the various roles that she participates in on campus and at home are constantly in dialogue with one another. To illustrate this dialogue, Jaime tells me an anecdote about going home to visit her family for a weekend shortly before our interview:

> When I was home this past weekend I told them I would not use a Styrofoam plate because of what I'd learned in this class and the NRC (Sustainable Living in the 21st Century) class, and I just learned a ton of information about how Styrofoam is terrible, it never fully decomposes, and all that. So I literally put my food on the tablecloth and ate from there, and everyone thought I was ridiculous but I was making a point. (Jaime Interview 3/4)

In this reflection, Jaime shows confidence in her ability to "make a point," even while she laughs at the absurdity of eating directly off the table. Jaime identifies as not being "environmentally-aware" before college, and notes that she has also started "forcing" her family to recycle and compost (something that she slyly attributes in part to her being the oldest of three children and having some degree of clout in the household). She says that her family, then, has also been "changed" by her experiences in the Eco-Rep program, believing that while they wouldn't have started practicing green habits at home without her influence, they now would continue to do so even if she wasn't there to monitor it. While Jaime expresses mostly positive emotions in response to sustainability, this does not result in her becoming complicit or lazy; rather, these reflections show a motivated activist who is experiencing positive reinforcement and wants to keep getting better at what she is doing.

In Ann's case, her emotional responses exist in a near-constant state of tension between feeling confidence in her work and guilt for her own participation in hurting the environment. Ann's understanding of sustainability is defined by what it reacts *against*, as she writes about her "fear for the day that nonrenewable resources are used up" and speaks for the human community by saying that "we are not giving back to the Earth." As with Zhi, however, these feelings of fear allow her to feel some degree of motivation, urging that "everybody must be educated in the destruction that we are creating and spread the *feeling of importance* everyone has on this Earth for making a change" (my emphasis). Ann also writes that attending the group events during Earth Day was "great" and "exciting... to see so many people interested and participating in the events that the university had to offer; it brought a sense of community" (Earth Day Reflection). Like Jaime, Ann's emotions help her to feel that sustainability itself creates a community which, among other things, helps its members feel like important actors toward positive change.

For Laura, the tension between emotions exists between her optimism regarding the work of sustainability and her disappointment at being met with low attendance at her outreach events. She writes that it was "difficult," a "tough turn-out for me to see" and, when some of her audience members were loud and disruptive, it was "hard to hear." She was, however, optimistic that while her projects did not reach a wide audience of students, she was able to talk to a large number of Resident Assistants at outreach events and Earth Day; as I suggested earlier, this led to her changing her concept of audience in performing outreach. She also eventually expressed positivity ("that was a good way of looking at it") and suggested ways to revise future work to reach a wider audience. Similarly, Laura found a "pleasant surprise" ("Earth Day Reflection") at the Earth Day events that allowed her to feel like part of a larger community.

Pat's emotional responses are perhaps the most consistently negative; much of their reflection in both the interview and their writing involves a degree of cynicism and pessimism, both about themselves and the campus community. Pat writes that they were "blown off" by the Resident Director of their chosen hall, and that the Earth Day events did not, for them, "foster a sense of community in the Eco-Rep program" ("Institutional Change Unit Reflection") because of low turnout at the events they attended. Connecting to their understanding of sustainability as ever-present, however, Pat is able to develop a sort of angry imperative regarding what it means to work in sustainability. Pat claims that the Eco-Rep class allows for a chance to learn "from other people," which they argue is important because "people here are following personal beliefs... generally people I know in other majors aren't all that cynical about themselves, they think of themselves as outside of these problems" (Interview 3/7). For Pat, cynicism is not an excuse for apathy, but rather a reason to continue learning and working.

Below is a summary of my findings of the "dominant emotions," which I define as those most commonly expressed, in each student's data set in their discourses around sustainability outreach.

Table 2.

	Dominant emotions	How emotions are used	Role of negative emotions	Role of positive emotions
Zhi	Disappointment, humility, guilt, anger, hope	To express imperatives: to reflect on what should be done	Disappointment leads to personal responsibility	Expressing connections between people
Jaime	Pride, inclusion	To teach others	Frustration at not being seen/public leads to desire to be more public	Welcoming others into the discourse community
Ann	Uncertainty, frustration, guilt, confidence, optimism	To self-reflect	Reflecting on challenges and trying to develop solutions; being motivated by fear	Gratitude and confidence at being informed
Pat	Cynicism, certainty, disillusionment	To imagine the kind of community that would be better	To reflect on personal failings and imagine change	To feel included in a community
Laura	Disappointment, excitement	To engage in self-reflection	To imagine solutions	To reflect on success and consider how to improve

So, in each of my case study participants, there are moments of emotional tension in their discourses that in some way reflect their understanding of sustainability-as-knowledge or sustainability-as-outreach. I suggest that these moments of emotional tension are productive learning experiences, fostered at least in part by intentional pedagogical choices made by the course facilitators and program managers. Furthermore, as I have suggested, in each of their own ways my case study participants balanced negative and positive emotional responses to help them find motivation to keep working. Lastly, for my student case study participants, the language of emotion works in conversation with their developing content knowledge of the discipline of sustainability to help them navigate moments of tension. For these students, when the content knowledge "matters" (as in, when it must be tangibly used outside of the classroom), it exceeds the sole realm of content knowledge and gains new complexity as it is re-contextualized in other settings. Whereas the course facilitators, as more advanced undergraduates, are able to draw more expertly on disciplinary content knowledge, the student Eco-Reps "fill in the gaps" with their more familiar language of emotion. As such, emotions may be given more credibility in classroom settings as something that, as Ahmed suggests, helps assign value to ideologies, bodies, and contexts.

Further, the primary difference that emerged from students' experience with expressions of positive or negative emotions is in the way their reflection is directed, typically either inwardly or outwardly. Students who express or encounter more negativity in their outreach express more inward-directed self-reflection, while students who express more positive emotional responses express more outwardly directed reflection, often towards how to teach or help others. In this regard, I hope to offer suggestions for complicating the conversation around student engagement to include a more holistic understanding of how engagement relates to emotion. The students who define sustainability in negative, pessimistic, or cynical ways are more likely to also express negative emotional responses to their outreach work, while students who define sustainability in positive or optimistic ways are more likely to perform such definitions through their outreach work. This has theoretical implications for the relationship between prior, existing knowledge and how students process new and learned information. This suggestion also has pedagogical implications regarding how teachers contextualize disciplinary knowledge.

As I have outlined, these students' emotional responses matter for this study because: emotional responses and content knowledge have a dialogic relationship; students use emotional responses to help them *navigate* moments of tension; students' willingness to perform outreach work is not seemingly affected by what kind of emotion they experience during their work, but rather these emotions affect where their reflections are typically directed. To repeat, in places where students experience negative emotions, they would engage more directly in inward reflections, considering questions about self-improvement and what else could be done in order to eventually reach positivity, and when experiencing positive emotions, students would reflect outward on their larger communities.

One final example of this outward reflection on a more macro-scale is a recurring Eco-Rep annual participation within the university's Earth Day activities. Each year, a number of student Eco-Reps and other members of the sustainable community at the university lie on the ground outside one of the university's busiest public walkways, as pictured in Figure 1:

Figure 1: "Earth Day Activism"

Each student has a piece of paper on their chest or back, with a word written on each that symbolizes people who have been killed, diseased, or displaced as a result of human failure to live sustainably, words like "flooding," "drought," or "pollution." This activity, which was started by a student Eco-Rep in 2013, continues to be one of the most visible and most popular of the students' options for participating in Earth Day events. Of my case study participants (students and facilitators), all but one of them chose to participate in this event. In their reflection on participating in this Earth Day activity, Pat explained that "this was one of the more directly and easily visible things we did… it made me feel like I was showing people in a way where we all need to come to terms with what we're doing to harm the environment" (Interview 3/7). This activity could be seen as an expression of the sense of frustration typically felt by many activists, and turned here by the Eco-Rep Program students into a hopeful teaching moment for their peers.

Discussion

Each in their own ways, my student case study participants found themselves experiencing *conflict* with their surrounding environments as part of their Eco-Rep work, or perhaps more broadly, simply by *being* Eco-Reps. In each case, this conflict led to them acting differently than they would have anticipated had the conflict not been a factor. I believe the program (and ones like it) would benefit by including more explicit focus on the tensions students are likely to encounter in outreach work. My findings are suggestive of WAC-oriented pedagogical moves that could allow a program like Eco-Reps to more formally recognize these tensions, and future research would examine the possibility to use emotional engagement, including negative emotions, as a way to enrichen students' learning experiences across the curriculum. Emotional labor, at least as it exists in our current social milieu, tends to be conflictive because it begins as invisible and then needs to be justified (often by those engaging in the labor) before it is recognized as valid. As such, these moments of either tension or even outright contradiction are ones that should be recognized institutionally and made visible so that the onus is not placed on the laborer to engage in the additional work of explanation and validation.

With regard to recognizing these tensions, I would no sooner suggest that Zhi is developmentally *behind* Jaime for having her first year as an engaged student be met with disappointment than I would suggest that Jaime is developmentally behind Zhi for *not* encountering disappointment in hers. What I might suggest, however, is that Zhi could have benefited from having a more supported, holistic network between her different contexts, and that Jaime could have benefited from having a bit more tension between hers. I'm reminded of Joe Harris' suggestion that we approach discussing community by allowing "for both consensus and conflict" (18). Within the Eco-Rep program, students design their own outreach activities based on how *they* assess the needs of the physical space on campus that *they* volunteer to cover, which is evocative of Harris, who writes that his work within universities has been universally accompanied by a "sense of difference, of overlap, of tense plurality, of being at once a member of several communities and yet never wholly a member of one" (11). The self-directed nature of the Eco-Rep work done in the classroom models the kind of work necessitated by the outreach and, for each of my case study participants, allowed them to craft their own individual relationships with that work.

In that sense, the student Eco-Reps and others doing similar work both use and need rhetoric to help them craft their persuasion to their audience and to understand their own role in the relationship. Bryan Garsten claims that the relationship between emotion and rhetoric exists as a criterion for the practice of judgment as "keen perceptivity and relatively steady habits of emotional response. When people have all these traits, they find that they can draw upon their various perceptions, feelings, and opinions to respond in a relatively deliberate way to whatever particular situation confronts them" (8-9). In this sense, I argue that through their emotional experiences, the students, while applying the disciplinary content knowledge of sustainability and performing outreach, complicated and enriched their ability to engage in a domain of rhetorical persuasion with their audiences. Garsten further draws this comparison between rhetoric and emotion in his reading of Aristotle, arguing that Aristotle "thought citizens tended to judge better in deliberative settings, where they were situated in *their own perspectives and experiences*...they exercised their judgment best when they could draw upon structures of perception and value acquired throughout their lives" (119, emphasis added). For the students, this gives their experience the kind of diversity characteristic of healthy ecosystems as defined by Greta Gaard (163) and, as the findings of this study suggest, allows for productive (if challenging) educational experiences as students negotiate their individual experiences, emotions, and outreach work with the disciplinary content knowledge of the classroom. Raúl Sánchez argues "for agency [implicated]... more thoroughly with the environment without immersing it entirely in that environment and thereby removing the possibility of responsibility" (31). The Eco-Rep program, by emphasizing students' own agency in choosing the sites for and makeup of their outreach work, allows for discursive participation outside of a pre-determined framework.

Applications for Pedagogy and Disciplinarity

What we can learn from these findings is that the unpredictable nature of outreach work does not make it a necessarily unacceptable risky learning environment for students. A teacher who shies away from assigning outreach-based projects because she is worried that her students will be met with resistance (or have difficulty being met with *anything at all*) can, by including in the work moments of critical self-reflection, help her students engage in productive learning opportunities regardless of audience reception. By its nature, outreach work involves a complex agentive subjectivity for students, helping them engage more directly and critically with their surrounding environments, and leading to productive learning experiences. Similarly, teachers may consider ways to upset the conflation of positive emotional experiences with success and negative emotional experiences with failure. Self-reflection and directed learning can help students synthesize their emotional experiences into effective learning moments, understanding how their negative emotions are just as valid and useful as positive ones. As with my participants (especially Pat and Jaime), negative emotional experiences can be especially useful as moments to understand and appreciate their own expertise and passions, as well as to reflect on their potential role as agents of change against an apathetic or unappreciative audience. Equipping students with this kind of rhetorical orientation potentially provides them with a strategy for negotiating and productively incorporating processes of failure into their learning and development rather than merely disengaging from negative emotional experiences.

This study was limited in its scope because of the small number of case study participants, although I believe a deep inquiry into students' writing, interview reflections, and classroom experiences was helpful in creating a complete picture of each students' lived experiences. While my recursive coding scheme helped me arrive at some important and exciting realizations, I believe this analysis could also have benefitted from additional coding to consider neutral emotion or the lack of emotion, as well as internally versus externally-oriented reflection. Lastly, future investigations into the relationship between science and emotion within Composition Studies would do well to draw more heavily and explicitly on feminist criticisms and methodologies, an area that lies beyond the present scope of this article.

While disciplinary knowledge might be external to public discussion, the public can and often does change the *stakes* of and consequences for disciplinary knowledge. Within the sciences, there have been discussions of both public intellectualism and popularizations of scientific thought. Drawing on Ulrich Beck's concept of the world risk society (the capacity for lay audiences to question foundational societal concepts as industrial and natural disasters increase), Robert Danisch claims that science functions to "produce uncertainty, fear, and danger" (173) in the general public. The management of risk, according to Danisch, has become more important to the function of society than the production of goods, and scientific discourse is how the public communicates discussions of managing risk. Furthermore, advancements in science and technology that seek "to improve the human condition is the central causal factor for the explosion of risks and the deepening of uncertainty" (179). Beck imagines a "public science" (Danisch 185) that would function as a sort of watchdog against some of the dangerous consequences of unchecked scientific discourse, which I would define as anthropocentric, and prone to both capitalist influence and misogynistic disciplinary traditions (see Merchant). Danisch contends that Beck's idea of a public science is limited because he offers "no generative conception of how this competence will emerge" (185). However, as Danisch suggests, a more practical (and possible) realization of this function may come from the field of rhetoric. Alan Gross claims that "rhetoric mediates not only the development of knowledge in all disciplines, including science, but also the existence of entities upon which this knowledge is developed" (285). Taking this assertion a step further, Heather Graves claims that "if we study the language that scientists use to conceptualize their objects of study... we can gain insight into the role that rhetoric plays in both the epistemology...and the ontology of science" (181). Graves further asserts that we should not "collapse the fields of study [rhetoric and science] into one another," (191) but rather look for places where rhetoric can be productively applied to scientific inquiry and epistemology. I would also suggest that scientists in other fields outside of sustainability look at the ways in which Sustainability Studies is emerging as a field both academic and public, precisely because of the way direct and actionable communication to their various publics is a crucial component of disciplinary knowledge production.

So how do rhetoric and emotion save science? In essence, they can help save it from itself: specifically, its most dogmatic and exclusionary ideological tendencies. Feminist scholars such as Patricia Sullivan have critiqued the "objective-subjective and rational-emotional dichotomies central to the scientific enterprise" (56) that make scientific inquiry tied to inherently masculine ideologies. Likewise, the publication practices of scientific genres (see Gross) creates an abstracted, idealized laboratory space that intentionally ignores the messy, human-centered and often emotional labor that are inherent to scientific progress (see Keller 34). By recognizing and even foregrounding emotion as a critical domain of scientific inquiry, I believe we are upsetting this masculinist dominance. Further, as scientific *outreach* relies inherently on persuasion (drawing as it does from modes of persuasion other than logos), outreach by nature is a subversive, agentive action. This is a further emphasis on what Sustainability as a field can offer the wider discipline of science. As such, I might generalize the theoretical *and* pedagogical takeaways of this project by making two interconnected suggestions: that rhetoric is necessary and needed in the realm of science, and that the study and teaching of emotion are necessary and needed in the realm of composition. As such, emotion and emotional labor become explicit throughlines for composition teachers and theorists to talk with our colleagues in the sciences. Our students are constantly engaging in visible and invisible labor: often the emotional labor is what our institutions and our disciplines, by their nature, make invisible. We may create richer educational opportunities for ourselves and our students the more we validate emotional labor as part of the educational process, and our academic disciplines will be the better for it.

Works Cited

Ahmed, Sara. *The Cultural Politics of Emotion*. Routledge, 2004.

Aristotle. *On Rhetoric*. *On Rhetoric: A Theory of Civic Discourse*, edited and translated by George A. Kennedy, Oxford UP, 1991, pp. 25-282.

Bacon, Nora. "The Trouble with Transfer: Lessons from a Study of Community Service Writing." *Michigan Journal of Community Service Learning* vol. 6, 1999, pp 53-62.

Clough, Patricia T. 'The Affective Turn: Political Economy, Biomedia and Bodies,' *Theory Culture & Society* vol. 25, no. 1, 2008, pp 1-22.

Danisch, Robert. "Political Rhetoric in a World Risk Society." *Rhetoric Society Quarterly*, vol. 40, no. 2, 2005, pp. 172-192.

Depalma, Michael-John. "Toward a Theory of Adaptive Transfer: Expanding Disciplinary Discussions of "Transfer" in Second-Language Writing and Composition Studies." *Journal of Second Language Writing*, vol. 20, no. 2, 2011, pp. 134-147.

Dobrin, Sidney and Christian Weisser. "Breaking Ground in Ecocomposition." *Relations, Locations, Positions: Composition Theory for Writing Teachers*, edited by Peter Vandenberg, Sue Hum, and Jennifer Clary-Lemon, NCTE, 2006, pp. 566-589.

Dobrin, Sidney and Christian Weisser. *Natural Discourse: Toward Ecocomposition*. SUNY Press, 2002.

Dyson, Anne Haas and Celia Genishi. *On the Case: Approaches to Language and Literacy Research*. Teachers College Press, 2008.

Erickson, Christina. "Student Sustainability Educators: A Guide to Creating and Maintaining an Eco-Rep Program on Your Campus." AASHE, NWF, April 2016. www.nwf.org/EcoLeaders/Campus-Ecology-Resource-Center/Reports/Student-Sustainability-Educators. Accessed 13 January, 2020.

Farmer, Frank. *After the Public Turn: Composition, Counterpublics, and the Citizen Bricoleur*. University Press of Colorado, 2013.

Gaard, Greta. "Ecofeminism and Ecocomposition." *Ecocomposition: Theoretical and Practical Approaches*, edited by Sidney Dobrin and Christian Weisser, SUNY Press, 2001. pp. 163-178.

Garsten, Bryan. *Saving Persuasion: A Defense of Rhetoric and Judgment*. Harvard UP, 2006.

Graves, Heather. "Rhetoric, Knowledge, and 'The Brute Facts of Nature' In Science Research." *Writing in Knowledge Societies*, edited by Doreen Starke-Meyerring, Anthony Paré, Natasha Artemeva, Miriam Horne, and Larissa Yousoubova, WAC Clearinghouse and Parlor Press, 2011, pp. 179-192.

Gross, Alan G. *The Rhetoric of Science*. Harvard University Press, 1996.

Gross, Alan G. and Arthur Walzer. "The Challenger Disaster and The Revival of Rhetoric in Organizational Life." *Argumentation*, vol. 11, no. 1, 1997, pp. 85-93.

Harris, Joseph. "The Idea of Community in the Study of Writing." *College Composition and Communication* vol. 40, no 1, 1989, pp. 11–22.

Keller, Evelyn Fox. "Gender and Science: Origin, History, and Politics." *Osiris*, vol. 10, 1995, pp. 26- 38.

Merchant, Carolyn. "The Scientific Revolution and The Death of Nature." *Isis*, vol. 97, no 3, 2006, pp. 513–533.

Micciche, Laura R. *Doing Emotion: Rhetoric, Writing, Teaching*. Boynton/Cook, 2007.

Sánchez, Raúl. *Inside the Subject: A Theory of Identity for the Study of Writing.* NCTE, 2017.

Spoel, Philippa and Barriault, Chantal. "Risk Knowledge and Risk Communication: The Rhetorical Challenge of Public Dialogue." Starke-Meyerring, Paré, Artemeva, Horne, and Yousoubova, pp. 87-112.

Starke-Meyerring, Doreen, Anthony Paré, Natasha Artemeva, Miriam Horne, and Larissa Yousoubova, editors. *Writing in Knowledge Societies.* WAC Clearinghouse and Parlor Press, 2011.

Sullivan, Patricia A. "Feminism and Methodology." *Methods and Methodology in Composition Research,* edited by Gesa Kirsch and Patricia A. Sullivan, Southern Illinois UP, 1992, pp. 37-58.

Tinberg, Howard. "2014 CCCC Chair's Address: The Loss of the Public." *College Composition and Communication,* vol. 66, no. 2, 2014, pp. 327-341.

Truana, Nancy. "Embedding Philosophers in the Practices of Science: Bringing Humanities to the Sciences." *Synthese,* vol. 190, 2013, pp. 1955-1973.

Warner, Michael. *Publics and Counterpublics.* Zone Books, 2005.

Wegner, Diana. "The Evolution of an Environmentalist Group Toward Public Participation: Civic Knowledge Construction and Transgressive Identities." Starke-Meyerring, Paré, Artemeva, Horne, and Yousoubova, pp. 113-138.

Zerbe, Michael. *Composition and the Rhetoric of Science: Engaging the Dominant Discourse.* Southern Illinois UP, 2007.

The Good Enough Teacher

Natalie Davey

Abstract: *This paper puts forward a pedagogical model of care for K-12 educators that is specifically focused on alternative classroom educators. In conversation with educational theorists and psychologists, a model of care that is translatable to both teachers and students in non-traditional classrooms is presented. Looking first at Arlie Hochschild's "emotion work" in the context of alternative classroom teaching, a link is made to Nel Noddings's "ethics of care" as a pedagogical starting point. The author then riffs on psychoanalyst D.W. Winnicott's notion of the "good enough mother," the one who "manages a difficult task: initiating the infant into a world in which he or she will feel both cared for and ready to deal with life's endless frustrations" (Alpert). Connecting Alpert's mobilizing of Winnicott to aspects of Noddings's "caring relation" builds a theoretical bridge that supports and scaffolds the construction of what the author calls the "good enough teacher." The author also suggests that this pedagogical model of care might also be replicable by students who need to take care of themselves. Throughout the paper examples are drawn from the author's experiences as a teacher and learner in a variety of alternative education classrooms.*

There has always been a place-based duality to my classroom assignments. With a career spanning twenty years in K-12 classrooms, I have worn many hats, sometimes all at once. The truth is that no teacher has ever played a singular role in her capacity as an educator. In whatever classroom iteration one teaches, there are competing forces at play: student needs, parental pressure, and the never ending top-down emphasis placed upon the facilitation of key outcomes regarding student skills.[1] Without negating the importance of skill building, and keeping in mind the multifaceted roles played by teachers, I believe more attention should be placed on the emotional space that exists between curriculum delivery and skill development. In that in-between space where teaching and learning occurs, educators are performing ongoing emotional work rendered invisible by the expectation that K-12 teachers simply know how to care for all of their students. Emotions must be considered *work* in order to obtain a fuller picture of what transpires between teachers and learners in the realm of public education, and a disservice is done to both parties when this labour is glossed over as obvious or natural. Without a pedagogy that is supported by an ethics of care, I believe that an educator's emotional labour risks not only going unseen but also untaught, leaving teachers without the explicit supports to

---

1. Different understandings are politically and philosophically embedded in loaded terms like "skills" and "outcomes." For the purpose of this paper I write from the stance that skills-based training and anticipated student outcomes are important base notes for public education but are by no means all-encompassing. Teaching the "whole student" means looking beyond the explicit curriculum to bigger pedagogical questions of that which is educational in education. For more on this topic see Davey, "Becoming."

make the care they show to and for their students as well as themselves enough.

To understand my own roots of caretaking and caregiving in the context of education, I look back to where I started my career: a prison. At 22 I did not yet have the language to define my educational practice or praxis-to-be. I had been given no opportunity to do any research about what sort of space I was walking into on my first day of class; I was hired on a weekend and started teaching on the Monday, naively assuming that I was "ready" for whomever I was to meet in what was then Toronto's central booking facility for youth awaiting trial. I learned quickly, from detention staff and the students themselves, that I was out of my depth. I had only taught for one full year prior to my youth detention centre assignment and had made assumptions about my ability as a teacher based on limited mainstream classroom experiences. I had never read anything by prison activists and scholars like Angela Davis or Ruth Wilson Gilmore. I had only just been introduced to Paulo Freire's *Pedagogy of the Oppressed*, a title mentioned in teacher's college (that one day I hoped to read). Looking back, I recognize that what sustained me through those challenging years was the care shown to me by my students who must have seen in me, in spite of all my inexperience, an authentic care for them.

Outside of the jail I felt alone. My teaching experiences in the detention centre were not translatable to friends or family, let alone to myself, which made for an isolating reality. Though I had two teacher colleagues at the detention centre whom I clumsily attempted to connect with outside the walls of our basement classrooms, the reality was that our sole commonality, our one point of connection, was located inside a space that we all desired to leave. We were teachers at different stages in our careers. I was a new teacher with no knowledge of alternative teaching in general, let alone teaching in prison, while my colleagues had taught for years in various alternative settings and felt jaded by the detention centre's limited educational resources. In two years at York Detention Centre no senior schoolboard administrator ever visited our prison classrooms, and so the message delivered through their absence was that we were on our own. Without school-based institutional supports, I worked to care for my students while they took care of me. They asked how I was feeling at the start of a day just as I checked in with them. In what was an emotionally charged environment, when moments of stress occurred in our classroom, students would work to protect me from violent words and actions even as I worked to create a safe learning environment for them.

Retrospectively, I can see that the student-to-teacher caregiving I received in the prison setting was located in an educational grey zone that today gives me some pause. The hesitation I feel is not because there is anything wrong with young people showing care for their teachers. Empathy building is in fact a soft skill to be celebrated (Stanbury, Bruce, Jain and Stellern). Instead, I question the narrative that suggests teachers should not need such care. This false narrative creates the myth that "good" educators have it all together with (or more often without) support and is damaging for teacher-candidates who feel the need to be "experts" when they have barely graduated from teacher's college (Allen). It is also damaging to young students who feel betrayed when unsupported teachers inevitably fail them. What if, in those early days of my career, I had been given the language to describe the care I needed to help sustain the difficult work of teaching in isolation? How would I have approached my students differently? How would I have approached a care of myself as an alternative educator?

Former Halifax Poet Laureate and activist El Jones writes of her prison activist work, saying, "We can't pretend this work doesn't take a toll." Jones' words resonate deeply with my memory of the prison classroom and of alternative classrooms in general, for inherent in the teacher's role is the emotional toll of working in these environments. I imagine the weight of this emotional burden to be heavier for those who work with and advocate for underserved students in alternative classrooms (see Corcoran). On the Toronto District School Board's website a sunny description defines an "alternative" classroom as, "schools where students need a new way—to find their way" ("Alternative Schools"). I find this spin doctoring of language deceiving in the face of what I have experienced and what other alternative educators have shared with me. Our stories fit with Richard Ashcroft's statement, "Teachers who work in institutional or alternative community settings typically receive no special training intended to equip them to serve their often difficult-to-teach students" (82). My experience of being hired without training for the detention centre position is a case in point.

If "alternative" is understood by what it is not—mainstream—then who is it that populates those alternative classrooms? How is an alternative student different from their counterpart in the mainstream classroom? Adam Jordan describes alternative schools as "popular interventions for marginalized students" (263). These spaces exist to facilitate schooling experiences for students who are living on the margins, set up in places such as children's hospitals, detention facilities, psychiatric out patient facilities and group homes. Citing work by Foley and Pang and Lehr, Tan, and Ysseldyke, Jordan goes on to note that "little research has focused on professionals in these settings... [even though] close to 11,000 public alternative schools or programs are believed to exist in the United States education system ... and as many as one million students are currently attending alternative learning programs [throughout the country]" (263). In the face of such large numbers, how are teachers able to sustain the emotional work inherent to the success of their marginalized students in these outlying educational spaces when, as educators, their own formal and informal structures of care are so limited—or were never there in the first place? Research around teacher attrition rates in the first five years of the profession suggests a stark truth[2]: Teachers are not receiving enough care to sustain a long career.

Building the Framework: Hochschild, Noddings, and Winnicott

In her interview with the *L.A. Review of Books* (LARB) about her recent work *Carceral Capitalism*, activist Jackie Wang says that she does not want to "glorify the informal structures of care that [end up] emerg[ing] in the crucible of a capitalist system that would grind us all to a pulp if it weren't for our friends" (Buna). With no systemic support available, Wang derives emotional support for her activist efforts from "informal structures of care." Similarly, under the present government in Ontario, governmental cuts to education highlight a systemic will to withdraw support from students and teachers who need it most (see "Education Funding Changes"). From this context I frame a

---

2. The attrition rate in Canada can be as high as 30 percent in the first five years of service (Karsenti & Collin).

159

theoretically-grounded pedagogical model of teacher and student care that goes beyond reliance on the "informal."

I begin with a reading of Arlie Hochschild's "emotion work," connecting the concept to the specific lived experience of an alternative education teacher working without mainstream supports. Then I look to Nel Noddings and her "ethics of care" as a pedagogical starting point for a model to do emotion work differently. Finally, I riff on how, in his Op-Ed for *The New York Times*, Avram Alpert has taken up psychoanalyst D.W. Winnicott's notion of the "good enough mother." Alpert describes her as one who "manages a difficult task: initiating the infant into a world in which he or she will feel both cared for and ready to deal with life's endless frustrations." Each of these thinkers helps to flesh out what I am calling the "good enough" teacher. Linking Alpert's Winnicottian translation to aspects of caring relation, I sketch out my version of the "good enough teacher" to be a model of teaching and learning that supports all teachers, but most specifically alternative educators, in the balanced and sustainable practice of what it means to be "good enough." I write from the stance of one who wants to be a better teacher than her 22 year-old self was. I want to be a "good enough teacher" with the experiences and nuanced vocabulary to better show care for others and for myself. I also consider the possibility of the "good enough teacher" as being a pedagogical model to teach students better care of themselves.

In *The Managed Heart: Commercialization of Human Feeling*, Arlie Hochschild describes "feeling rules" concerning the "emotion work" that is owed from one to another in a wide range of social interactions (49, 52). She explains acts of "emotion management" as determining the appropriate responses due to that range of interpersonal exchange (60). As observed in her study of public-contact workers, Hochschild notes the complex feeling rules and "gift of exchange" centered in the work of those for whom interpersonal connection defines the job, for example the classroom teacher (78). Andy Hargreaves' work on the emotional geographies of teachers in relationship with both students and colleagues further highlights the complexity of that exchange. In his study of 53 teachers in a variety of elementary and secondary schools, Hargreaves' interviews draw on "methodological procedures used by Hochschild" with the end goal being to highlight how "teachers draw upon [personal and past] emotional understanding…to interpret the emotional experiences and responses of others" (507-508). Megan Watkins refers to Hargreaves' work in her investigation of teachers' tears in the affective geography of the classroom. Watkins says it is "important to consider the particular spatiality of classrooms and how they function as affectively charged sites … contained spaces with a specific interiority where teachers and students are grouped together, interacting for sustained periods of time" (138). In the affectively charged site of the alternative education classroom, enhanced feeling rules dominate that very particular educational space, not unlike the cramped airplane space of Hochschild's airline workers. These rules warrant attention and require unpacking.

Even as these and other studies have taken up Hochschild's emotion work in their classroom research, there are others who would disagree about using her concept in regards to teaching. In a literature review analyzing 19 different educational articles focused on how Hochschild's concept does or does not fit within the realm of teaching, Kwok Tsang highlights the complexity inherent in Hochschild's term in the context of the classroom and boils the confusion down to interpretation of vocabulary, specifically looking at the difference between emotional labour and emotion work. According to Tsang's study, educational researchers commonly agree that teaching involves emotional labor "because teachers' emotional activities are governed by the emotional rules of teaching" (1314). For the purpose of this paper, I use the term "emotion work" to look more generally at how the practice of emotion management is key to a sustained career in teaching for alternative educators. I see that work of emotion management as an even greater quandary for educators whose classrooms fall outside of the traditional school-based support systems.

Current research[3] that looks to the benefits of supporting teachers in their professional learning makes a direct connection to mentorship. Mentoring relationships are not easily formed, for the emotion work and feeling rules at play are loaded with and layered by the complex relationships that exist within the school community. The student population requires ongoing care, collegial competition can rear its head in the form of workplace lateral violence (Davey, "Breaking Out" 232), and administrative hierarchies further complicate the already emotionally-laden school environment. Finding a healthy mentoring relationship outside of a traditional school in an alternative classroom comes with even more place-based challenges. For example, within the partnership-driven world of post-secondary education (PSE), my current alternative classroom situates me on a college campus teaching parallel to but not directly with colleagues who are kept separate because of institutional divisions. I have seen these divisions make the feeling rules harder to decipher and have experienced the way they breed feelings of isolation and resentment in teachers. As Hochschild suggests, we can become estranged from the very emotion work performed to mitigate work stresses, resulting in the loss of feelings that connect us to others (91). In the educational realm, emotional estrangement negatively affects the student/teacher relationship, especially those students most systemically underserved. As previously stated, many of those students are learning in alternative programs and classrooms (Bullough 25). A "good" teacher will try to care for her students with all she has to give, but what is the end result for her and her students if she loses herself along the way? I believe that the "good enough" teacher will, instead, find a way to strike a balance between the work of emotion and care for both others and herself through a pedagogy of care.

Carol Gilligan writes, "the ideal of care is … an activity of relationship, of seeing and responding to need, taking care of the world by sustaining the web of connection so that no one is left alone" (62). Noddings builds upon Gilligan's work and fleshes out a full-fledged "ethics of care" from the stance that, "One who attempts to ignore or to climb above the human affect at the heart of ethicality may well be guilty of romantic rationalism" (*A Relational Approach* 3). Noddings further explains,

> [Care ethics are] interested in maintaining and enhancing caring relations—attending to those we encounter, listening to their expressed needs, and responding positively if possible. But even when we must deny the need expressed, we try to do so in a way that will preserve the caring relation. (*A Relational Approach* xvi)

---

3. See Campbell, Clinton, Fullan, Hargreaves, James, and Longboat.

Similar to Hochschild's emotion work that is embedded in the very act of teaching, Nodding's "caring relations" are intrinsic to classroom dynamics. The goal of teachers is to respond to the learning needs of their students, and to do so may require engaging with, listening to, and responding to those needs that the student names. The emphasis is placed on listening in the teacher/student relation, for "the teacher as carer is interested in the *expressed* needs of the cared-for, not simply the needs assumed by the school as an institution" (Noddings, "Caring Relation in Teaching" 772). Working in alternative classroom settings with students of extremely diverse learning needs makes honing an ability to respond with care all the more necessary. Without school-based institutional supports like guidance counselors and social workers, the caring relation is dependent solely on the teacher.

Noddings's premise for the "caring relation" that "we recognize human encounter and affective response as a basic fact of human existence" (*A Relational Approach* 4) provides pedagogical potential for alternative educators. She expands by stating that, "Caring is a relationship that contains another, the cared-for … [for] the world is not divided into carers and cared-fors as separate and permanent classes" (xxi). For Noddings studying conditions that make it possible for caring relations to flourish should occur from a relational perspective. In consideration of the alternative classroom, I especially focus on her contribution of the cared-for in the relation. Noddings uses examples of contributions made by the infant to the parent-child relation, the patient to the physician-patient relation and, in the educational space, the student to the teacher-student relation. In the context of my own alternative classroom teaching, I have found the interchanging nature of carer and cared-for to be strikingly impermanent. The role of teacher or student in a classroom depends on shifting factors in the lives of those who enter the educational space. Mitigating the aforementioned "grey zone" of student-to-teacher care requires explicit guidance, for example asking students for help when maneuvering the physical space of the classroom or sharing with students small classroom-based administrative responsibilities. Sharing aspects of classroom work, be it arranging tables for a group discussion or asking a student to write the class agenda on the white board, makes more transparent the many micro-tasks that need to happen to make a school day run smoothly.

For students to take on roles as carers, Noddings believes that young people need "to develop as caring persons, … [so they] must have supervised practice in caring" (*A Relational Approach* xviii). Noddings goes on to write,

> The caring attitude, that attitude which expresses our earliest memories of both caring and being cared for is universally accessible…[and thus] we must nurture that ideal in all of our educational encounters…The primary aim of all education must be nurturance of the ethical ideal. (6)

In this paper, I push toward a pedagogical model of care that extends the same need for a nurturance of care ethics to support teachers in training and educators in general. Such a model requires that caring and caregiving not be equated. Andrea Lobb writes of Noddings's complex unpacking of care-giving as she works to dissect the concept of empathy through a critical feminist lens.[4] She makes the point that empathy, like caregiving, is not implicitly selfless and points out that a recognition of what is received in the giving of empathetic care has the potential to benefit both parties. She leans on Noddings to make this point. Therefore, caregiving is an important element in care ethics, but technically, as a set of activities or occupation, it can be done with or without caring. Teaching, for example, can be done with or without caring. It is only with awareness and acknowledgement of the difference between the two that the need for care support in education can be unpacked. It is at this juncture where I see a bridge to be built connecting Noddings to Winnicott.

For Noddings there is an important distinction to be made between *caring about* and *caring for*. The former expresses concern but without the guarantee of a response to one who needs care. The latter is characterized by direct attention and response, requiring the "establishment of a caring relation [and] person-to-person contact of some sort" (*A Relational Approach* xiv). Such a distinction is important when considering the function of institutions and large organizations in supporting caring. A traditional school, for example, or in the case of my alternative education focus, an off-site classroom, cannot necessarily care for everyone directly—or can it? Noddings would suggest that it can work toward "establishing an environment in which caring-for can flourish" (xv) but cautions that "a primary message of *Caring* is that we cannot justify ourselves as carers by claiming 'we care.' If the recipients of our care insist that 'nobody cares,' caring relations do not exist." When considering how we "develop communities that will support, not destroy, caring relations" (xxiii), I turn to Alpert's reading of Winnicott's "good enough mother" when he writes, "To fully become good enough is to grow up into a world that is itself good enough, that is as full of care and love as it is suffering and frustration." Alpert's summation of Winnicott's important concept extends, in locus parentis, to a teacher's desire for her students.

The turn to a psychologist for pedagogical guidance speaks to the interdisciplinary impact of a thinker whose ideas have shaped and stretched processes of meaning-making across various fields. Steven Tuber writes, "Winnicott evokes a parallel process in which reading his work resonates on multiple levels" (7). Tuber begins his primer of Winnicott's extensive body of work by reminding the reader that Winnicott was first trained as a pediatrician before moving into psychoanalytical care. In Helen Stein's review of Tuber's book, she describes the author's reading of the psychoanalyst to hinge upon Winnicottian paradoxes that "are sub-varieties of a central one, the capacity to be alone and the need for [human] relatedness" (2). One such paradox is "the impossibility of teaching mothers what is natural about mothering along with the need to help them when things go wrong" (2). To engage with such an impossibility, Tuber writes of Winnicott's certainty that "there was a psychology of babyhood, and that the baby was an inherently psychological being" (18). According to Tuber, an explanation of this infant psychology is unpacked in Winnicott's paper "Primitive Emotional Development," where he describes what he calls the baby's "instinctual urges and predatory ideas" of their mother's breast. Tuber's reading of Winnicott values the doctor's refer-

---

4. In Lobb's essay she highlights a connection to Winnicott in a footnote with a reference to "the maternal variety [of care] famously theorized by DW Winnicott (1958)."

163

ence to "urges" as "keeping true to his psychoanalytic training" but believes the addition of "predatory ideas" to be ground-breaking psychoanalytic language, for Winnicott "gives the baby a mind and a motivational force distinct from his urges. Being predatory, moreover, implies being related and relationship-seeking" (19). Winnicott's careful and deliberate word choice helps to unpack what is a nuanced explanation of the paradoxical interrelatedness of the infant and the mother. The one needs and at the same time must learn to be without the other.

It is from that paradoxical stance, in an effort to understand how the "good enough mother" is released from the unreasonable burden of perfection, that I find clarity in the words of Martha Nussbaum who writes that for Winnicott the central cultural and personal problem "is how to bear the exposure of being imperfectly human" (388). Nussbaum suggests that Winnicott's understanding of the relatedness inherent in the mother/infant dyad has "a distinctively ethical heart…for only through developing the capacity to imagine its mother's feelings does the child become capable of generous and reparative acts" (389). Thus, according to both Tuber and Nussbaum's readings of Winnicott, what makes the notion of the "good enough mother" and the mother/infant dyad a useful cross-disciplinary metaphor is its relatability – we are all imperfect and we all need care.

From an educator's perspective the ethical heart of Winnicott's dyad forms a natural link to Nodding's care ethic. I am by no means the first to work with the concept of the "good enough mother" in the teaching environment, nor to connect Noddings and Winnicott in educational research. Isca Salzberger, Giana Henry, and Elsie Osborne look to Winnicott's mother figure in their study of senior teaching staff who are interviewed in a counseling and education professional development course. Going into their sessions with the teachers, Salzberger, Henry, and Osborne wonder if teachers tend "to overrate or underrate the part they play in the development of their pupils" (3). What emerges from their conversations with the teachers is an awareness in the interviewees of the shared human experience of anxiety that impacts both those teaching and those taught. That anxiety does not stop in childhood but continues to exist at some level throughout life is a surprise to some of the teachers. A psychoanalytic understanding of that anxiety is introduced to them via the teachings of Winnicott as he "drew attention to the need of an infant to be held both physically and emotionally by the mother" (3). Within the counseling course the important role of the teacher is tied to Winnicott's "mother" as the educator-participants come to see that "if painful emotions can be received by another [i.e. a teacher] and understood, it allows for growth and development" in students (3).

Guy Allen also interprets Winnicott in his own educational research as he incorporates the notion of a "good-enough mother" with what he calls a "good-enough teacher" into his pedagogical effort to change a university introductory writing course from the inside out. A professor of literature and writing, Allen sees his practice as a "good enough" teacher in the highly competitive university environment as "creat[ing] an environment where students can make meaning or discover for themselves" (150). The "facilitating environment" that he can provide for his writing students depends on the "potential space" that is created for play, where "the 'work' of childhood" occurs (151). Allen's educational mobilizing of Winnicott, specifically regarding the physical and psychic space of the classroom as well as the course structure, "depends on the 'good enough' caregiver making and maintaining that space" of both independent and creative play (151). To ensure that their writing course is not simply "a space without potential" (170), Allen says that a teacher becomes a "good-enough other who offers the good-enough environment," thus "setting the minimal conditions for the subject's development of capacities for both autonomy and connection" (173). The way that Allen utilizes and applies the "good-enough" label to a teacher is pedagogically valuable in the writing classroom, and I pick up on some of his ideas in my own work with Winnicott's language. I take up the term "good-enough" in relation to alternative educators to shift exclusive focus away from the role of the teacher, as my turn to an ethics of care explicitly includes the student as being "good-enough" and, in fact, necessary to the care that needs to be lived out in the alternative classroom.

Sandra Chang-Kredl makes a direct connection between Winnicott and Noddings in her discussion of "portrait segments" of early-year teacher experiences, framed by Noddings's discussion of care in connection with Winnicott's notion of transitional spaces. Chang-Kredl writes, "We all struggle with the demand of an unsettled subjective and social existence. According to Winnicott ..., 'relief from this strain is provided by an intermediate area of experience'" (155). That illusory space of relief, what Winnicott calls the "resting place for the individual engaged in the perpetual human task of keeping inner and outer reality separate yet interrelated" (qtd. in Chang-Kredl 155) is an intermediate area of experience that I believe, for the "good enough teacher," is situated in the classroom. Likewise, Jodi MacQuarrie theorizes Noddings and Winnicott in tandem when the author calls into question the "progressive approaches of education that encourage teachers to analyze and interpret as a means to an end of coming to know students well" (40). She works with what she calls Winnicott's "use of an object" and investigates teacher-student relationships through the lens of Noddings and other educational philosophers, suggesting that the "progressive" teacher's eye has been analyzing students instead of turning the gaze inwards where she believes it belongs. At the end of her article she conceptually marries aspects of both Winnicott and Noddings, telling a story of her own classroom where she cares for a student who, through his relational response to her care, chooses to care for her and himself in the process. She writes, "Our challenge as teachers, then, is to strive to always first be in relation with our students so that they may transform and flourish" (49). Both MacQuarrie and Chang-Kredl focus on social interaction and interrelation as inherent to the teacher's experience, and both gesture to care as the necessary centre of what they analyze to be healthy educational relationships.

The interrelated and relation-based roles of Winnicott's dyad are important to the development of my pedagogy of care. To connect the mother/child dyad with Noddings's "ethics of care" and Hochschild's emotion work, I use Winnicott's "good enough mother" to ground the development of a pedagogical model for teaching in the alternative classroom. Three quotations from Winnicott drive the pedagogical model's development. The first is taken from his paper "Mirror-Role of Mother and Family in Child Development." In what is essentially a free-verse poem, Winnicott writes,

> When I look I am seen, so I exist.
>
> I can now afford to look and see.

I now look creatively and what I apperceive I also perceive. (217)

The second quotation comes from his paper "Group Influences and the Maladjusted Child" where he writes,

> I suggest that this I AM moment is a raw moment; the new individual feels infinitely exposed. Only if someone has her arms round the infant at this time can the I AM moment be endured, or perhaps risked. (48)

The third quotation comes from his paper "Mind and Its Relation to the Psyche-Soma." In it he writes, "What releases the mother from her need to be near-perfect is the infant's understanding" (204).

Winnicott's mother/infant dyad is defined by their interrelation: by seeing themself through the eyes of the mother, the new one therefore sees themself, that is to say, recognizes their own existence. Not only does the infant recognize that they exist in her eyes, they can "now afford to look and see." According to Winnicott that seeing means the infant can rest in the knowledge of their mother's care and, therefore, take the risk to look beyond her face to "perceive" the world that they are now a part of. The infant's perception of the world directly links to their apperception of their own existence by virtue of their mother's care. The infant can then start to "creatively" make a place for themself in the world where they will not simply exist in it as a created thing but as a creator themself. All of this self-perception and awareness is connected to the care given to the infant by their "good enough" mother. She is the one who enables the "I AM moment[s]" to be "endured, or perhaps risked" by her child as they create space for themself in the world, confident that her arms are always within reach. And the "good enough" mother is released from "her need to be near-perfect" because of the infant's "understanding" of her care. The "I AM" moments of isolation, lived by both mother and child, keep them simultaneously together and separate, creating a healthy balance of care given and received.

The pivot from psychoanalysis to pedagogy is educationally intuitive for one who learns and teaches in a non-traditional classroom. The ethics of care that Noddings has developed hinges on her notion of the "caring relation" and that relation, like Winnicott's mother/infant dyad, is interpersonal. She writes, "The one-caring and cared-for are reciprocally dependent... we are all inevitably cared-fors at many times and, ideally, most of us are carers" (*A Relational Approach* xxi). In a mainstream highschool with a large staff and an administration team, teachers have the opportunity to be cared for by students but also by various colleagues and educational management. The caring relation manifests differently in the alternative setting where only one or two teachers work with limited direction from offsite administrators who are not physically present to provide support. The reciprocal dependence that exists between teacher and learner in the alternative environment is the foundation upon which the pedagogy of the "good enough" teacher is built.

Key Tenets: A Pedagogical Model of Care

The key tenets of this tri-part pedagogical model are:

1. The teacher and student acknowledge their co-dependence for educational progress to be made in the classroom, what I call the "student/teacher binary"(see Davey, "Student/Teacher Binary").
2. The teacher strives for a balance of both student care and self-care.
3. The teacher facilitates space for students to creatively engage the educational process.

These three tenets can be lived out by any "good enough" teacher—and I believe *should* be lived out for an alternative educator to do more than simply survive her classroom life. I suggest that it is all the more important for alternative educators to have this pedagogical foundation upon which to build a thriving teaching practice. If we want teachers to last beyond the first five years while performing the profession's intense emotion work, external and internal systems need to be put into place to make it possible for them to thrive in the long run.

To help explain how this pedagogy might play out in the real time alternative classroom in 2019, I find inspiration in the words of Katherine McKittrick. In her exploration of colour and hue, inspired by singer Nina Simone's *Pastel Blues* album, she writes, "We must live with seeing and knowing something (blue) that we cannot accurately chronicle or express. Put otherwise, the unexplained, the undescribed, unfold into a kind of promising inaccuracy" (2). McKittrick's description of knowing something that "we cannot accurately chronicle" speaks to my educational journey. I take solace in the "promising inaccuracy" of a pedagogical practice that strives for balance and self-care, brought about through both teacher facilitation and student engagement. A pedagogy of care holds within its very description a sort of impossibility, for certainly, like teaching itself, a balanced provision of care for self and others will be a very individualized practice as it plays out in the classroom. And yet, the definitive naming of such a pedagogical approach obligates a discursive awareness of the emotion work that occurs in alternative educative spaces. That awareness has the potential to facilitate a working through of the three tenets to be lived out by "good enough" teachers for whom, if an ongoing balance is achieved, may feel released from the pressure of doing educational emotion work in isolation. That release may then, in turn, create space for pedagogical growth in both teachers and their students.

Tenet One

The first tenet speaks to the need for the teacher and student to acknowledge their co-dependence for educational progress to be made in the classroom. The "teacher/student binary" can be described as a gift that must be given and also received (Davey, "Teacher/Student Binary" 75). The importance of this gift is bound up in the interrelational nature of the teacher and student as needing the other to exist. There is no teacher without the student and no student without the teacher. The emotion work that comes with teaching in the alternative classroom can feel all the more difficult because of the isolation inherent to the job. But if teachers can see their students as partnering with them in the task of teaching and learning, their sense of isolation may be mitigated.

An example of this tenet is found in the alternative classroom in which I have taught and learned for the last four years. My student cohorts are made up of youth aged 18 to 20 years old, all who are completing different high school credits that were failed at one point or another on their individual academic journeys. Some have failed by a mere percent or two, while others have a long way to go to pass. I am an English Literature teacher and a Sociology teacher, not a teacher of math or science. Therefore I cannot be a subject matter expert for most of what these students need to learn. But in my role as a credit recovery teacher, I am to provide the students with the necessary material for them to succeed in all courses. The gift of the partnership that is necessitated with this paradoxical set-up is that both teacher and student must work together. Students must work with me to guide me towards their prior knowledge in a specific course that needs recovering, direct me to resources they found effective, and steer me away from those they did not like. Areas of subject specific interest must be explicitly named by the student so that she might be engaged as we co-create new assignments for the credit to finally be recovered.

Acknowledging this teacher/student partnership reduces the pressure to be all things for my class – teacher, guidance counselor, social worker, lawyer. The student's role is key here to create a cascade effect. Said another way, the credit recovery educator might ask herself, "If we are developing assignments as a team, what else can I count on in terms of my students' abilities?" By transparently naming the need for student expertise and lived experience to make the credit recovery process function, the paradigm shifts away from a deficit mindset, so often connected to "at-risk" students, towards one that is strengths-based.

Tenet Two

The second tenet that is built into a pedagogy of care necessitates that the teacher establish and practice a consistent balance of both student care and self-care. Current academic research and educational blogs speak to the need for teachers to practice self-care so that they can be the best teachers for students. Jennifer Gunn emphasises the importance for teachers to work on "self-preservation mindsets" and "building a strong peer network," both of which are good suggestions for all educators. For alternative educators who may not have the possibility of a school-based peer network, self-preservation mindsets are necessary but, I would suggest, are too focused on the "I" of the teacher without acknowledging the potentially positive impact of the student on the teacher. In the prison, working with youth who were deemed by the education and legal systems to be a hard-to-serve population, students proved to be carers of me and of each other. For example, students would support each other in literacy skill building at one table, while I worked to quell any number of emotional crises in another corner of the room. The general understanding was that in our classroom there would be no fights, and throughout my two years in the prison there was only ever one. I look back to that time and see that, even in my naïve state as a new teacher, the trust I had instilled in my students had helped to set us all up for success. We relied on each other and were, therefore, a community of sorts. The second tenet of a pedagogy of care points to the "good enough" teacher's balancing of emotion work that, as Noddings says, "develop[s] communities that will support, not destroy, caring relations" (xxiii). The balance of living in a world that is itself good enough, that is as full of care and love as it is suffering and frustration, is connected to an emphasis on community.

Tenet Three

Finally, community building is also inherent to the third tenet that requires the teacher to facilitate space for students to creatively engage with the educational process. Winnicott's use of the word "create" gives power to the infant who is connected to and also isolated from the "good enough" mother. To create means having agency. For agency to play out in the lives of small alternative classrooms, teachers must release control over the care given and received by those students to each other and themselves. The students will become active participants in creating a class culture, for good or bad. From the stance of one practicing a pedagogy of care in her own alternative classroom, community-building means de-emphasizing the "I" of the traditionally teacher-focused classroom by centering the "we" of teacher and students creating community together. An example of such community creating is examined by Paul Pedota when he explores how teacher support of student academic success and positive self-image also benefits teacher retention. That pedagogical perspective aligns with what I am suggesting regarding the good enough teacher's partnership with her students in the alternative classroom. Pedota writes, "It would do well to remember that we must look at the whole individual when planning how to support success so that the effort, energy, and persistence of an activity, for both students and teachers, will increase their performance and satisfaction" (61). He provides ten strategies that I agree with in principal, ranging from establishing a supportive classroom climate to deemphasizing grades so as to promote learning "that has meaning to students" (59). My focus on the student/teacher partnership falls within those quotation marks. In the case of my present day credit recovery classroom, if we are to get the job done—that job being credit accumulation with the long game being high school graduation—for us to succeed as a teacher/student team, we must emphasize "that [which] has meaning to [my] students" and learn from each other. As the students guide me towards their prior knowledge in the subject, teaching me about what units or components of the course they did not complete in their first attempt, we then build assignments from scratch that hit on those missing pieces. What we put together is essentially a course-based puzzle that simply needs to be completed. For there to be true buy-in from the student who has struggled academically in school, they must feel heard in this process. To summarize, the student needs the guidance of the teacher and, equally important, the teacher needs the expertise of the student.

Barriers

One of the barriers to such a care-driven pedagogical mindset is that though school-aged students are no longer infants, as in the Winnicottian mother/infant dyad, educational systems can and do infantilize their student bodies. Infantilizing occurs in the teacher-centered negation of students and the potential of their creative power within the educational space. Once students enter their secondary school years where teachers are pushed to deliver content to satisfy top-down pressures from educational authorities, experiential opportunities for students to engage with their own learning disappear. The embedded play that exists, for example, in Ontario's 2016 kindergarten curriculum is essentially removed by the time students have reached secondary school (see "The Ontario Curriculum"). That removal means students lose creative agency in their schools and classrooms. Recently proposed changes to the Ontario Secondary School Diploma will require all students to take four e-learning courses to graduate (see Farhadi). When only 12 of the 30 credits required to graduate are electives, the significant number of online courses being added to the compulsory diploma requirements is a decision that is rife with inequities. Beyond the socioeconomic realities that will affect access for some students, because of the imposed obligation to fill their timetable with these online compulsory courses, all students will end up with less choice regarding elective courses, often specialized and connected to the arts. With a care-based pedagogy in mind, this example points to a systemic devaluing of student agency and an overall infantilization of them in public schools.

An Anticipated Future of Educational Care

With some hope I return to Jackie Wang's interview with M. Buna where she describes an "interdisciplinary…approach to unpacking issues related to the carceral state [as a way] to attack a set of problems on multiple levels of analysis." While Wang is working to dismantle the prison system, I am looking to present a pedagogical approach for isolated alternative educators, but perhaps the two ideas are not so far apart. Each one requires that systemic changes be made from the inside out. In the case of a pedagogy of care where a shift occurs within an alternative teacher's own praxis, Wang's desire rings true: the need for community and reaching out so as to "spark conversations and organizing efforts." This paper's conceptual conversations with Hochschild, Noddings and Winnicott work together to add "multiple levels of analysis" needed in the realm of education for changes to occur. For alternative educators to practice a pedagogy of care, they need to look for support from unlikely allies. Such allies can take many forms such as interdisciplinary works of literature, community resources, mainstream school colleagues with access to educational supports and—most importantly—the students themselves. These allies can help attack the problem of isolated emotion work with the "promising inaccuracy" (McKittrick) of a pedagogical practice that strives for balance, self-care, teacher facilitation and student agency in the alternative classroom.

Works Cited

Allen, Guy. "The 'Good-Enough' Teacher and the Authentic Student." *Pedagogy of Becoming,* edited by Jon Mills, Rodopi, 2002, pp. 143-176.
Allen, Jeanne M. "Valuing Practice Over Theory: How Beginning Teachers Re-orient Their Practice in the Transition from the University to the Workplace." *Teaching and Teacher Education*, vol. 25, no. 5, 2009, pp. 647-654. doi.org/10.1016/j.tate.2008.11.011.
Alpert, Avram. "The Good Enough Life." Editorial. *The New York Times,* 20 Feb. 2019.
"Alternative Schools." The Toronto District School Board, 2014, https://www.tdsb.on.ca/Findyour/School/Alternative-Schools.

Ashcroft, Richard. "Training and Professional Identity for Educators in Alternative Education Settings." *The Clearing House: A Journal of Educational Strategies, Issues and Ideas*, vol. 73, no. 2, 1999, pp. 82-85, doi: 10.1080/00098659909600153.

Bullough, Robert. "Teacher Vulnerability and Teachability: A Case Study of One Mentor and Two Interns." *Teacher Education Quarterly*, vol. 32, no. 2, 2005, pp. 23-39.

Buna, M. "Carceral Capitalism: An Interview with Jackie Wang." *Los Angeles Review of Books*, 3 May 2018, lareviewofbooks.org/article/carceral-capitalism-conversation-jackie-wang/.

Campbell, Carol, Jean Clinton, Michael Fullan, Andy Hargreaves, Carl James, and Kahontakwas Diane Longboat. "Ontario: A Learning Province, Findings and Recommendations from. the Independent Review of Assessment and Reporting," Education Advisors to the Premier of Ontario, 2018, www.oise.utoronto.ca/preview/ihae/UserFiles/File/OntarioLearningProvince2018.pdf.

Chang-Kredl, Sandra. "Transitional Spaces and Displaced Truths of the EarlyYears Teacher." *Canadian Curriculum Studies: A Metissage of Inspiration/Imagination/Interconnection*, edited by Erika Hasebe-Ludt and Carl Leggo Canadian Scholars, 2018, pp. 152-158.

Corcoran, Roisin. "Teacher Emotions." *IRINSTITUTES*, 5 Jun. 2017, https://irinstitutes.org/teacher-emotions/.

Davey, Natalie. "Breaking Out: The Institutionalized Practices of Youth Prison Guards and the Inmates Who Set Them Free." *Exploring the Toxicity of Lateral Violence and Microaggressions: Poison in the Water Cooler*, edited by Christine Cho, Julie Corkett and Astrid Steele, Palgrave, 2018, pp. 231-245.

—. "On 'Becoming': The 'Educational' Quandary of Teaching Incarcerated Youth." *Review of Education, Pedagogy and Cultural Studies*, vol. 39, no. 4, 2017, pp. 391-409.

—. "The Student/Teacher Binary: A 'Gift' to Consider." *The Leader Reader: Narratives of Experience*, edited by Darrin Griffiths, Word & Deed Publishing Inc., 2018, pp. 74-76.

"Education Funding Changes Continue to Have an Impact." People for Education, 10 Oct. 2019, peopleforeducation.ca/our-work/education-funding-changes-continue-to-have-impact/.

Farhady, Beyhan. "Mandatory Online Courses for Highschool Students a 'terrible idea' Expert Says." CBC News, 26 Mar. 2019, www.cbc.ca/news/canada/toronto/mandatoryonline-courses-ontario-high-school_students-terrible-idea-e-learning-1.5072018.

Gilligan, Carol. *In a Different Voice: Psychological Theory and Women's Development.* Harvard University Press, 1982.

Gunn, Jennifer. "Self-care for Teachers of Traumatized Students." *Room 241*, 22 June 2018, https://www.crisisprevention.com/enCA/Blog/March-2018/The-Case-for-a-Culture-of-Caring-in-Schools.

Hargreaves, Andy. "The Emotional Geographies of Teachers' Relations With Colleagues." *International Journal of Educational Research*, vol. 35, 2001, pp.503-527.

Hochschild, Arlie. *The Managed Heart: Commercialization of Human Feeling.* University of California Press, 1983.

Jones, El. "We Gon Be Alright," *The Halifax Examiner*, https://www.halifaxexaminer.ca/featured/we-gon-be-alright-on-activism-death-and-survival/.

Jordan, Adam, Kasey H. Jordan and Todd S. Hawley. "Purpose and Passion: The Rationales of Public Alternative Educators." *The Journal of Social Studies Research*, vol. 41, no 4, 2017, pp. 263-273, doi.org/10.1016/j.jssr.2017.01.004.

Karsenti, Thierry and Simon Collin. "Why Are New Teachers Leaving the Profession?: Results of a Canada-wide Survey." *Education*, vol. 3, 2013, pp.141-149. doi: 10.5923/j.edu.20130303.01.

Lobb, Andrea. "The Agony and the Empathy: The Ambivalence of Empathy in Feminist Psychology." *Feminism and Psychology*, vol. 23, no. 4, 2013, pp. 426-441.

MacQuarrie, Jodi. "Against Interpretation." *Journal of Thought*, vol. 41, no. 2, 2006, pp. 39–50. JSTOR, www.jstor.org/stable/42589866.

McKittrick, Katherine. "Pastel Blue." *Don't Wear Down*, http://www.katherinemckittrick.com/wornout/.

Noddings, Nel. *Caring: A Relational Approach to Ethics and Moral Education*. Los Angeles: University of California Press, 1986.

—. "The Caring Relation in Teaching." *Oxford Review of Education,* vol. 38, no. 6, 2012, pp. 771-781.

Nussbaum, Martha. "Winnicott on the Surprises of the Self." *The Massachusetts Review,* vol. 47, no. 2, 2006, pp. 375-393.

Pedota Paul. "How Can Student Success Support Teacher Self-Efficacy and Retention?" *Clearing House: A Journal of Educational Strategies, Issues and Ideas*, vol. 88, no. 2, 2015, pp. 54-61. doi: 10.1080/00098655.2014.998600.

Salzberger, Isca, Gianna Henry, and Elsie Osborne. *The Emotional Experience of Learning and Teaching*, Karnac Books, 1993.

Stanbury, Stacey, Mary Alice Bruce, Sachin Jain, and John Stellern. "The Effects of an Empathy Building Program on Bullying Behavior." *Journal of School Counseling*, vol. 7, no. 2, 2009, pp. 1-27.

Stein, Helen. "Steven Tuber: Attachment, Play, and Authenticity: A Winnicott Primer." *Clinical Social Work Journal*, vol. 38, no. 2, 2010, pp. 248-249. doi:10.1007/s10615-0100276-3.

"The Ontario Curriculum: Elementary." Ontario Ministry of Education, 2016, www.edu.gov.on.ca/eng/curriculum/elementary/kindergarten.html

Tsang, Kwok. "Emotional Labor of Teaching." *Educational Research*, vol. 2, no. 8, 2011, pp. 1312-1316.

Watkins, Megan. "Teachers' Tears and the Affective Geography of the Classroom." *Emotion, Space and Society.* Vol. 4, no. 3, 2011, pp. 137-143.

Winnicott, D.W. "Group Influences and the Maladjusted Child." *The Collected Works of D.W.Winnicott*, edited by Lesley Caldwell and Helen Taylor Robinson, vol. 5, 1955-1959, Oxford University Press, 2016, pp. 45-54.

—. "Mind and its Relation to the Psyche-Soma." *British Journal of Medical Psychology*, vol. 27, no. 4, 1954, pp. 201-209.

—. "Mirror-Role of Mother and Family in Child Development." *The Collected Works of D.W.Winnicott*, edited by Lesley Caldwell and Helen Taylor Robinson, vol. 8, 1967-1968, Oxford University Press, 2016, pp. 211-220.

BOOK REVIEWS

Varieties of Solace

Irene Papoulis

All of this year's books circle around issues of healing, a richly faceted subject always dear to members of the Assembly for Expanded Perspectives on Learning. Nate Mickelson reviews Burt Bradley's *After Following*, in which the poet takes solace in writing his own meditations on the work of other poets; Paul Puccio responds to Peter Khost's *Rhetor Response: A Theory and Practice of Literary Affordance*, which explores the potential connections to life that literature could provide readers in our classrooms and beyond; Erin Frymire addresses Jessica Restaino's *Surrender: Feminist Rhetoric and Ethics in Love and Illness*, which combines rhetorical analysis and personal writing to address the agony of terminal illness; and Tracy Lassiter reviews Terese Marie Mailhot's *Heart Berries*, a memoir in which the writer finds catharsis in exploring her traumas by writing about them.

While the authors and reviewers of these books have a diverse range of interests, they have all inspired me to reflect on how much the brutality of the world gets to all of us, inevitably, and how much we need outlets and support for acknowledging our reactions. They've made me think about the fact that as a teacher I sometimes focus too narrowly on the tasks I assign to students, and the skills they will acquire by performing those tasks. They remind me of what I know but sometimes forget: that acknowledging underlying emotions and life-realities can make our classrooms, as well as our lives in general, more life-affirming, more nurturing, and ultimately more productive.

These books all point to the profound value of writing and storytelling. As many students spend less and less time reading for pleasure, schools can be the one place where they learn to respond deeply to the stories of others, and to be able to compose and rethink their own stories. These books encourage us, and our students, to embrace and enter written stories, and to view the practice of doing so as an emotional as well as an intellectual exercise.

In theory, we in the academic world have become increasingly aware that the emotional and the theoretical are very much entwined. Yet it can be a giant step from that awareness to an actual welcoming of real emotions into our own as well as our students' writing and thinking. These writers demonstrate the complexity, the difficulty, and the rewards of doing so, and our reviewers provide careful and interesting readings of the process. Both authors and reviewers inspire us to approach the intimacy of storytelling with care and empathy, being fearless in our openness to ourselves and others.

Many *JAEPL* readers deeply understand already the need to acknowledge students' emotional lives in the classroom. These wonderful books not only offer reminders of the need for healing practices; they also provide nuanced approaches that can be useful for living as well as teaching. They inspire me, and I hope you, to take another step from wherever we are toward a richer understanding of the solace that reading and writing can offer us.

Bradley, Burt. *After Following: Poems.* Homebound Publications, 2019

Portrait of a Western Poet in Progress

Nate Mickelson
New York University

The town of Powell is located in Wyoming's northwest quadrant, midway between the Big Horn National Forest and Yellowstone National Park, twenty-five miles south of the Montana border. Home to slightly more than 6,000, the town sits on desert land reclaimed for agriculture in the early twentieth century. It is named for explorer and engineer John Wesley Powell though he never visited the region. (Somewhat more troublingly, the town is also near-neighbor to the site of Heart Mountain Relocation Camp, one of ten camps where the US government interned Japanese Americans during World War II.) Summer is Powell's best season. Dry, hot days stretch into cool evenings, and light lingers past 10 PM late into August. The town smells of sugar beets in the fall as farmers stockpile their harvest for shipment and processing elsewhere. In winter—even through early spring—temperatures drop well below 0° Fahrenheit and bright white snow stretches toward mountains in all directions.

Burt Bradley explores these and other aspects of Powell and its surrounding region in *After Following*, his ambitious and charming first collection of poems. Winner of the 2018 Homebound Publications Poetry Prize, the collection honors a pantheon of the poet's influences and inspirations. Bradley names his mentors in his poem's titles and then transforms their characteristic styles to suit a rural Western context. In "Sagebrush Sutra (after Allen Ginsberg)," for example, the poet refigures the high desert around Powell as an epic backdrop by injecting some of Ginsberg's playful disruptiveness:

> It has something to do with jet engines
> and a little with unmarked cars.
> It is the absolute proof of $E=MC^2$,
> the certitude in the uncertainty principle,
> and concrete evidence of God's existence.

Even if the desert "doesn't care a fig about us," the poem concludes, "if we ignore it, we miss / one of the gateless gates to heaven / on earth." The poem "Falling (after Keats)" achieves a similar effect by retooling the British poet's dense abstractions via multisensory immersion in a Wyoming sunset:

> sealed and unsealed with a whiff
> of some primeval perfume,
> vermillion scented, a hint of plum
> dissipating into the deep red end
> of things turning purple, indigo,
> these last swaths of color on the horizon.

To write "after" another writer is to bring their characteristic style to bear on new subject matter through sometimes appreciative, sometimes rivalrous affiliation. In addition to Ginsberg and Keats, Bradley writes "after" Neruda, Picasso, T.S. Eliot, Edgar Allen Poe, and Jack Kerouac, among others. (Los Angeles poet Wanda Coleman's "Retro Rogue Anthology," rewriting Mark Strand's influential, and predominantly white male, anthology *The Contemporary Poets: American Poetry Since 1940* from a woman-of-color perspective, is perhaps the most transformative example of this technique.) "Following" another writer's example is doing something different and perhaps less fraught. As Bradley observes in the closing lines of "In the Footprints of Whitman," *After Following*'s final poem: "It's not about catching up with me or him, / it's just about following." No doubt the Brooklyn poet would welcome this kind of following, especially given his admonition in *Leaves of Grass* that "He most honors my style who learns under it to destroy the teacher," if it breaks new ground. If Bradley celebrates the writers and artists he names, he also shows his independence from their tutelage through the poems he has created under their influence.

Imitating models is a generative practice with a long history. The classical rhetorician Quintilian, for example, proposes *imitatio* as method for using model texts to generate writerly invention (Kalbfleisch 41). As Elizabeth Kalbfleisch explains in a recent essay for *Pedagogy*, Quintilian's concept, if not the term or its classical meanings, continues to inform the ways reading and writing are taught, in particular in college composition. She describes imitative reading strategies such as memorizing, reciting, and paraphrasing as "fluid practice[s]" that enable students to understand and internalize other writer's techniques and ideas (48). John Muckelbauer theorizes a further possibility that mirrors Bradley's experiments. Applying insights from Derrida and Deleuze, he notes that imitating models involves two simultaneous moves: repeating their methods and introducing variations. Recognizing the generative tensions between these moves, Muckelbauer advocates for having student writers approach model texts as sources of inspiration: "what is propagated in inspiration's infectious movement from the model to its copy, is precisely the dynamic of losing oneself in response to a model, of becoming something other than oneself" (74). Indeed, as Bradley demonstrates, imitation allows writers to immerse themselves in the "singular, affirmative rhythm of transformation" brought into being by the text they are considering (Muckelbauer 75).

After Following tells the story of Bradley's development as a poet through his engagement with transformative models. As the poet notes in "An Open Apology to Robert Haas on the 25th Anniversary of Janis Joplin's Death," he started writing in earnest while "driving a forklift in and out / of refrigerated warehouses" during a first job after high school. Soon after, he entered a years-long period of searching for form "head first, ass up like some Looney Tunes character, spinning the contraption [of poems] into a cocoon" ("Belated Letter to James Wright"). Encountering the everyday speech rhythms and intimate subject matter of James Wright's poems proved a decisive influence. As he signals in a poem written "after" one of Wright's own influences, William Carlos Williams, the older poet's work helped him gain confidence: "The work day still panting / after me . . . // I feel for a few words, all ill-fitting / but enough for this to depend upon" ("After Work (after William Carlos Williams)." Looking back over his years of writing, Bradley notes that perhaps the most important lesson he has learned from his mentors is to embrace the possibility of "sitting in the pure poetry / of this Being all alone" ("A Long Way from Amherst (following Emily Dickinson)."

Bradley taught writing at Powell's Northwest College, one of Wyoming's seven community colleges, for more than 30 years before retiring in 2016. His tender appreciation for Wright, Williams, Dickinson, and others suggests he values imitation just as much as a teaching method as a practice of writing. Further evidence of this possibility comes in a poem titled "Why No One Writes Like Thomas Wolfe." As the poem builds steam, Bradley decries the warping effect of some writing programs:

> We've got nice, accredited creative
> writing programs now, where you learn
> all about hooks and pithy topic-sentenced
> short paragraphs, suddenly bereft of adverbs,
> and for God's sake keep it succinct. Remember
> the real work lies in the pitch, the query
> letter, the marketing strategy.

Kalbfleisch and Muckelbauer (not to mention Quintilian) would likely agree to the alternative Bradley models: Have students read, and then have them imitate as a way to discover techniques and rhythms that will open up new possibilities for their work!

A few of Bradley's poems fall flat, in particular those that play too neatly with their model's well-known elements. "Sometimes a Raven (after Poe)," for example, aspires to Poe's dense, haunting, repetitive sounds but offers what I hear as a distracting muddle of l's: "It's difficult to imagine / my day life, the kids, wife, bills. / my dull job in a fluorescent office, / and bills, hells bells! bills." And the collection's opening poem, an invocation of Yeats's remarkable "The Second Coming," jangles with faux-earnestness: "So, I pray for your help, my dear Yeats. / I'll take one fake fairy, or one occult fib, / even some mumbo-jumbo automatic writing— / new metaphors or dead—for any vision: / even with glasses, rose-colored or cracked / is better than no vision at all" ("An Open Prayer to W.B. Yeats").

Despite these wrong notes, *After Following* is filled with moments when Bradley's imitation of his mentors and his careful attention to his corner of the West combine to wonderful effect. His dexterous evocations of the Wyoming wind are a case in point. "Blizzard (following Katagiri Roshi)" immerses the reader in a chilling winter gale:

> Strung out like shredded sheets, this snow
> unnerves things, a whitened wind
> at full strength: seen! at last.
> . . .
> Even with squinting eyes
> and grimacing face, with numbed hands
> and frozen feet I feel this constant
> manifestation of beauty itself.

"The Beat Season (after Jack Kerouac)," the title a play on Powell's sugar beet harvest, fills the page with a fall breeze:

> In the grace and beauty of the dying season,

the wind glasses into light in clear rectangular sheets,
while the light brilliances back into wind,
of serrated ocher, the stuff of lost leaves
losing their sense of limbs, disembarked and sap free—
a woodless vision that torments ex-lumberjacks and ex-squirrels.

One hopes that Bradley's students are busy, somewhere, imitating his imitations, transferring and transforming the techniques they developed in his classes to the contexts and purposes that matter for them now. Poets and writing teachers alike have much to gain from *After Following*'s careful mirroring of such a wide range of poetic styles and preoccupations, as well as from its encyclopedia of influences. Indeed, Bradley invites us to visit two vast libraries in these poems: one stocked with books and art and music he learned from as he developed his craft and one that expands from horizon to horizon and mountain peak to mountain peak around Powell. Both are worth the trip.

Works Cited

Coleman, Wanda. "Retro Rogue Anthology." *Mercurochrome*, Black Sparrow Press, 2001, pp. 163-244.

Kalbfleisch, Elizabeth. "*Imitatio* Reconsidered: Notes toward a Reading Pedagogy for the Writing Classroom." *Pedagogy*, vol. 16, no. 1., Jan. 2016, pp. 39-51.

Muckelbauer, John. *The Future of Invention: Rhetoric, Postmodernism, and the Problem of Change.* SUNY Press, 2008.

✦

Khost, Peter H. *Rhetor Response: A Theory and Practice of Literary Affordance*. Utah State UP, 2018

Paul Puccio
Bloomfield College

> I've dreamt in my life dreams that have stayed with me ever after, and changed my ideas: they've gone through and through me, like wine through water, and altered the colour of my mind.
>
> —Emily Brontë, *Wuthering Heights*

This epigraph, borrowed from a book that has long figured in my imaginative life, expresses, by way of analogy, how literature lingers and unfurls in my mind. Like actual dreams, literary texts generate many of the landscapes and persons and situations that materialize in my consciousness. I may close a book after reading, but I rarely close out what breathed and pulsed in me as I read. Ever since I was a boy, my reading has washed over the rest of my life, shaping how I understand myself and the world, and also crossing, in analogies and references, into my acts of communication. Peter Khost describes this particular form of bookishness as "the wakeful dreaminess of living through texts that change us" (179).

Khost's *Rhetor Response: A Theory and Practice of Literary Affordance* is broadly concerned with readers who find meaning or pleasure in literary material and how they may use those materials for their own rhetorical purposes. Literary affordances are "applications of features of literary texts to unrelated rhetorical situations" (6). Occurring consciously or unconsciously, these applications emerge in the process of reading and writing. When we make a literary affordance, we respond not *to* but *through* a text, without concern for the text's critical reception, the author's intention (if that is even knowable), or the text's meaning (46). Khost focuses on literature because "people are already inclined to make affordances of nonfictional texts" (12); we don't hesitate "using" nonfiction, but the discipline of literary studies (at least since the twentieth century) has taught us to favor interpretation above any other kind of engagement with a text. Furthermore, readers are more inclined to become invested personally with literature because it "[moves] our emotions, [stretches] our imaginations, and [becomes] interwoven with or assimilated into our own life narratives" (13).

This is more than a matter of relatability (*e.g.*, "My family is right out of a Dickens novel," or "I'm just like Emma Bovary"—a declaration that would be particularly tangled because Emma Bovary herself understands her life through the romantic novels she's read). Relatability is a one-way street, while a literary affordance reflects (or creates) a dynamic relationship with a text, "toggling between real and fictional worlds" (93). To extend the traffic metaphor, a literary affordance is more like a roundabout, with multiple entrances and exits and the endless possibility of returns, re-circlings, and recursions. "Something about our relationship to certain literary features holds us in a special way," Khost explains, "which I suspect is partly a result of the dialogic nature of the nearness and distance of these textual features to our lives" (179).

One of the most familiar literary affordances, as Khost points out, is Freud's use of the Oedipus myth to explain a child's unconscious desire for the parent of the other sex. Freud is no more concerned with interpreting *Oedipus Rex* than Sophocles wrote with an eye on psychosexual development. Nevertheless, Oedipus and Jocasta are the narrative "traffic" through which Freud develops and proposes his theory. Another handy example of a literary affordance is the epigraph at the top of this review, a sentence that I slipped out of its original context (Catherine Earnshaw explaining why she will always love Heathcliff, despite her marrying Edgar Linton) and into my own quite different rhetorical situation.

Khost describes *Rhetor Response* as "a humble guide and companion" (211); in that spirit it does not argue for a theory or practice that comprehensively supersedes any other; rather, it invites readers, as Peter Elbow might say, simply to *believe* in this distinctive form of textual engagement. In prose that is lucid, colorful, and, as we might expect, full of illuminating literary affordances, this book gracefully balances the personal with the theoretical and the pedagogical. Throughout, Khost explores the "fuzzy energy" (xi) that vibrates between his life and his reading; particularly in a series of "interchapters," he engages in a practice that he calls "autotextography" (a neologism that is cousin to "autoethnography"). In these sections, he explains, "I briefly narrate and analyze what a particular literary text or set of texts has done for me and how these effects have become assimilated into my rhetorical and pedagogical repertoire" (12).

The book situates its subject within several theoretical frames. Khost provides an overview of affordance theory as articulated by James Gibson and other ecological psychologists who emphasize that an affordance occurs within the relationship between a person (or animal) and the environment. One may make an affordance of an object that was never intended by its creator (*e.g.* standing on a chair to reach my copy of *Wuthering Heights* on a high shelf). Khost also reviews the major theoretical claims in reader response criticism and in ethical criticism, both of which explore the relationships between reader and text. For me what is most compelling about Khost's work is that he developed it "primarily by reflecting on [his] own experiences and later by observing those of [his] students and . . . only thereafter wandering (and wondering) about scholarly references" (39). This attentiveness to his students and to his own literacy practices, as well as his trust in intuition (xi), embodies a way of knowing that is increasingly necessary in higher education, occupied as institutions have become by quantitative inquiry and judgment.

I will explore the institutional and pedagogical possibilities for literary affordance later in this review. But here I'd like to respond to his invitational spirit by offering an "interchapter" with an autotextography of my own.

* * *

Ever since I was 11 or 12, I've been reading Gothic literature. Throughout grammar school and high school I read this genre indiscriminately, hardly distinguishing between properly literary tales like "The Turn of the Screw" and *Jane Eyre*, popular novels like *The Haunting of Hill House* and *Burnt Offerings*, and Gothic romances like *Rebecca* and *Nine Coaches Waiting*. I particularly enjoyed what I later learned literary critics named the "female Gothic" narrative: a young orphaned woman secures a position as governess (or librarian or secretary) in an isolated (and usually castellated) house full of mysterious rooms and menacing characters, one of whom typically marries her at the end.

What would attract a young boy to these books?

The answer to this question—as in so many Gothic novels with their tangled domestic histories—lies in my own family's story. After having lived for many years in a cozy ethnic neighborhood in Philadelphia, my parents moved to a new suburban development in New Jersey. A foreign and frightening place it appeared to them, especially my mother who had neither car nor job. She was a stay-at-home mom, and I was her stay-at-home son. New Jersey seemed perilous to her, with its wide streets, its vacant fields, its unfamiliar people. Her anxiety over this strange new place made her very protective of me, especially after my Byronic brother enlisted in the navy when I was ten years old, and I was the only child at home. It didn't help that I was small, unathletic, bespectacled, and skittish—in other words, ostentatiously defenseless.

In her excitably maternal imagination, nameless dangers lurked behind shrubs and at the bottom of cul de sacs and in the vast stretches of parking lots. These were no places for me; after all, I wouldn't even be able to *see* an assailant if I lost my glasses. There were no other children my age close by, and she considered any destination that required my crossing a road far too dangerous. The only safety was inside the ten rooms of our house and within our fenced back yard.

When not in school, I spent my days converting games for "two or more players" into activities for one child; reading books and imagining myself in their landscapes; and exploring every corner of the house that my mother daily cleaned. I knew precisely what was stored in each box neatly piled in the hall closet; I rearranged the bottles of shampoo and lotion in the bathroom by color; I alphabetized my parents' LPs; I organized my books according to height. Like those orphaned governesses, I was trapped in a house with nothing to do but uncover mysteries. The only problem was that there were no mysteries in my family's house.

Gothic fiction invited me into other houses where I could lose myself amidst hidden passages and cobwebby attics and forbidden doorways that led to unused wings with rooms where mirrors reflected dusty and shadowy corners; houses with rooms even whose names suggested the secrecy and quiet inscrutability of the past—the drawing room, the library, the morning room, the west tower, the conservatory. I read these books both for what they mirrored of my life and for what they offered that was so totally different. The frisson created by all the ambiguities in the Gothic moreover gave me a heuristic through which I would many years later come to understand my own childhood experiences: how home can be both a haven and a prison, how the flip-side of safety is suffocation, how rescue may only come in the arms of something (or someone) forbidden and allegedly dangerous.

These books also cultivated my reading tastes: as an undergraduate, I enrolled in every available course in nineteenth-century British literature; my doctoral dissertation focused on Victorian and Edwardian fiction. The impact of Romantic and Victorian writing on my prose I leave to you, dear reader, to discern.

* * *

Khost's institutional and pedagogical context is writing studies, and he compellingly argues that the practice of literary affordance not only broadens the scope of challenging assignments for students but also welcomes the expertise and passions of (especially non-tenure-track) faculty trained in literature who teach largely composition courses. He provides an astute analysis of the administrative predicament faced by writing program administrators and by work-seeking teachers with advanced degrees in literary studies, and he offers "literary affordance as an agreeable compromise," grounded in "the togetherness in support of the greater good" (119). His hope that "non-writing expertise" can be brought to "the service of writing" (121) reflects a strategic resourcefulness and a generous spirit of collaboration that can advance this professional field in collegial and intellectually inclusive ways.

I read this book, however, from a somewhat different perspective, namely that of a literature professor (albeit one whose teaching has been steeped in composition pedagogy). Over the past decade I've witnessed a dizzying decline in English majors, as well as a widening gap between student interests and abilities, on the one hand, and college-level reading and writing expectations, on the other. This has given me recurring doubts about the value of traditional engagements with my subject (such as "research" papers, argument-based analyses, and reviews of critical material). How effective are these assignments for the majority of my students who struggle to read any literary text longer than 150 pages, who are unlikely to pursue an advanced degree in English, and who may take only one college-level literature course (mine)? To what extent do these traditional assignments interfere with a goal that I can't help but believe may be far more vital: encouraging them to regard the reading of literature as a regular, productive, and enjoyable practice?

In recent years I have developed writing assignments that, having read *Rhetor Response*, I would now say invite literary affordance. I've asked students to reflect on how literature has complicated or refocused their insights about issues important to them, how their lives help them understand elements of a literary text and how that text helps them understand elements of their lives, how they see the world differently because of a story or poem or play. I have wanted these assignments to prompt what Khost (after Richard Rorty) calls "unmethodical" reading, a response that is "inspired" by, in Rorty's words, "an encounter with an author, character, plot, stanza, line or archaic torso which has made a difference to the critic's conception of who she is" (52). We can't easily calibrate inspiration on a rubric, but that's no reason to exclude it from our teaching goals. Rorty's own literary affordance—his reference to Rainer Maria Rilke's poem, "Archaic Torso of Apollo"—reminds us of the super-charged potential of our engagements with art, in which contact can produce transformation: "You must change your life."

Peter Khost helps me appreciate just how valuable these "unmethodical" writing activities can be, and how they also participate in a history of readerly uses of literature. He also confirms my hope that once a reader "has done something desirable with or through a text, then this person may be more inclined to consider the text's meaning" (178). Perhaps one remedy to the crisis in the Humanities is to give our students the opportunity to experience just how much literature can alter the color of their minds.

✦

Restaino, Jessica. *Surrender: Feminist Rhetoric and Ethics in Love and Illness.* **Southern Illinois UP, 2019.**

Erin Frymire
Trinity College

I will admit I was, at first, reluctant to begin reading Jessica Restaino's book. I am interested in rhetorics of the body and am planning on a new course focused on rhetorics of health, so it seemed a valuable resource, but I was worried it would be too sad. *Surrender* is an ethnography of Restaino's deep friendship with Susan Lundy Maute, focused on the last few years of Maute's life with terminal breast cancer. Together, Restaino and Maute seek to understand a rhetoric of terminal illness and the role language plays in experiences that seem beyond words. Though there are indeed passages of the book in which Restaino's frank discussion of Maute's symptoms and vivid expressions of her grief make for emotionally difficult reading, one also gains a fuller sense of both Restaino and Maute, and the book is ultimately as much about friendship as it is about illness. Restaino's book is an engaging read that expands the boundaries of the scholarly monograph, traditional research methodology, and the very topics that we in academia are allowed to consider. Though I *was* at times overwhelmed by the grief and sorrow at the center of the book, Restaino's emotional honesty is what exemplifies the importance of personal investment in research and what can be achieved when we let go of the strictures of traditional research methods and allow ourselves to be deeply immersed.

Though worthwhile for its depiction of this friendship and research project, I found Restaino's book most valuable in how it questions long-accepted research methodologies and challenges readers to undertake similar projects and "make space for research and writing work that confounds or overwhelms us" (145). *Surrender* weaves together personal memoir with reviews of the scholarly literature and Restaino's arguments for new methodologies and ways of thinking the field might pursue. After the introduction, there are four chapters named "Stage IV" through "Stage I" to "In Situ," reflective of the classifications of cancer. Between chapters, Restaino includes interludes she titles "Bloodwork," which are brief excerpts of Maute's writings, interview transcripts, or bits of text message conversations. These sections display the intimacy of Restaino and Maute's friendship and provide a further glimpse into the ways in which they worked together to grapple with the challenges of Maute's illness and the questions hovering at the end of life. She explains that the title "Bloodwork" is used "to indicate this human flow as well as the experience of 'getting bloodwork,' a routine process in the life of any cancer patient" (7). In reflecting on my reading, it seems to me that "bloodwork" might also characterize Restaino's methodology. This work is, at times, quite literally bloody. She describes helping to care for Maute when she is hospitalized toward the end of her life and dealing with internal bleeding. Yet, beyond the very literal bloodiness, the depth and intensely personal nature of this research also makes this work "bloody." Restaino allows the research to go far beneath the surface; her pages expose intimate moments of friendship and personal reflections on grief.

Some of these intimate moments relate directly to Maute's experience of cancer and the various effects she suffered toward the end of her life. It is the effort to put language to these experiences that motivates Restaino's research in the first place. Together, Restaino and Maute cultivate a rhetoric of terminal illness. Physical pain, limited mobility, and the inevitability of an untimely death are areas of human experience that often lie beyond words. It is this inexpressibility that Restaino examines in partnership with Maute. She writes: "such struggle through loss in words is, indeed, worthy research, worthy of our attention if we want to understand how language functions to usher us through some of the most necessary, most profound experiences of our lives" (25). Rather than shying away from such difficult and physical work—work that may seem beyond the scope of writing and rhetoric—Restaino dives into this difficult territory and encourages readers to follow. Together, Restaino and Maute seek ways of talking about their experiences that move beyond common cultural metaphors of the valiant warrior fighting disease—a trope that Maute soundly rejects. In exploring the function of language in navigating terminal illness, they do not come to any firm conclusions, but instead find value in the questions themselves.

This valuing of uncertainty extends beyond the subject matter of Restaino's work and into the methodology itself. It is here that the book makes its most important contribution. Restaino's exploration of research methodologies is valuable reading for anyone involved in qualitative research and would be especially useful for those interested in health humanities, disability studies, feminist methodologies, or those who engage in ethnographic and/or community-based research.

The origin point of Restaino's project is inviting Maute to speak to her Rhetoric of Sport class and discuss her experience of her body as both an avid and talented athlete and a person with terminal cancer. This leads to what appears to have been, at least initially, a fairly standard qualitative research project. Restaino records interviews and gathers her and Maute's writings in response to her questions. However, Restaino soon feels the inadequacy of these methods: "While I had initially positioned myself as the qualitative researcher I vaguely knew how to be... I soon found myself struggling within the strictures of that role. I wrote interview questions, but we went off the script quickly" (26). It is this being "off script" that seems to best characterize the methodology that develops. Rather than sticking to her original plan—and the traditional boundaries and processes in ethnographic research—Restaino allows the process to unfold more naturally. While it still involves a great deal of writing and recording, she finds that she cannot maintain that kind of objective researcher position if she wants to be able to get at the experiences of terminal illness, friendship, and loss at the core of her project. Traditional methods are simply inadequate when research includes the bodily care Restaino provides for her friend. Rather than a scholarly distance, this work requires "increased focus on the researcher role in itself. My argument is thus that when we constrain ourselves methodologically we are also likely to constrain ourselves subjectively" (65). In freeing the project from such constraints, rather than a researcher-subject relationship, Restaino and Maute evolve into co-investigators in a project in which both are subjects. Restaino argues that the research subject "might be *both* researcher and participant, or perhaps even multiple, complex, and entwined subjectivities of each" (35). Their friendship and desire to understand and help one another become central to the methodology of the project, in which self-reflection or self-study are crucial for understanding the linguistic dimensions of the experience of terminal illness.

Though the book seems to spend rather too much time attempting to define itself—there are moments in each chapter in which Restaino rearticulates exactly what this book is doing—it becomes apparent that these efforts are necessary in Restaino's questioning and expansion of a research methodology that embraces uncertainty. Restaino hopes to carve out a path for others to follow—not necessarily or not only in the subject-matter, but in both carefully considering and thoughtfully incorporating love (and "blood") into one's research. Such research requires breaking down the traditional boundaries and rejecting any illusions of objectivity. Restaino explains that her "hope is that my sharing this project might encourage others to embrace similar kinds of research collaborations when they arise rather than to dismiss these exigencies as too emotional, too personal, or just not 'real' research" (15). Her book goes further than merely encouraging readers to take up this challenge. In her final chapter, she provides questions to scaffold a project like hers that "welcomes uncertainty, weakness, or even awfulness as valued, usable data toward the generation of particular kinds of texts and knowledge" (148). By providing guiding questions, Restaino may help future researchers to feel somewhat more comfortable with the potential discomfort of this kind of research.

Questions like, "Do I feel at times helpless?" (149) may be a source of encouragement for researchers to continue through feelings of helplessness or confusion, rather than abandoning a project as too difficult—or even "unacademic."

Restaino boldly puts her blood on the page in *Surrender* and leaves the reader thinking about the expanded possibilities for academic work and research methodology. By tackling difficult subjects with such care and humanity, Restaino shows us the value in pursuing the personal—of love itself—as a methodology. Thus, Restaino's work is taboo not (or not only) for openly discussing the bodily realities of terminal illness, but for her advocacy of love, loss, and friendship as topics deserving of serious scholarly attention.

✦

Mailhot, Terese Marie. *Heart Berries: A Memoir.* Counterpoint, 2018.

Tracy Lassiter
University of New Mexico

This was a difficult book to read.

It's not because the book is too long; it's a slender book of only 141 pages, including the transcript of an interview at the end. And it's certainly not because Terese Marie Mailhot's prose style is inaccessible—quite the contrary. With her writing, Mailhot easily draws you in and makes you feel every nuance of emotion she's expressing. What makes this book challenging is the impulse—the need—to stop constantly to make note of lines that hit like a boxer with a one-two punch. Consider these: "I punctured a friend's chest with a fork. He heard me when I said no" (104). "I wanted to know what I looked like to you. A sin committed and a prayer answered, you said" (10). "You were different from the men who made a challenge out of hurting me" (56). "I was the third generation of things we didn't talk about" (110). Even if I hadn't been making notes for this review, I would have been making note of these lines for their sheer intensity and lyricism.

In *Heart Berries*, Mailhot has created a memoir that's part journal, part postmodern expression. It sometimes reads like it's dispelling proverbs ("If transgressions were all bad, people wouldn't do them" [17]), sometimes like stream-of-consciousness, but these impressions are crafted. Her talent was polished by creative writing classes at New Mexico State University and an MFA writing program at the Institute of American Indian Arts. At one point, she signals this intentional crafting to her readers, stating, "I don't like neat narratives or formulas" (22). Hence, the book unfolds loosely in chronological order, interspersed with memories or flashbacks. But more than writing classes, perhaps what shaped Mailhot most was her difficult childhood, one of abusive parents, neglect, and hunger. She indicates this to her readers in the first chapter of the book, saying, "I'm a river widened by misery, and the potency of my language is more than human" (7).

Mailhot grew up in British Columbia on the Seabird Island Indian Reservation. Her father, artist Ken Mailhot, was an abusive alcoholic who was often absent from the home. Her mother, Karen Joyce Bobb, met Mailhot while he was in prison for abducting a young girl. Her mother also was an alcoholic who frequently was absent from the home, leaving Terese and her brothers to fend for themselves. Eventually during her teens, Mailhot was in and out of foster care (Lederman). She escaped her home environment to live with a man she married in her late teens; later, he would win custody of their first son while leaving her to raise their second son alone.

Heart Berries details these experiences and her on-again, off-again intense relationship with writer Casey Gray. It was after one of her breakups with Gray that Mailhot checked herself into a mental institution where she was later diagnosed with post-traumatic stress disorder, an eating disorder, and bipolar II disorder. At the facility, someone gave her a notebook, and the writing she began there eventually became *Heart Berries*, a New York *Times* bestselling book. It's true that Mailhot is unafraid to depict the difficult events that happened to her, but she also is unabashed about sharing her own behavior during the course of her life. She doesn't shirk, for example, from telling us "I remembered I hit myself until there were bruises on both sides of my head…Those nights, I wasn't convinced I was crazy" (61). Through her story, Mailhot asserts that the raw and the dark stories are no less worthy of being heard in the world than any other, particularly because they reveal the lived experiences of those who endured traumatic experiences.

Scholars of various disciplines—including the humanities—are paying attention to trauma lately as the number of child and adult learners experiencing one or more form of traumatic experience enter our classrooms and workplaces. Trauma often is a factor in poor educational outcomes, work and classroom absenteeism, and the connection to other risky behaviors like drug use. The extreme end of untreated traumas is suicide, and the CDC reports that American Indian/Alaskan Natives (AIAN) are the highest population at risk of suicide in the country. Indeed, statistics from a recent CDC study indicate that, since World War II, AIAN men are 71% more at risk of suicide than any other population. For AIAN women, that increased rate is 139% (Bunker). Mailhot's story, then, becomes one of urgency, something she indicates when she says "Crafting truth to be bare as it feels was important" in an effort for her to feel "redeemed" and proclaim her survival (128, 127). In the interview that follows the memoir, Mailhot explains that one of her impetuses in writing her book was to refute the criticism about the "sentimentality" of trauma writing. Mailhot dives into writing about trauma head-on, saying "I took the voice out of my head that said writing about abuse is too much… by resisting the pushback, I was able to write more fully, and, at times, less artfully about what happened" (131). I was reminded here of the work of Melissa Febos, who also shares her story in gritty realism. Like Mailhot, Febos feels that despite the similarity in stories of abuse and trauma, every survivor's story is different. As Febos explains, "We are telling the stories that no one else can tell, and we are giving this proof of our survival to one another" (Febos 51). But don't call Mailhot's story one of "resilience." "It's an Indian condition to be proud of survival, but reluctant to call it resilience," she states. "Resilience seems ascribed to a human conditioning in white people" (7). Whatever she chooses to call it, *Heart Berries* becomes a powerful declaration: "Words I never knew to be—I am," Mailhot tells us. This sentiment makes me want to run to a dictionary, to discover new words I, too, can aspire to be.

Beyond serving as testimony to her survival, it appears Mailhot has another purpose. She relates the gritty details of her relationships because she feels her story, which is similar to so many other Indigenous women's stories, needs to be told. She feels her work is an effort against the "continuum of erasure" that tries to silence their voices (111). She makes a similar claim in the opening of the book when she states, "The thing about women from the river is that our currents are endless," and the stories emerging from those currents are a form of women's empowerment. Mailhot additionally remarks, "When I gained the faculty to speak my story, I realized I had given men too much…I stopped answering men's questions or their calls" (3). The theme of empowerment echoes in other comments Mailhot makes that are unapologetic about herself, such as when she says, "I wanted as much of the world as I could take, and I didn't have the conscience to be ashamed" (10). She eventually comes to grips with her past, her parents' treatment, her relationship with Gray, and her relationship with her sons. She currently teaches creative writing at Purdue University where she likely dispenses hard-earned bits of writerly wisdom, like this one: "Nothing is too ugly for this world" (22). Let us commence, then, in being brave, in telling our own tales, sullied and sordid though they may be.

Works Cited

Bunker, Theodore. "CDC: US Suicide Rates Highest Since WWII." *Newsmax*. 30 June 2019. https://www.newsmax.com/newsfront/suicide-rates-cdc-report/ 2019/06/20/id/921269/.

Febos, Melissa. "The Heart-Work: Writing About Trauma as a Subversive Act." *Poets & Writers*, Jan.-Feb 2017, pp. 48-51.

Lederman, Marsha. "Writer Terese Marie Mailhot's Journey from Devastation to Voice of a Generation." *Globe and Mail*, 5 May 2018. https://www.theglobeandmail.com/arts/books/article-writer-terese-marie-mailhots-journey-from-devastation-to-voice-of-a/

CONNECTING

On "Showing Up" in Teaching, Tutoring, and Writing: A Search for Humanity

Christy I. Wenger

When I teach my upper-level students about the theories and practices of rhetoric and composition, I often start the semester by taking an informal poll. I ask students to choose which is more important in college writing classes: a focus on conventions and structure, or a focus on voice or individual expression. This is a trick question, of course, since I hope to prove to students that both are necessary, though the degrees to which they are necessary and in which contexts and at which times is the challenge I present for them to investigate throughout the semester.

A few outliers recognize the philosophical query presented by this poll and refuse to choose one over the other. But most students eagerly choose a "side" on the first day of class, approaching my challenge as a debate, as they've been well-trained to do over the course of their education. The majority of students side with conventions. As the semester progresses, we talk about why. We talk about how they are expected to master author-evacuated prose as English majors and minors and to avoid personal pronouns in their writing. We talk about their success mastering these conventions, continual achievements that paved the way for students' entry to my upper-level writing seminar. We talk about how they often feel pressure to write papers on topics their teachers "like" and frame arguments in ways consistent with their teachers' readings of texts. We talk about where that pressure comes from and how it shapes their writing. As we read more and more composition theory, including Joseph Harris and Michele Eodice but also David Bartholomae and James Berlin, the majority of my students revise their original viewpoints.

Time and again, the same majority that ardently supported conventions at the beginning end the semester championing voice. Students don't simply abandon the importance of conventions—they confirm their desire to be read and understood—but they do develop a hearty respect for voice. This shift is a hallmark of the class likely because of how it is situated in our program as one of the first and few courses to ask students to come to terms with who they are as writers and who they want to be; to question and analyze writing and not only to do it.

This semester, I asked my students who shifted their views to tell me *why* voice is important. They collectively described voiced writing as "real" and "full" and "meaningful." When I asked them what those descriptors meant, they admitted they were abstract but nonetheless important. Naming voice in writing is hard. Peter Elbow agrees and has called voice variously a "warm and fuzzy word" (1), raising suspicion in a university that valorizes defined and discrete skills, and, even worse, a "swamp" (11), particularly when it is used as a measure of authenticity.

When supporting the importance of voice, my students aren't so much arguing for authenticity as they are pointing to another term Elbow uses: resonance. Resonant writing reveals and connects with lasting impact. The "sound of resonance" in writing is "the sound of more of a person behind the words" (12). When I mentioned Nicole Wallack's recent naming of voice as a "showing up" in our writing to these students, they agreed that Wallack's term felt less abstract and somehow more modern. Showing up means being present in our writing, being a presence on the page. We can do this in many ways: by including personal experience as evidence; creating a distinctive voice; owning a sense of identity or self and connecting that to our ideas and arguments; other distinctive moves that explicitly suggest the writer behind the text (Wallack 28-31). This isn't a search for authenticity so much as it is one for humanity, a present person behind and within the text who connects to the present reader.

The pieces collected in this section of *Connecting* all exhibit ways of "showing up" in writing. They do so by modeling how we might claim very specific, very material conditions of learning and thinking and speak from the authority of personal experience. They are full of voice. They show up by revealing the presence of their writers and by making intentional space for readers to show up in response, as a writer's presence begets the readers'. The writing contained within this section also offers practices that might help us think through the dynamics of a pedagogical praxis of "showing up."

First up is "Sylvia Wynter Over Tea." Coauthors and graduate research assistants Nicole Wilson, Angela Montez, and Sara Yiseul Chung write a triple-voiced narrative about their experiences working with black studies scholar and humanist philosopher Dr. Sylvia Wynter, O.J. in order to curate her archive. In this process of curation, they find inspiration to fashion their own, bricolaging their graduate studies experiences, their reading of field texts, and their personal experiences. Their effort to create an authorial harmony with solo parts instead of a chorus is their intentional means of "showing up." As they note: "This work is a practice in collective sameness-in-difference that opens the table to multifaceted voices and perspectives." These women's stories diverge, but their voices coalesce around the need to find a sense of presence in their fields of study and their commitment to a project that allowed them to get to know an author as specific and real, which affirmed their own presence as scholars and writers.

Like Wilson, Montez, and Chung, Christina M. LaVecchia and Cristina D. Ramírez also find meaning for their academic career pathways and studies outside of the narrow scope of scholarly study, outside of the university's formal structures. They also "show up" by joining their voices to explore the bridges between alternative-academic, "alt-ac," and academic work, bridges they argue that can be traversed both ways, so that alt-ac becomes a pathway for a dual-directional transfer of skills and not a way out. Because of their alt-ac experiences, LaVecchia and Ramírez "show up" dynamically in their present academic lives, since those experiences, they say, allow them "to engage in different and meaningful work, learn more about writing practices outside the discipline, and most importantly, operate in highly collaborative environments" where they feel "valued … as scholars/professionals."

Student voices pepper the last piece by Patricia Pytleski. Student writing tutors voice their experiences tutoring each other and outline the benefits of being on the "other side" of the tutoring table in this reflection on a novel method of tutor training, what Pytleski calls "Tutor to Tutor Teaching." Notably, students featured in this essay echo the importance of helping other students, tutors or not, find and establish their voice in their writing regardless of its generic function as a graduate application, academic essay, and beyond. Pytleski argues that tutor's individual reflections on their experiences tutoring each other form the most persuasive argument for including this sort of training alongside more conventional models such as observations and workshops.

Individuality and investment are evident in these pieces, testaments to these expert writers' ability to generate authorial presence. As my students would say, these pieces are full of voice, are "real" and "full." As teachers of our craft, this collection of essays in Connecting makes us think about how we might better invite our students to show up in their own writing, of how we might help students approach authorial presence as an invitation to appear as individuals, and to use their voices to address the connections between their lives and their ideas.

Works Cited

Elbow, Peter. "What Do We Mean When We Talk About Voice in Texts?" *Voices on Voice: Perspectives, Definitions, Inquiry*, edited by K. B. Yancey, NCTE, 1994, pp. l-35.

Wallack, Nicole B. *Crafting Presence: The American Essay and the Future of Writing Studies.* Utah State UP, 2017.

✦

Sylvia Wynter Over Tea

Nicole Wilson, Angela Montez, and Sara Yiseul Chung

Throughout the Spring and Summer of 2018, we fled the bounds of the university to sit at the kitchen table of esteemed Black Studies scholar and Humanist Philosopher Dr. Sylvia Wynter, O.J.[1] We were selected to work with Dr. Wynter through the Texas A&M "Wynter Project," following her flight from California to Texas, where she sought to continue her productions of critical work as a retired Stanford professor. As graduate research assistants, our charge was to help Dr. Wynter curate her archive, which included locating and assembling her research materials, as well as reading, editing, and revising her most recent scholarship.

Over many warm cups of tea, we conversed, worked, and moved in excess of these scholarly tasks. Our many conversations led us to see Dr. Wynter as a mentor and aca-

---

1. Sylvia Wynter, a Caribbean philosopher, playwright, novelist, and dancer, is an influential critical thinker whose work draws on Black studies, history, economics, literature, philosophy, and material science. Wynter's oeuvre is an ongoing project built since her participation in the anti-colonial struggles of the Caribbean between the 1940s and early 60s. She unpacks and critiques the ways in which the "ethnoclass" mode of our present global humanity misrepresents the human, by limiting it to specifically the European Man. Her theoretical framework urges us to move away from the colonized idea of modernity and the modern man that is deeply ingrained in Eurocentrism and seeks to de-colonize our minds and our modes of thinking.

demic mother who encouraged and inspired us to unsettle the university. At Dr. Wynter's home, we were able to escape, even if temporarily, the structures of power that can create a toxic environment for those of us who are considered *other* leading to unbalanced working hours, neglected care towards students of color, and discriminatory practices that favor individual productivity over communal labor and effort. At Dr. Wynter's home, we were freed from these structures of power that precipitated our complex feelings of scholarly inadequacy and anger.

Here, we share our inspiring conversations to reflect on our active engagement with each other and Dr. Wynter's decolonial praxis. We acknowledge that this collaborative piece could have been filtered through the voice of singularity, but utilizing the collective voice speaks to the ethos of the Wynter Project, which brought together divergent voices and peoples under the banner of mentorship, care, and fugitive scholarship. There is power in collective difference, in sitting together as one over tea, while maintaining our distinct positionality and interests. This work is a practice in collective sameness-in-difference that opens the table to multifaceted voices and perspectives. As laborers para-external to the university, we experienced a more rich and fruitful production of knowledge through the supportive communal environment of a non-traditional space. Together, we produced care-oriented work in the undercommons.

Tasting Grief: Herbal Tea and Sylvia Wynter's Necessary Bread

Nearly two years after the commencement of the Sylvia Wynter Project, I continue to parse Black women's kitchen table gatherings as a complex aesthetic. What grammar, I have wondered, fully expresses the dynamism of Black women meeting, laboring, and conversing at the kitchen table? As the origin narrative of the pioneering Kitchen Table: Women of Color Press suggests, for Black women always already at the edge of their "symbolic integrity," the kitchen table remains a force of personal, political, and social change (Spillers 66). While I have been meeting Black women (my mother, sister, aunts, and grandmothers) at the kitchen table for conversation, Sunday morning hairdos, and to learn and teach since girlhood, what did it mean to flee the university, enter the interior of Dr. Sylvia Wynter's home, and be seated at her kitchen table? What did it mean, to share time, space, energy, and the most delectable tea as Dr. Wynter and I moved through grief? In paying homage to Dr. Wynter, this reflection attends to the paradoxical conditions of possibility that precipitated being mentored and mothered by her even as she mourned the loss of community (upon relocating to Texas from California) and even as I mourned the loss of my womb.

In Spring 2016, I found Sylvia Wynter somewhere between fatigue and mayhem caused by microaggressions and growing health concerns. I found the critical theorist and humanist philosopher as I had found her contemporaries, Hortense Spillers and Saidiya Hartman, at a predominantly white institution (PWI). I found Sylvia Wynter while I was making peace with the reality that I had, in fact, lost the lone brilliant Black woman professor in the Department of English. In short, I found Sylvia Wynter on the page and while mourning what felt like compounding loss.

A Gender Theory course would serve as my initial introduction to Dr. Wynter. My excitement would be short-lived, as an advanced Sociology graduate student fractured the gravitas of the course's inclusive pedagogical design. "Do you find it strange," my colleague whispered, "that the only assigned reading by a Black woman is not written by her; instead, it is written *about* her?" Well sure I found this strange.

My colleague and I were both determined to discuss the omission during the next class session. Our objective was not to challenge course design, but, as the next generation of Black women academics, we did not want to ignore the silence. We wished to engage an organizing logic that allowed many amazing theorists (Foucalt, Lacan, Butler, Fausto-Sterling, Spivak and Rodriguez) to critique society, shape conversation, and challenge classroom praxes while absenting others. We sought to understand why Wynter's own work was voiced by Alexander Weheliye (a Black male academic and critical theorist) and other women of color theorists were entirely eliminated. That discussion never happened.

I was hospitalized, as exceptional pain, massive bleeding, and growing fibroids had attached to and crowded my uterus. I was unable to return to work, class, and life as I had known it. I would have a surgically invasive abdominal hysterectomy or, what I aptly mark, theft of my uterus, cervix, and fallopian tubes. During the recovery process, I would seek the voices of those Black women my professor had chosen to silence. Outside of that classroom and away from the university, Wynter, Spillers, and Hartman's texts were a healing salve allowing me to closely parse their words, trace their insurgent rhetorics, place my tongue on their theories, voice their discontent, and make audible the blues embedded in their discourses. But it was Wynter's description of the global "jobless archipelago," and its population of "life/unworthy of life," that bequeathed me a language to narrate the impact of medical apartheid in my own family and thereby transform silence into utterance. That is, bringing Dr. Wynter's texts and theorizing to my working-class mother's kitchen table helped me name the tyrannies my mother, grandmother, and great-grandmother were made to swallow as they navigated the fine line between abdominal hysterectomy as necessary medical intervention and a long history of Black women and forced sterilization. While seated at my mother's table, I gained intimate knowledge of what it means to experience myself through a lineage of wombless women. Three generations before me. Three unnamed and silenced Black women, and how lucky I am/was to be number four.

Two years after meeting Dr. Wynter on the page, and two years after losing my uterus, cervix, and fallopian tubes, I was standing in her kitchen. I was seated at her table. She encouraged me to reimagine my origin story—to locate a space where joy abides in the messiness of grief. Over herbal tea and sometimes through tears, I consumed Sylvia Wynter's "necessary bread." In her "Necessary Bread: Black Women's Literature" chapter, Akasha Gloria T. Hull states, "For a Black woman, being face-to-face with another Black woman makes the most cruel and beautiful mirror" (194). Especially when the moment is fleeting, reparative, effectual, transformative, and precipitates the sharing of deep, vast knowledge. And most certainly when Sylvia Wynter, the teacher you have waited your whole life to meet names you: Daughter.

I am convinced that Dr. Wynter and my meeting in the center of her home and in the middle of our grief, as we expanded the restorative power of words and consumed the healing power of tea, was part prophecy, part foresight, and wholly necessary.

English Breakfast: Studying Nineteenth-Century Literature as Praxis

A warm cup of tea with Dr. Wynter allowed me to reconsider my position as an emerging literary scholar. As a Korean student studying nineteenth-century British novels, I follow the footpath of Dr. Wynter and many scholars who aim to decolonize and disorient the Eurocentric standpoints of humanism and humanist studies. With them, I lament that the multifaceted and colorful variety of human groups and their origin stories are condensed and homogenized to a single genre, and I am concerned with how our society readily accepts the categories structured according to "evolutionarily pre-selected degrees of eugenic 'worth' between human groups at the level of race, culture, religion, class, ethnicity, sexuality, and sex" (Wynter 54). Thus, I want to add voice to unsettling our ways of reading and consuming literature. I believe in the power of literature being a primary platform where we can reflect the effort to decolonize our ways of perceiving the world. I see my attempt not as singular, but as a communal effort and a gesture of ethical care for others who want to unsettle norms.

Literature reflects our humanist history and philosophy as a set of knowledge based on "story-telling"; literature itself functions as a mode of telling origin stories, establishing certain images and ideas of human life. At times, these stories function as records and depictions of lives that enhance the image of the world that certain people *wanted* to represent. In this context, I believe that tracing the systematic operations of these divisions and classifications of humans in past literary works can help us understand how these literary productions contributed to solidifying systematic operations. Specifically, the nineteenth century and its novels are accomplices in producing the problematic idea and notion of "Man," making the white liberalist figure of "Man" as the default figure of human while the others are defined as being the Other; it is when people expanded on the idea of the liberal human, conflicts over social classes, gender, and de-humanizing institutions such as slavery and child labor persisted. The characters' categorization according to nineteenth-century norms of social class, gender, and race is a symptomatic function of the overrepresentation of valuable peoples of biological and economic standards.

Based on this perspective, my scholarly commitment goes to the "othered" characters that are neglected, orphaned, oppressed, gendered, marginalized and foreign. I want to examine how their otherness works to reify a certain type of humanness that society is willing to accept; I want to study how these othered characters are often gothicized and to understand their ontological functions. Approaching literary works from this angle and committing to the othered characters, I hope to build upon Dr. Wynter's theorizations and explore how reading literature of the past with a decolonized mind can be a process of re-illuminating different origin stories; it should provide the modern reader with a horizon of stories that we did not encounter before.

The expression "being human as praxis" (McKittrick 4) is what I want to hold on to while pursuing my research in literature. It leads us to question our lives, our knowledges and discourses because if we acknowledge that our beings are *praxes*, we also see that our productions of humanist history and philosophy are open to being (re)read and (re)viewed, to yield new meanings and values.

Rather than consuming literary works as a reflection and an engagement of humanity in the past, I suggest that we read them as *praxis* and trace how they continually work to foreground the existence of the "othered" to aid the narratological representation of "Man." I believe it is right to recognize this "always already" existence of the othered characters, and this knowledge should be the basis of our aim to disorient, destruct and re-construct ways of thinking and viewing our worlds, incorporating the voices of people from all kinds of groups; it is an ethical gesture and a work of care and love. Rediscovering the existence of others could potentially offer us a version of a story that open up a new literary horizon. I want to engage the othered imaginatively and question how the humanities would look if we are not basing our ontologies on the figure of the "Man" but rather on the ghostly, the monstrous, the fleshy, and the gothicized. As such, through literature, we can (re)write our understanding of ourselves as the collective "we" and multiple "genres of humans," unsettling the oversaturated and colonized modes of thinking. To quote Dr. Wynter, "this task – to set the human free – therefore demands that we must begin, for the first time, to track a complete version of our species' history as it had been performatively enacted from its origins" (Wynter and McKittrick 63).

Doing so, if I am to be fugitive in conventional academia, I proudly acknowledge that. And I urge and reach out to others to take part in this project, to (re)read and write literature as praxis, with the lens of care, ethics, and love of our multifaceted and beautiful humanist fruits of creativity.

Rooibos Tea: Dr. Wynter's Care as Critical Analysis

Before participating in the Wynter Project, I did not understand the integral relationship between community, care, and scholarship. Though I understood that intersecting research interests brought colleagues and professors together, I did not understand how these intersections produced communities of belonging, yet alone care, in the academy. Rather, pessimistically, I tended towards framing most professional interactions as strategies of advantage – another line on a CV, another publication, another potential job placement. Yet, even with an intense drive to do whatever I needed to succeed, I wondered about the value of human life in the academy, including my own deteriorating mental health, my friend, who had just attempted suicide, and the lives of Black Americans, which I studied and sought to represent.

In a system founded upon heteronormative, Western, White, Male scholarly formations of cold logic and rationality, I questioned if there were sites for emotionality and care within the university that were not simultaneously sites of racialized female denigration. It was alienating to wonder about the value of human life in the academy. As a result, I was bitter and exhausted. I did not want to live as as fractured being, negotiating the parameters of logic and care, within the university. So I was determined to leave this space, until I met Dr. Wynter.

It is perhaps telling that I found reprieve outside the university—in the home of a scholar while assisting in an archival project that moved beyond academic research into mentorship and care. From Dr. Wynter, I learned that the best and most radical of research demands care and community, even as these facets of research are disavowed in the popular imaginary of academic life.

Here, I share my journey to a better understanding of the integral relationship between community, care, and scholarship through the reproduction of two inspiring conversations I had with Dr. Wynter. Both conversations taught me to analyze the world in a ~~(non)~~*scholarly*, affective manner that focused on WE (rather than ME).

During our first meeting: Dr. Wynter advised that "we return to the 60s." Initially, I did not understand her suggestion. My confusion was not a result of misrecognizing the impact the 60s had on American civil society. But in the wake of Rodney King, Eric Garner, and Trayvon Martin, it seemed to me that the 60s were dead. When prompted, she explained that the 60s had a revolutionary atmosphere—"We" were rising together. The "we" referencing the global community of black scholars, artists, politicians, and laborers coming together to fight for their common humanity. I understood then and agreed—We should return to the 60s. I learned then that the best scholarship does not happen alone, absent of care or community. Rather, it is communities of belonging and communities of care that drive scholarship. Despite their status as scholars, artists, or laborers, the scholarship produced then and now is for them. It is for us. So that we may rise together.

The Parkland, Florida Shooting: Out of the concern Dr. Wynter expressed for Parkland, Florida students, she told me "Watch those kids." She said: "They are the future. They have the potential for so much change because they have gone through an experience that has changed each of them and brought them together indefinitely." I was silent. I felt in that moment that Dr. Wynter understood and knew something (about scholarship and life) that no one else would ever understand. Powerfully and affectively, she understood that the Parklands students were doing much more than politically protesting gun violence. They were coming together as a community. They were bringing the 60s to us. From this interaction, I learned that care allows us to access fugitive possibilities and ways of thinking. Dr. Wynter's care for the Parkland students and for humanity as a whole sharpened her insight in the Parkland protests. Her analysis was a (re)orientation of analysis: a way of understanding the world and people in a manner that did not dissect but rather blurred the lines between feeling, care, and intellect.

Soon after the culmination of the Wynter Project, Nicole asked, "What are you learning from the project?" I shared with her and Sara these two moments. From Dr. Wynter, I learned that community and care are integral to the production of knowledge—or at least, integral to the types of knowledges that open us up to fugitive understandings and critical lenses of analysis. While the toxicity of the university attempts to fragment us, care (for each other and for our fields of study) brings us together. In this way and in many more, care can be an affective/effective mode of critical analysis to unsettle the logics of the university that positions scholarship as individualistic, cold-blooded, and detached.

More Tea, Please

Through communion with each other and esteemed critical theorist Sylvia Wynter, we have witnessed the underbelly of the academy. The criminality of care is that it ruptures the Capitalist Machiavellian logics of the university to produce pockets of *otherwise* being and knowing. The narratives shared here textualize our fugitive journeys to care and community for the (re)production of an affective scholarship. Over one cup of tea, we discussed literature. Sara brought up the idea if it is possible to read literature in a different way, and together we asked, can we decolonize the way we read and think about literature of the past? Over the next, we discussed discourses of displacement. Nicole parsed the conditions that made meeting Dr. Wynter at the intersections of race, class, gender, nationality, and grief possible. Over another, we discussed care and its relationship to scholarship. Angela challenged the notion that scholarship need only be framed through a Western, White, Male understanding of attachment and analysis. As emerging female scholars of color, we hope our reflections have set the table for extended contemplations on the future of humanities scholarship that invites multifaceted voices and perspectives and brings into being an ethos of care. We invite all to enter, to sit, to share with us a cup of tea.

Works Cited

Hull, Gloria T. Hull. "Researching Alice Dunbar-Nelson: A Persona and Literary Perspective." *But Some of Us Are Brave: Black Women's Studies*, edited by Gloria T. Hull, Patricia Bell-Scott, and Barbara Smith, 2nd ed., Feminist Press at the City University of New York, 1982, pp 189-95.

McKittrick, Katherine. "Yours in the Intellectual Struggle: Sylvia Wynter and the Realization of the Living." *Sylvia Wynter: On Being Human as Praxis*, edited by Katherine McKittrick, Duke University Press, 2015, pp. 1-8.

Scott, David. "The Re-Enchantment of Humanism: An Interview with Sylvia Wynter." *Small Axe*, no. 8, 2000, pp. 119-207.

Spillers, Hortense. "Mama's Baby, Papa's Maybe: An American Grammar Book." *Diacritics*, vol. 17, no. 2, 1987, pp. 64-81.

Wynter, Sylvia. "Forum N. H. I. Knowledge for the 21st Century," *Knowledge on Trial*, vol.1, no. 1, Giant Horse, Inc., 1994, pp. 42-73.

Wynter, Sylvia and Katherine McKittrick. "Unparalleled Catastrophe for Our Species? Or, to Give Humanness a Different Future: Conversations." *Sylvia Wynter: On Being Human as Praxis*, edited by Katherine McKittrick, Duke University Press, 2015, pp. 9-89.

✢

The Versatility of a Rhetoric and Composition Degree: Tales from Former Postdocs Outside the Field

Christina M. LaVecchia and Cristina D. Ramírez

As rhetoric and composition doctoral students head out onto the job market each fall, they are understandably anxious about what their future holds. In the past decade, the academic job market has shifted from a traditional timeline with predictable openings to an unpredictable space with fewer opportunities. According to Jim Ridolfo's rhetmap, only 220 jobs were listed in 2018-19, compared to the 287.8 average number of jobs annually posted over the last 5 years.[2]

Those seeking jobs each year may ask themselves, what jobs will I qualify for—where I can truly utilize my skills and passion for teaching, learning, and research? Although it's often assumed that most job seekers will envision an R1 tenure-track position as the answer to these questions, some may see themselves looking at jobs not just outside of the traditional tenure-track lines, but outside of academe altogether. Others may be prioritizing personal and/or family choices that necessitate casting a wider net in terms of institutional and job types. In this piece, we seek to normalize a wider set of pathways for rhetoric and composition graduates and show that the skills they acquire during their graduate careers are highly valued outside academe.

We are two former postdocs who took this road less traveled. We reflect here on the unusual, out-of-field places our careers have taken us in order to (re)consider:

- What can we do with rhetoric and composition knowledge, expertise, and training? Further, what *is* the work of our discipline, and what can it become?
- How might rhet/comp training and skills transfer outside of the traditional higher ed faculty position? What does that work look like in other contexts?
- How could such work benefit you if you do return to the academy?

Both of our postdocs might be described as "alt-ac"—as, while they involved research, writing, and teaching/mentoring, they were not the typical higher ed position, let alone the kind of position advertised on the MLA *JIL* or rhetmap. At the time, being in these positions outside of our academic training seemed "less than" what was expected of us as doctoral graduates in our field. However, we came to realize that these were not "step down" positions, but adjacent, rewarding opportunities that enabled us to engage in different and meaningful work, learn more about writing practices outside the discipline, and most importantly, operate in highly collaborative environments in which we felt valued as scholars/professionals.

Looking back from our current positions (tenure-track at the University of Arizona and full-time at a small private university without a tenure system), we see how working in non-traditional and fast-paced settings enhanced our careers more than we could have imagined. We bolstered our critical thinking, maneuvered strategically in our work spaces and with colleagues, and imagined different and noncongruent ways to utilize our writing and research skills—specifically, in healthcare and federal think tank research, as you will read below. At first, thinking outside our comfort zones made us nervous, and at times, we felt unprepared for our situations because traditional graduate school pathways don't typically ask students to think outside the academy. But quite contrary to our fears, our skills in rhetoric and composition gave us the edge in being able to perceive work situations, projects, and studies from a writing perspective.

---

2. However, we recognize limitations on direct comparison of data from rhetmap year-to-year, as rhetmap's data sources have changed (from purely mirroring the MLA *Job Information List* composition/rhetoric category to later including the technical and business writing category; it also increasingly includes jobs listed only on rhetmap). In short, it's important to know that rhetmap is only a partial snapshot of the job market.

Through these experiences and in recognition of the shifting realities of the job market, we hold a vested interest in sharing and examining the many ways that rhetoric and composition graduates can not only work outside the discipline, but excel in many high-level roles and positions.

Our Stories

LaVecchia: Strong geographic constraints led me to consider a wide range of positions when I finished my PhD and went on the market: traditional tenure-track assistant professorships at SLACs; a WAC staff position; an online teaching position in graduate education for a department of Teaching, Learning, and Leadership; and staff positions in instructional design or research and college grant offices, to name a few. After a two year search, I was hired as a postdoc by a healthcare research unit at Mayo Clinic.

The Mayo Clinic Knowledge and Evaluation Research—or KER (pronounced "care")—Unit is a space that thrives on interdisciplinarity: clinicians, healthcare services researchers, clinical researchers, designers, statisticians, social scientists, study coordinators, and patient advisors, among others, all contribute to the work of the KER Unit. That work is the advancement of patient-centered care through researching and developing interventions for shared decision making, evidence-based medicine, and minimally disruptive medicine. Due to that interdisciplinary culture, I found a comfortable collaborative home in this fast-paced environment.

Before coming to Mayo, I didn't have a research background in health and medicine. So, what got me hired? At the time, KER was looking for a qualitative researcher and my doctoral coursework, attendance at the Dartmouth Summer Seminar, and orientation in a humanistic field with social science influences qualified me. More importantly, I conducted an informational interview with a unit member—which persuaded my principal investigator of my enthusiasm for the position and that I would fit well with the culture of the KER Unit. Looking back, it's tempting to attribute getting this opportunity to the luck of stumbling upon a place with the right culture and local need that also valued interdisciplinary perspectives. Yet, these same conditions land us jobs *inside* the field, too.

KER often operates like a think tank, and my rhetorical perspective was highly valued during brainstorming conversations, weekly huddles, and project meetings. Within KER we were encouraged to be involved in multiple projects (turn around, enter into a conversation about a problem someone is trying to solve, and all of a sudden you're an author, I'd joke), and I soon found myself pulled into a wide range of conversations. These included patients' experiences with care for unexplained and/or contested illnesses, the range of purposes of shared decision-making, the nature of conversations about cost or diagnostics in clinical encounters, measuring high-quality diabetes care, end-of-life decision making, and more. I often helped to advocate for storytelling and qualitative approaches; my perspective on communication was valued; my meta-understanding of my discipline and research practices was recognized; and it was seen as highly desirable that not only did I come ready to write and present on my own, but I could mentor other trainees in the unit on those critical skills.

Once I got my foot in the door with my postdoctoral appointment at KER, I found further opportunities to contribute my disciplinary perspective. Attending a welcome lunch hosted by the Mayo Research Fellows Association (a group supporting postdoc professionalization and socialization similar to many English graduate organizations), I let slip to one of the organization's officers that I was a writing specialist. She immediately asked if I would deliver a lunchtime workshop for their monthly series. I agreed and a few months later delivered an interactive talk in a dimmed lecture hall (that was also broadcast to the Florida and Arizona campuses) that demystified the common writing metaphor of "flow" and reviewed strategies for improving coherence at the document, paragraph, and sentence levels.

The director of the Office of Postdoctoral Affairs and Research Training attended my talk, remarked with enthusiasm on the "high added value" of my writing expertise, and invited me to offer additional "deeper dive" programming. Their office, I came to learn, was inundated with requests for writing support from postdocs, trainees, and graduate students—and crucially the director, an alumnus of a small liberal arts college, recognized the importance of our field's work. Thus I designed a four-workshop series on scientific writing in which I introduced participants to key ideas from rhetoric and writing studies (writing as a situated and social act; writing as a process); coached productive feedback practices and engaged participants in peer review; and explicitly discussed the expected conventions and moves of the IMRaD (introduction, methods, results, and discussion) genre, section by section. Much to my initial surprise, our discussions on the scientific paper genre were the most valuable part of the workshop for my participants. I had assumed that my (insider) participants knew more about this genre than I did as a humanist and would find such discussion a waste of time, but I soon (re)learned the value of my ability to analyze and demystify writing genres. This experience taught me about how scientists write and think. I also learned that writing teachers sometimes have allies in surprising places.

Ramírez: The domino effect of greater social and economic influences in the spring of 2009 that unfolded over a course of a year led to my failed national job search. Going on the job market outside the field, I wanted a position that would incorporate my research skills and experiences as a rhetoric and writing studies scholar. Not giving up the search, I became aware of a postdoctoral position opened on my home campus of The University of Texas at El Paso with a federally funded Center of Excellence, The National Center for Border Security and Immigration. With a focus on conducting research into the newest technologies along the border, the Center had just opened, and they were hiring for a postdoctoral full-time research position. The Center was also seeking to improve the experience and education of those who worked within the ranks of the Department of Homeland Security (DHS), such as Border Patrol and the Transportation Security Administration (TSA). With another researcher who held a doctorate in criminal justice, this post-doc was marked to conduct an education needs assessment of the entire Department of Homeland Security within a year's time. The Center valued not just the doctoral degree, but the skills that accompanied it. While this position was at the University, it was in a community foreign to rhetoric and composition.

In my first week, the committee noted that my skills in writing, reporting research, and developing curriculum, along with an understanding of educational programs—all grounded in my degree in rhetoric and writing studies—signaled the primary reason I was hired for the position. Further, they mentioned that my vast experience in presenting at national conferences was attractive to them because the findings of our research had to be reported to federal governmental agencies. I had found a position in which I could use the skills I had and also grow in terms of using them in a different setting.

The task that was placed before my research partner and me was to survey all five agencies of the Department of Homeland Security and, from the survey results, develop a curriculum for an associate's, and eventually a bachelor's, degree. A background in rhetoric and writing studies was immensely valuable at every stage of the research project, from developing and framing the questions of the study to testing the survey questions. As we were developing the survey questions, my research partner with a doctorate in criminal science had some understanding of the educational needs and desires of federal workers. We developed an instrument that contained fifty-two courses and subjects from five academic areas, such as mathematics and ethics, politics and the world, laws and law enforcement, public relations, and planning. While developing the survey, my co-researcher had not considered writing skills as a subject to include in the survey. Yet, with my background in rhetoric and writing studies, I knew that writing would be a valued skill among the federal workers, and so we included various iterations of writing skills from critical thinking/analytical skills to ethics, technical writing, interviewing skills, and English composition.

In the process of collecting the survey data, we visited forty-five DHS sites across the country, speaking to hundreds of groups of workers about the survey and what we intended to create from the data (Ramírez and Rioux 8). Conducting this kind of research was not included in my training as a graduate student; however, speaking to ten to fifty people or more and having to carefully explain the process of an assignment resonated with being in the composition classroom. By the end of the study, we had collected 5,122 surveys (Ramírez and Rioux 12). Graduate student assistants entered the data into a qualitative data software collection database, and as the numbers emerged, we were surprised at what they showed. Among the top listed subjects of the fifty-two listed, the surveyors ranked the top six subjects as critical thinking/analytical skills, ethics, technical writing, and English composition. As these numbers emerged in the data analysis, we had to shift our perception and conclusion about what educational skills are valued in the federal workplace. As noted, we predicted that criminal justice or management would rise to the top of educational needs. On the contrary, writing and communication skills were most valued. A quote from the published report of this study notes, "Two subjects that are consistently among the top twenty for these agencies are Technical Writing and English Composition. Also consistently listed is the subject Informational and Descriptive Oral Communication. The importance of these topics was reinforced through the informal interviews, roundtable discussions and focus groups. The researchers were told repeatedly about the importance of these skills" (23). The experience in this research gave even me a new understanding of my own skills and how they can function in the workforce. During our analysis and presentation of these results, my skill set in writing studies felt validated at every turn.

I brought these expert skills to the table in my postdoctoral position, and so the contributions I was able to provide when writing up and proposing some of the curriculum served the team well. At the end of the study, my research partner, Dr. Gail Rioux, also had a newfound understanding of the importance of writing and communication skills.

What We Learned

Beyond gaining invaluable skills outside of the normal composition educational setting, we were surprised, and our thinking was enriched, by a number of aspects of these experiences. First, in order to succeed, we learned how to denormalize our ways of thinking, writing, and doing—to more acutely understand what we bring to the table that's valuable outside the traditional disciplinary imagination of a writing classroom. Disciplinary enculturation can blind us to our skills and worth, making this a challenging shift in thinking. But we soon learned to articulate our value and to anticipate the ways in which we might contribute to a project—say, the impact a bread-and-butter rhetorical perspective can have on a conversation about a study (like, "Is the true purpose of coding these videos to *evaluate* or to *describe* this clinical interaction?" or "What kinds of questions are we asking?").

Learning how to be the outside disciplinary expert in the room who thinks in a different way than everyone else proved to be the true challenge of this work, but also one of its deepest rewards. Often, we were not merely the sole rhetorician or writing specialist but indeed the sole *humanist* in a conversation. This challenge isn't unique to those working outside the field—faculty at small schools who routinely have to collaborate across disciplines, WPAs and WAC directors, and grant and industry proposal writers also know this role well, to name a few. However, we soon realized that making a place for ourselves in unfamiliar work spaces, in which we often felt we were an ambiguous fit, involved critical rhetorical skills: evaluating the writing or research situation and figuring out why the groups were approaching a project in a particular way. For example, Cristina Ramírez was able to see the explicit need to ask a question about writing needs within the survey, which the political science researcher had not even considered. And in hindsight, had this focus to the questions been left off of the survey, the most important aspects of the educational needs assessment would have been left off and the curriculum would have been structured much differently.

What fortified our courage in these situations was discovering that the threshold for "expertise" plays out differently when you're in an out-of-field or industry context compared to when you're inside of the field. Inside the field, we typically don't make claims to expertise without years of research and (sometimes extensive) publications. However, outside the field, colleagues can (at times) grant an immediate recognition of the value of our most basic skills—writing up reports from raw data, asking questions from the perspective of a writer, tracking the congruency of the written word—which may allow us to bravely jump into arenas we might otherwise consider related to yet outside our skillset. For instance, Christina LaVecchia had little research or teaching background in scientific rhetoric and writing, apart from teaching two semesters of undergraduate technical writing and taking a graduate seminar in professional writing theory. Yet she was seen as an expert in scientific writing at Mayo and was able to leverage the opportunity to develop a scientific writing workshop series, as described above.

As a whole, we were impressed with the extent to which our colleagues outside the field were using rhetoric and writing in sophisticated ways. Indeed, while we in rhet/comp certainly develop expertise in and deep knowledge of rhetoric and writing, our field does not have exclusive knowledge of these domains and professionals outside of our field highly value these practices. Nonetheless, we want to stress that those schooled in rhetoric and composition have skills in teaching writing, structuring and producing writing, collaborative work, and peer mentoring others through writing projects small and large that are welcomed in industry and address their needs. Bringing the classroom to the boardroom—being able to pinpoint the use of the rhetorical lens in settings outside the academy, explain it, and harness it—was indeed seen as an incredibly valuable skill in our experience.

In short, we both found our skills and everyday work of writing were highly valued outside the field—at times, we perhaps felt more valued than at any other time in our careers. We found traction and thrived in these unusual spaces because we were able to contribute as mentors, project managers, grant writers, collaborators, co-authors, sounding boards, readers and responders of writing, and qualitative data collectors and analysts. While both of us have returned to traditional paths in the academy for rhetoric and composition graduates, we look back on our experiences not as detours but as important, formative, and beneficial periods of our careers and encourage others to follow in our footsteps.

Works Cited

Ramírez, Cristina D. and Gail A. Rioux. "Advancing curricula development for homeland security education through a survey of DHS personnel." *Journal of Homeland Security Education*, vol. 1, 2012, pp. 6-25. https://ijspre.org/advancing-curricula-development-for-homeland-security-education-through-a-survey-of-dhs-personnel

Ridolfo, Jim. "Market comparison." *Rhetmap: Mapping Rhetoric and Composition.* 2019. http://rhetmap.org/market-comparison/

✢

Writing Center Reflections: The Impact of Tutor to Tutor Teaching

Patricia Pytleski

Besides accessible locations, ample resources, and sufficient funding, an essential consideration for a successful writing center involves content knowledge and pedagogical training of the undergraduate and graduate student tutors. Most centers train their tutors with classes or programs highlighting best practices in writing and tutoring instruction and also encourage tutors to observe experienced tutors' sessions. Tutor training, tutors' observations of tutoring sessions, and the discussions that follow are useful to writing center training; students witness varied tutoring styles and methods and then can discuss and analyze their own tutoring process and choices. Even once tutors begin tutoring, their training continues, through ongoing meetings and discussions, guest speakers, and assigned scholarship.

As Kenneth Bruffee states, "Tutors learn tutoring 'techniques' by working with each other as writers and critics... As peer critics, in fact, they are genuinely responsible for each other's academic growth, and for each other's well-being in the class" (79). This collaborative sharing of perspectives and practices and their responsibilities to each other and to their tutees demonstrate the mission of my writing center of supporting scholarship, creativity, and composition on campus. As Director at Kutztown University's Writing Center (UWC), I have begun to supplement all of this conventional training with what I call "Tutor to Tutor Teaching." Tutors should draw from their own writing choices and experiences inside and outside of the center and share their knowledge and practices with student writers *and* other tutors during sessions. By tutoring each other, tutors create and enhance the shared practices of the writing center.

Here I hope to demonstrate the benefits of Tutor to Tutor Teaching. Essential to my reflection on this training method is not only relevant scholarship from sources such as Anne Ellen Geller and Elizabeth Boquet but also tutors' experiences as voiced by themselves, in their own words. The inclusion of a variety of voices, scholars, graduate and undergraduate tutors, as well as my own as director, is intentional: to literally voice the importance of Tutor to Tutor Teaching writing sessions on the success of campus writing centers.

In our UWC, tutors are encouraged to experience Tutor to Tutor Teaching, a hands-on authentic training that engages them in tutoring with other tutors, as they work together on their writing within sessions. Pedagogically, this training has proven that students often learn better or at least differently, collaboratively, from one another. I have begun encouraging all tutors to sign up for writing sessions after seeing its beneficial effect on the center's community and in later tutoring sessions.

Through their experiences working with students and with their peer tutors' writing, tutors start to learn what a difference they can make in the lives of writers as they are also improving their own writing and reflecting on their writing choices. In Bruffee's speech to peer tutors, in "What Being A Writing Peer Tutor Can Do for You," he states, "Being a writing peer tutor is related to all kinds of productive relationships among human beings. Your tutees learn from you, you learn from your tutees, you learn from the writing peer tutors you work with, and they learn from you" (5). Through tutoring collaboration, tutors and tutees reap personal and intellectual benefits, and tutors benefit from working with each other. In Tutor to Tutor Teaching, tutors put themselves on the receiving end of a tutoring session and benefit as writers *and* as tutors.

It is essential that tutors think about themselves as writers and draw from their own writing processes and writerly choices within their tutoring sessions, whether they are the tutor or the tutee. As Gellar and her coauthors note, "Those of us who educate tutors must be mindful as well, as we are in danger of forgetting one (at least one) powerful motivating factor that brings tutors to their work in writing centers: namely, their senses of themselves as writers... we believe their identities as writers can, will, and should influence their tutoring" (Gellar, Eodice, Condon, Carroll, and Boquet 72-3). Sudents should incorporate their writing selves, choices, and reasoning behind these choices into their tutoring sessions. In reminding our tutors that they were chosen as tutors partially due to their own writing experiences and successes and encouraging them to never leave their roles as writers out of sessions with other students, we are helping them to formulate their feedback to students around what has worked for them as writers.

When tutors put themselves in the receiving end of a tutoring session, they benefit as writers and as tutors. Most indicative of the success of Tutor to Tutor Teaching are the testimonies of KU's writing center tutors.[3] Heather was with the writing center first as an undergraduate student, then as a master's graduate assistant, and eventually as the GA Research Assistant and GA Manager of the writing center. Heather used Tutor to Tutor Training because of the pressure to perfect graduate applications: "As I was preparing my PhD applications in the fall of 2017, I wanted to make sure my writing sample was as clean as possible." She made two appointments with different peer tutors to focus on two different things within her writing: organization/ content and "narrative flow of the piece …[to] smooth out any areas of clunky sentence structure and mixed metaphor." Due to her knowledge of tutoring sessions to begin with, she was able to determine that she needed two different sessions to get the type of feedback she felt would be beneficial. Her prior knowledge and personal tutoring experiences in these two sessions helped her encourage students to tackle a few things at a time and perhaps return for more sessions to work on all writing areas of concern. Her experience as a tutor first, and then as a tutee, helped inform her tutoring processes immensely to encourage students to focus on a few things within each session.

Eddie, who held the same undergraduate and then graduate status as Heather, and also as the Research Assistant and eventual Manager, determined that his experience as a tutee informed his tutoring strategies afterwards and also improved the camaraderie and trust within the center; he shared, "If the staff understands that the singular goal is to help students find their voice through their writing, they will be able to support each other as they support their fellow students in their sessions." As an additional benefit, he said, "[when] the tutors all signed up for sessions with each other for their own work… not only does this reinforce the need for the UWC overall, but it shows the trust the tutors have in each other." Eddie's comments demonstrate the impact Tutor to Tutor Teaching can have on the environment and on the center's welcoming and trusting community. Tutor to Tutor Teaching of these two graduate assistants highlighted different experiences and revealed various benefits from their sessions as tutees: focusing on a few things within each session and the impact of the center's environment and tutors' sense of trust. Yet it is not only the graduate student tutors that engage in this practice and have shared their positive experiences; an undergraduate tutor, Greg, also shared his experience from the student side of the tutoring session as well.

Greg, a former undergraduate KU student now working on his MA at another university, stated that "One of the most important lessons I learned as a tutor … was to know when to ask for help on my own writing … I learned that there is no such thing as having 'mastery' over writing." Greg shared that even the students trained to teach others benefited from writing help and a tutor's objective look at his work. Greg stated that he benefitted when the tutor "helped me out of writer's block by going over my ideas … in brainstorming sessions… [and] helped me feel more and more confident in

---

3. All student testimony is IRB approved.

my writing and my voice by being both an encouraging tutor and an engaged audience for my work." Through Greg's experience being tutored, he saw firsthand the value of the writing process and of discussing voice and audience as a tutor. Through Tutor to Tutor Teaching, pedagogies were validated, writing choices were considered, analyzed, and discussed, and these tutors saw the positive impact of these sessions on the writing centers' sense of community and on its practices within sessions.

The testimonies of two graduate and one undergraduate writing center tutors, the related scholarship on collaborative learning and peer tutoring and my own prolonged study of its effect on the Kutztown University Writing Center all demonstrate that Tutor to Tutor Teaching benefits tutors' tutoring practices, their own writing, and the overall writing center community. I encourage all writing center directors to promote Tutor to Tutor Teaching within their centers as an essential supplement to their training but also as a pedagogical service to their tutors.

Works Cited

Bruffee, Kenneth A. "Two Related Issues in Peer Tutoring: Program Structure and Tutor Training." *College Composition and Communication*, vol. 31, no. 1, 1980, pp. 76–80.

— "What Being A Writing Peer Tutor Can Do for You." *The Writing Center Journal*, vol. 28, no. 2, 2008, pp. 5–10.

Geller, Anne Ellen, Michele Eodice, Frankie Condon, Meg Carroll, and Elizabeth H. Boquet. "Straighten Up and Fly Right: Writers as Tutors, Tutors as Writers." *Everyday Writing Center: A Community of Practice*. University Press of Colorado, 2007, pp. 72–86.

Contributors

Kathleen Tamayo Alves is Associate Professor of English at Queensborough Community College of The City University of New York where she teaches literature and composition. Her research centers on eighteenth-century literature and culture, biopolitics, and literary history. She has published and presented portions of her book-length project, *Body Language: Medicine and the Eighteenth-Century Comic Novel*, which explains how medicine shaped and is shaped by comic language through fictional dramatizations of female-specific medical phenomena, such as menstruation, hysteria, and pregnancy. (kalves@qcc.cuny.edu)

Kelly Blewett is an assistant professor of English at Indiana University East, where she directs the undergraduate writing program and teaches writing and pedagogy courses. Her essays, which explore writing pedagogy, reading, editorial practices, and feedback in the writing classroom, have appeared in *College English*, *CEA Critic*, *Peitho*, and *Journal of Teaching Writing*, as well as several edited collections. (keblewet@iu.edu)

Sara Yiseul Chung is a Ph.D. student in English at Texas A&M University. Her research examines how the "human" is imagined with depictions of otherness in realist and gothic fiction in the long nineteenth century. She is interested in finding possibilities of re-conceiving human ontology in fiction through theoretical engagements with critical race studies and lenses of the body and flesh, affect, and ghostliness. (yssarachung@tamu.edu)

Hella Bloom Cohen is an assistant professor of English specializing in postcolonial theory and Anglophone global literature, and serves as affiliated faculty with Critical Studies of Race and Ethnicity and Women's Studies at St. Catherine University in St. Paul, Minnesota. She is the author of *The Literary Imagination in Israel-Palestine: Orientalism, Poetry, and Biopolitics* (Palgrave Macmillan, 2016). Her current research entails reconciling posthumanist concerns with the historically humanist practices within postcolonial studies. (hrcohen2@stkate.edu)

Natalie Davey is a Toronto-based teacher researcher who has taught in mainstream and alternative classrooms at the secondary and post-secondary levels for two decades. She currently teaches in Humber College's School Within A College (SWAC) program. Davey's research and writing interests include Narrative Analysis, Arts-Based Research practices, and alternative pathways to post-secondary education. (natalie.davey@tdsb.on.ca)

Jared Featherstone directs the University Writing Center and teaches in the School of Writing, Rhetoric, and Technical Communication at James Madison University in Virginia. He has been practicing meditation for 24 years and teaching mindfulness for over a decade. Both his teaching and his research involve the integration of mindfulness practices in learning environments. (feathejj@jmu.edu)

Erin Leigh Frymire is a Lecturer in the Allan K. Smith Center for Writing and Rhetoric at Trinity College in Hartford, Connecticut. She teaches courses in rhetorics of law, activism, and medicine, as well as first-year composition and writing in the disciplines, and co-directs the Global Health Humanities Gateway. Her scholarship focuses on systemic violence and examines the process by which states use violence to transform human bodies into unwilling rhetorical resources. (erinfrymire@trincoll.edu)

Tracy Lassiter is an Assistant Professor of English and the current English Coordinator at the University of New Mexico-Gallup. She has presented several times on trauma's impact on students, including at the 2018 NCTE conference and the 2018 and 2019 AEPL conferences. Her other research areas are information literacy, comics/graphic novels, and petrofiction. (tlassiter@unm.edu)

Christina M. LaVecchia is Director of Writing Across the Curriculum and Assistant Professor of English at Neumann University. Her work on professional practices, composing pedagogies, and digital literacies appears in *College English*, *Composition Forum*, and *Harlot*; the edited collections *Explanation Points* and *Showcasing the Best of CIWIC/DMAC*; and the textbook *How Writing Works*. Her healthcare collaborations appear in *Patient Education and Counseling* and *Health Expectations*. (lavecchc@neumann.edu)

Nate Mickelson is Clinical Associate Professor and Director of Faculty Development in the Expository Writing Program at New York University. He is the author *City Poems and American Urban Crisis, 1945 - Present* (Bloomsbury) and editor of *Writing as a Way of Staying Human in a Time that Isn't* (Vernon Press). His scholarly writing has also appeared in *The Journal of Urban Cultural Studies*, *Learning Communities Research & Practice*, *Transformative Dialogues*, and *The Journal of College Literacy and Learning*. A native of Wyoming, Nate is currently working on a study of reading practices and theories of justice in innovative American writing by Gloria Anzaldúa, CAConrad, Rachel Blau DuPlessis, and Leslie Scalapino. (nate.mickelson@nyu.edu)

Angela Montez is a May 2020 graduate from the MA program in English Literature at Texas A&M University. Her scholarly work focuses on Black Existentialism and African American Poetry and Poetics. She works full-time as an academic advisor in the Department of Mechanical Engineering at Texas A&M. She is highly interested in thinking about the intersections of care and academia in both her scholarly and administrative work. (angelali.montez@gmail.com ; almontez@tamu.edu)

Jesse Priest received his BA from the University of Maine, his MA from the University of Massachusetts Boston, and PhD in English Composition and Rhetoric from the University of Massachusetts Amherst. He is currently an Assistant Professor of English at the New Mexico Institute of Mining and Technology, where he teaches undergraduate and graduate classes in technical communication, science writing, and the rhetoric of video games. He also directs the Writing & Communication Lab at NMT. (priest.jesse@gmail.com)

Paul Puccio is a Professor of English and the Cyrus H. Holley Professor of Applied Ethics at Bloomfield College, where he teaches courses in British literature, children's literature, and Gothic literature. He has published articles on contemplative teaching practices, Victorian schoolboys, music drama, and ghosts in *CCC Online, Writing on the Edge, Dialogue, JAEPL, Reading Stephen Sondheim, The Encyclopedia of Catholic Literature, Modern Language Studies*, and other publications. (Paul_Puccio@Bloomfield.edu)

Patricia D. Pytleski is an Assistant Professor of English/ Composition and Rhetoric and Director of the Kutztown University Writing Center, where she teaches courses in writing and secondary English education and supervises English student teachers in the secondary education classroom. She is the author of "Contact Zones and Contingent Faculty: An Argument for Conversion" and "Crossing the Ideological Borders of Writing: The Fundamental Nature of Personal Writing (and Academic Discourse) In the First Year Writing Classroom." (pytleski@kutztown.edu)

Cristina D. Ramírez is Director of Rhetoric, Composition, and the Teaching of English and Associate Professor at the University of Arizona. Her cross-disciplinary work has appeared in *College English, Technical Communication Quarterly, The Journal of Homeland Security Education*, and *Latinx Writing and Rhetoric Studies*. She is the national award-winning author of *Occupying Our Space: The Mestiza Rhetorics of Mexican Women Journalists and Activists, 1875-1942* (U of Arizona Press, 2015), and co-author with Jessica Enoch of *Mestiza Rhetorics: An Anthology of Mexicana Activism in the Spanish Language Press, 1875-1922* (SIUP, 2019). She has traveled extensively through Mexico researching in non-digitized archives. (cristinaramirez@email.arizona.edu)

Keith Rhodes, between following his spouse's career and switching between professing composition and practicing law, has gotten around. He has been a WPA of some sort at Northwest Missouri State University, Missouri Western State University, and Grand Valley State University. He has also had fulltime faculty positions at Hastings College and now at the University of Denver. Since returning to the field in 2008, his scholarship has focused on style. (keith.rhodes@du.edu)

Jeff Ringer is Associate Professor of Rhetoric, Writing, and Linguistics at the University of Tennessee, Knoxville, where he directs the first-year composition program. He is the author of *Vernacular Christian Rhetoric and Civil Discourse* and co-editor, with Mike DePalma, of *Mapping Christian Rhetorics*. His research interests include evangelical Christian rhetoric and writing transfer. (jeff.ringer@utk.edu)

Sarah Seeley is an Assistant Professor, Teaching Stream at University of Toronto Mississauga. She teaches first-year writing as a member of the Institute for the Study of University Pedagogy. Seeley holds a Ph.D. in anthropology, and her research interests include language ideology, writing pedagogy, critical literacies, and the anthropology of education. (sarahseeley@utoronto.ca)

Anna Sicari, Ph.D, is an Assistant Professor of English and Director of the Writing Center at Oklahoma State University. Her scholarship focuses on writing centers, writing program administration, and feminist theory. Anna is a co-editor of the 2019 IWCA Outstanding Book Award, *Out in the Center: Public Controversies and Private Strug-*

gles with Utah State University Press and her work has appeared in *Praxis*, *The Writing Center Journal*, and *Composition Studies*. (anna.sicari@okstate.edu)

Kerri-Ann M. Smith is an Assistant Professor of English at Queensborough Community College (CUNY). Her work focuses on curriculum and instruction and culturally responsive pedagogy. She has conducted professional development training for educators in New York, Nigeria, and Ghana. An award-winning educator, Smith was recognized by the *New York Times* as a Teacher Who Makes a Difference and was honored by Caribbean Life Newspaper as a 40 Under 40 person of Caribbean descent. She is the co-author of the textbook *Writing Identities: A Guide to Writing Through Reading*. (ksmith@qcc.cuny.edu)

Irvin Weathersby is a Brooklyn-based writer and professor of literature and creative writing from New Orleans. He has published three biographies in *Notable Black American Men, Book II* and written for *Esquire*, *The Atlantic*, *EBONY*, *Killens Review*, and other outlets. In 2019, he was named the Bernard O'Keefe Scholar in Nonfiction at the Bread Loaf Writers' Conference. He has earned degrees in English, Education, and Creative Writing from Morehouse College, Morgan State University, and the New School. Before joining the faculty at Queensborough Community College, he was the education coordinator at a reentry program in the South Bronx and Harlem. (iweathersby@qcc.cuny.edu)

Nicole Jackson Wilson is a PhD candidate at Texas A&M University. Her dissertation project studies how working-class Black women academics construct their online identities and conceptualize their work as a form of online activism that has material effects beyond the digital world. (njwilsonphd@tamu.edu)

John D. Yi is a Lecturer of English at Queensborough Community College, CUNY. As a native New Yorker and a graduate of CUNY (Brooklyn College, BA and MA), he is dedicated to his students and hopes to pay forward the first-rate education he has received at CUNY. His pedagogical work and research includes, but is not limited to, culturally relevant pedagogy, multimedia studies and Asian American literature. He is currently pursuing a PhD in English Education at Teachers College, Columbia University. (jyi@qcc.cuny.edu)

Announcement

Journal of Teaching Writing

Now Accepting Submissions from K-12 Teachers for *JTW's* Fall 2020 Guest Edited Teacher-to-Teacher Section

THEME: Social Comprehension

Carrie Gaffney, Guest Editor

During regular times as teachers of writing, we are tasked to build our students' repertoires as academic writers. A quick check of the Common Core standards confirms that to be academic writers, students must adopt a formal style and objective tone (CCSS.ELA-LITERACY. W.11-12.1.D), use data and objective evidence to support ideas (CCSS.ELA-LITERACY.W.11-12.2.B), and always include a strong conclusion (CCSS.ELA-LITERACY.W.11-12.2.F). But these are not regular times. At the time of this writing, the majority of teachers across the globe have gone several months without seeing their students in person. Our plans for end-of-year research papers and fun narratives have been abandoned for what I can only describe as "survival teaching" during the COVID-19 pandemic. Furthermore, we are once again experiencing a summer of protests after the death of another Black man while in police custody. And although the world has always changed in real time, now—more than ever—we see the changes as they are happening.

Writing teachers have always been in a unique position to help students make sense of the world. And as we return (or don't return) to our buildings, we know the foreseeable future will almost certainly mean using writing to help students understand themselves and their world better. In the introduction to her book *Being the Change*, teacher, researcher, and writer Sara K. Ahmed writes that "social comprehension, like academic comprehension, is how we make meaning from and mediate our relationship with the world" (xxv). With no tangible end to the pandemic or civil rights abuses in sight, I would like for us to reflect on how we have made space for students to process their experiences through the written word. In what ways have you used writing to cultivate social comprehension? What tensions have you felt teaching social comprehension in an institution where test prep writing and response take precedence over writing to make meaning? How have you worked with colleagues and building leadership to prioritize social comprehension in the writing classroom across grade levels? In what ways have you observed growth in student writing as a result of teaching social comprehension?

Brief submissions (roughly 750-1200 words) that reflect on classroom practices that address this theme should be sent as a Word document to jtw@iupui.edu with the subject heading "K-12 Teacher to Teacher." The deadline for submission for our fall 2020 issue is November 1. All submissions will be reviewed by Carrie Gaffney, Guest Editor, in consultation with the *JTW* Editor. Contributors will be notified of the Guest Editor's decisions by November 30, 2020.

Questions? Please contact Carrie Gaffney, Guest Editor, Teacher to Teacher, at carolyn_gaffney@nobl.k12.in.us.

PARLOR PRESS
EQUIPMENT FOR LIVING

New Releases

A Genre Analysis of Social Change: Uptake of the Housing-First Solution to Homelessness in Canada by Diana Wegner

The Naylor Report on Undergraduate Research in Writing Studies edited by Dominic DelliCarpini, Jenn Fishman, and Jane Greer

Internationalizing the Writing Center: A Guide for Developing a Multilingual Writing Center by Noreen Lape

Socrates at Verse and Other Philosophical Poems by Christopher Norris

Writing Spaces: Readings on Writing Volume 3 edited by Dana Driscoll, Mary Stewart, and Matthew Vetter

Forthcoming

Collaborative Writing Playbook: An Instructor's Guide to Designing Writing Projects for Student Teams by Joe Moses and Jason Tham

The Art of Public Writing by Zachary Michael Jack

Check Out Our New Website!

Discounts, open access titles, instant ebook downloads, and more.

And new series:

Comics and Graphic Narratives. Series Editors: Sergio Figueiredo, Jason Helms, and Anastasia Salter

Inkshed: Writing Studies in Canada. Series Editors: Heather Graves and Roger Graves

www.parlorpress.com

JAEPL **Discount:** Use JAEPL20 at checkout to receive a 20% discount on all titles not on sale through October 1, 2020.

www.ingramcontent.com/pod-product-compliance
Lightning Source LLC
Chambersburg PA
CBHW031317160426
43196CB00007B/571